Anthropology:

CULTURE
PATTERNS
&
PROCESSES

Anthropology:

CULTURE
PATTERNS
&
PROCESSES

A. L. Kroeber

A Harvest/HBJ Book
Harcourt Brace Jovanovich
New York and London

First Harbinger Books edition 1963.
Culture Patterns and Processes consists of Chapters 1, 6, 7, 8, 9, and 10
of the author's complete ANTHROPOLOGY: *Revised Edition,* 1948.

ISBN 0-15-607805-8

IJKLM

Library of Congress Catalog Card Number: 63-12160

Printed in the United States of America

Contents

WHAT ANTHROPOLOGY IS ABOUT

LANGUAGE

THE NATURE OF CULTURE

PATTERNS

CULTURE PROCESSES

CULTURE CHANGE

List of Figures

EDITOR'S NOTE

This volume offers a selection of those chapters of Alfred L. Kroeber's classic work ANTHROPOLOGY that deal specifically with matters of *Culture Patterns and Processes*.

If no selection can ever take the place of the complete work from which it is drawn, this holds doubly true of a work as closely integrated as Kroeber's ANTHROPOLOGY, which covers a vast area of knowledge, illumines each of its parts from a single fundamental point of view, and subjects an entire field of scholarship to the searching inquiry of one mind of uncommon scope.

The present selection (and its companion volumes, which contain other selections) claims no more than that it will serve the convenience of those readers who wish to study the narrower topic only. However, the section numbers, and with them the many cross references, that run throughout the parent volume have been retained unchanged—to point up how much Kroeber's ANTHROPOLOGY is a work that is of one piece, and indivisible.

Anthropology:

CULTURE
PATTERNS
&
PROCESSES

What Anthropology Is About

I. ANTHROPOLOGY, BIOLOGY, HISTORY

ANTHROPOLOGY is the science of man. Of course, this literal, etymological meaning is too broad and general. More precise would be: "the science of man and his works and behavior." But even this needs an addition to make it sufficiently specific, since no one means to claim sciences like physiology and psychology as parts of anthropology. Now physiology and psychology focus their attention on particular men, whom they examine as individuals. This gives a clue to the additional limitation we are seeking. Anthropology obviously is concerned not with particular men as such, but with men in groups, with races and peoples and their happenings and doings. So let us take as our provisional basic definition the following: "Anthropology is the science of groups of men and their behavior and productions." This will include any findings on the total human species, since this constitutes an aggregate of races or peoples, a sort of supergroup or total society.

However, man is an animal or organism and he is also a civilized being having a history and social qualities. Thus he is investigated—different aspects of him are investigated—both by the organic or biological or life sciences and by what are sometimes called the historical and more generally the social sciences. True, this latter term, "the social sciences," though commonly used, is not easy to define satisfactorily. But we can leave this difficulty for the philosopher of science. In practice, anthropology is mostly classified as being both a biological science and a social science. Some universities recognize this fact by having certain courses of anthropological study count as the one and certain as the other, or perhaps even the same course counting either way. Such a situation of double participation is unusual among the sciences. If anthropology is not concerned so predominantly with man as an animal, or with man as a social human having a history, that it can be set outright in either the life or the social-historical science category, both aspects are evidently represented significantly in its subject matter. Could it be that the specific subject of anthropology is the interrelation of what is biological in man and what is social and historical in him? The answer is Yes. Or, more broadly, anthropology does at least concern itself with both organic and social factors in man, whereas nearly all other sciences and studies deal with one or the other. Anthropology concerns itself with both sets of factors because these come associated in human beings in nature. Often they are even inter-twined in one and the same phenomenon, as when a person is born with heredi-tary musical capacity and develops this further by study and training. They are not always easy to disentangle; but they must be separated if the processes at work are to be understood. That job is peculiarly the anthropologist's.

2. ORGANIC AND SOCIOCULTURAL ELEMENTS

To the question why a Louisiana Negro is black and longheaded, the answer is ready. He was born so. As cows produce calves, and lions, cubs, so Negro springs from Negro and Caucasian from Caucasian. We call the force at work heredity. Our same Negro is reputed amiable and easy-going. Is this too an innate quality? Offhand most of us might reply Yes. He sings at his corn-hoeing more frequently than the white man across the fence. Is this also because of his heredity? "Of course—he is made so," might be a common answer, "Probably—why not?" a more cautious one. But now our Negro is singing the "Memphis Blues," which his great-grandfather in Africa assuredly did not sing As for the specific song, heredity can obviously no longer be the cause. Our Negro may have learned it from an uncle, or perhaps from his schoolmates; quite likely he acquired it from human beings who were not his ancestors, or over the radio, acquired it as part of his customs, like being a member of the Baptist Church and wearing overalls, and the thousand other things that come to him from without instead of from within. At these points heredity is dis-placed by tradition, nature by nurture, to use a familiar jingle. The efficient forces now are quite different from those which made his skin black and his head long. They are causes of another order.

The particular song of the Negro and his complexion represent the clear-cut extremes of the matter. Between them lie the good nature and the inclination to melody. Obviously these traits may also be the result of human example, of "social environment," of contemporary tradition. There are those who so be-lieve, as well as those who see in them chiefly the effects of inborn biological impulse. Perhaps these intermediate dubious traits are the results of a blending of nature and nurture, the strength of each varying according to the trait or the individual examined. Clearly, at any rate, there is room here for investigation and weighing of evidence. A genuine problem exists. This problem cannot be solved by the historical or social sciences alone, because they do not concern themselves with heredity. Nor can it be solved by biology, which deals with heredity and allied factors but does not go on to operate with the nonbiological principle of tradition or with what is acquired by men when they live in societies.

Here, then, is one distinctive task for anthropology: the interpretation of those phenomena into which both innate organic factors and "social" or acquired factors enter or may enter.

The word "social" is the customary untechnical one for the nonorganic or more-than-organic phenomena referred to. It is, however, an ambiguous word and therefore sometimes a confusing one. As will shortly be pointed out, "social" refers to both social and cultural phenomena. Until the distinction between them has been made, we shall either put "social" into quotation marks or use "sociocultural" instead.

3. ORGANIC OR "PHYSICAL" ANTHROPOLOGY

The organic sciences underlie the sociocultural ones. They are more immediately "natural," less "humanized" in their concern. Anthropology therefore accepts and uses the general principles of biology: the laws of heredity and the doctrines of cell development and evolution, for instance, and all the findings of anatomy, physiology, embryology, zoology, palaeontology, and the rest. Its business has been to ascertain how far these principles apply to man, what forms they take in his particular case. This has meant a concentration of attention, the devising of special methods of inquiry. Many biological problems, including most physiological and hereditary ones, can be most profitably attacked in the laboratory, or at least under experimental conditions. The experimental method, however, is but rarely available for human beings living in groups. Sociocultural phenomena have to be taken as they come and laboriously sifted and resifted afterward, instead of being artificially simplified in advance, as is done in laboratory experimentation.

Then, too, since anthropology is operating biologically within the narrow limits of one species, it has sometimes been driven to concern itself with minute traits, such as the zoologist is rarely troubled with: the proportions of the length and the breadth of the skull—the famous cephalic index—for instance; the number of degrees the arm bones are twisted, and the like. Also, as these data had to be used in the gross, unmodifiable by artificially varied conditions, it has been necessary to secure them from all possible varieties of men, different races, sexes, ages, and their nearest brute analogues. The result is that biological or physical anthropology—"somatology" it is sometimes called in Anglo-Saxon countries, and sometimes simply "anthropology" in continental Europe—has in part constituted a sort of specialization or sharpening of certain aspects of general biology. It has become absorbed to a considerable degree in certain particular phenomena, such as human species or subraces and methods of studying them, about which general biologists, physiologists, and students of medicine are usually but vaguely informed.

4. SOCIOCULTURAL ANTHROPOLOGY

The sociocultural sciences, usually, but somewhat loosely, called the social sciences, overlie the organic sciences. Men's bodies and inborn equipment are back of their deeds and accomplishments as shaped by tradition, and are primary to their culture or civilization as well as to their aggregations in societies. The relation of anthropology to sociocultural science has therefore been in a sense the opposite of its relation to biological science. Instead of specializing, anthropology has been occupied with trying to generalize the findings of history. Historians can never experiment; sociologists, economists, and other social scientists only rarely. Historians deal with the unique; for to a degree every historical or social or cultural event has something unparalleled about it. They do not lay down laws, nor do they verify them by the artificial trials of experiment. But anthropology looks for such general and recurrent processes as may occur in the multifarious events of history and in the diverse societies, institutions, customs, and beliefs of mankind. So far as such processes can be extricated or formulated, they are generalizations.

It has sometimes been said that social and cultural anthropology—that part of the subject which is concerned with the more-than-merely-organic aspects of human behavior—seems preoccupied with ancient and savage and exotic and extinct peoples. The cause is a desire to understand better all civilizations, irrespective of time and place, in the abstract, or as generalized principles if possible. It is not that cave men are more illuminating than Romans, or flint knives more interesting than fine porcelains or the art of printing, which has led anthropology to bear heavily on the former, but the fact that it wanted to know about cave men and flint knives, which no one else was studying, as well as about the Romans and printing presses that history tells us about so fully. It would be arbitrary to prefer the exotic and remote to the familiar, and in principle anthropology has never accepted the adjudication sometimes tacitly rendered that its proper field should be restricted to the primitive as such. As well might zoology confine its interest to eggs or to protozoans. It is probably true that some researches into early and savage history, especially in the initial stages of anthropology, have sprung from an emotional predilection for the forgotten or the neglected, the obscure and the strange, the unwonted and the mysterious. But such occasional personal aesthetic trends cannot delimit the range of a science or determine its aims and methods. Innumerable historians have been inveterate gossips, but one does not therefore insist that the only proper subject of history is backstairs intimacies.

This, then, is the reason for the special development of those subdivisions of anthropology known as *archaeology,* "the science of what is old" in the career of humanity, especially as revealed by excavations of the sites of prehistoric occupation, and *ethnology*, "the science of peoples" and their cultures and life histories as groups, irrespective of their degree of advancement.[1]

5. EVOLUTIONARY PROCESSES AND EVOLUTIONISTIC FANCIES

In their more elementary aspects the two strands of the organic or hereditary and the sociocultural or "environmental" run through all human life. They are distinct as mechanisms, and their products are distinct. Thus a comparison of the acquisition of the power of flight respectively by birds in their organic development out of the ancestral reptile stem millions of years ago, and by men as a result of cultural progress in the field of invention during the past generation, reveals at once the profound differences of *process* that inhere in the ambiguous concept of "evolution." The bird gave up a pair of walking limbs to acquire wings. It added a new faculty by transforming part of an old one. The sum total of its parts or organs was not greater than before. The change was transmitted only to the blood descendants of the altered individuals. The reptile line went on as it had been before, or if it altered, did so for causes unconnected with the evolution of the birds. The airplane, on the contrary, gave men a new faculty without diminishing or even impairing any of those they had previously possessed. It led to no visible bodily changes, no alterations of mental capacity. The invention has been transmitted to individuals and groups not derived by descent from the inventors; in fact, it has already influenced the fortunes of all of us. Theoretically, the invention is transmissible to ancestors if they happen to be still living. In sum, it represents an accretion to the stock of existing civilization rather than a transformation.

Once the broad implications of the distinction which this example illustrates have been grasped, many common errors are guarded against. The program of eugenics, for instance, loses much of its force. There is certainly much to be said in favor of intelligence and discrimination in mating, as in everything else. There is need for the acquisition of more exact knowledge on human heredity. But, in the main, the claims sometimes made that eugenics is necessary to preserve civilization from dissolution, or to maintain the flourishing of this or that nationality, rest on the fallacy of recognizing only organic causes as operative, when sociocultural as well as organic ones are active—when indeed the superhereditary factors may be much the more powerful ones. So, in what are miscalled race problems, the average thought of the day still reasons confusedly between sociocultural and organic causes and effects.[2] Anthropology is not yet

---

[1] Ethnography is sometimes separated, as more descriptive, from ethnology, as more theoretically or more historically inclined.

[2] An example is the still lingering fallacy that individual development of organs by use somehow gets incorporated into the heredity of descendants. This fallacy rests on the misapplication to organic situations of a valid sociocultural mechanism. An example in reverse

in a position always to state just where the boundary lies between the contributing organic causes and the superorganic or "sociocultural" causes of such phenomena. But it does hold to their fundamental distinctness and to the importance of their distinction, if true understanding is the aim. Without sure grasp of this principle, many of the arguments and conclusions in the present volume will lose their significance.

Accordingly, a designation of anthropology as "the child of Darwin" is misleading. Darwin's essential achievement was that he imagined, and substantiated by much indirect evidence, a mechanism through which organic evolution appeared to be taking place. The whole history of man, however, being much more than an organic matter, a merely or strictly Darwinian anthropology would be largely misapplied biology. One might almost as justly speak of a Copernican or a Newtonian anthropology.

What has greatly influenced some of the earlier anthropology, mainly to its damage, has been not Darwinism, but the vague idea of progress, to the organic aspect of which Darwin happened incidentally to give such support and apparent substance that the whole group of evolutionistic ideas, sound and unsound, has luxuriated rankly ever since. It became common practice in the older anthropology to "explain" any part of human civilization by arranging its several forms in an evolutionary sequence from lowest to highest and allowing each successive stage to flow spontaneously, without specific cause, from the preceding one. At bottom this logical procedure was astonishingly naïve. In these schemes we of our land and day stood at the summit of the ascent. Whatever seemed most different from our customs was therefore reckoned as earliest, and other phenomena were disposed wherever they would best contribute to the straight evenness of the climb upward. The relative occurrence of phenomena in time and space was disregarded in favor of their logical fitting into a plan. It was argued that since we hold to definitely monogamous marriage, the beginnings of human sexual union probably lay in the opposite condition of indiscriminate promiscuity. Since we accord precedence to descent from the father, and generally know him, early society must have reckoned descent from the mother and no one knew his own father. We abhor incest; therefore the most primitive men normally married their sisters. These are fair samples of the conclusions or assumptions of the classic evolutionistic school of anthropology of, say, 1860 to 1890, which still believed that primal origins or ultimate causes could be determined, and that they could be discovered by speculative reasoning. The roster of this evolutionistic-speculative school was graced by some illustrious names. Needless to say, these men tempered the basic crudity of their opinions by wide knowledge, acuity or charm of presentation, and frequent insight and sound sense in concrete particulars. In their day, two generations or three ago, under the spell of the concept of evolution in its first flush, and of the postulate of

is the ascription of environmentally or historically produced cultural backwardness to organic and hereditary inferiority.

progress at its strongest, such methods of reasoning were almost inevitable. Today they are long since threadbare; they have descended to the level of newspaper science or have become matter for idle amateur guessing. They are evidence of a tendency toward the easy smugness of feeling oneself superior to all the past. These ways of thought are mentioned here only as an example of the beclouding that results from bad transference of biologically legitimate concepts into the realm of the history of human society and culture, or viewing these as unfolding according to a simple scheme of progress.

6. SOCIETY AND CULTURE

The relation between what is biological and what is sociocultural has just been said to be a sort of central pivot of anthropology, from which the range of the subject then extends outward on both sides, into the organic and into the more-than-organic. It is now necessary to consider the more precise relation of society and culture within the "organic-plus." In man, social and cultural phenomena normally occur associated much as the joint sociocultural phenomena co-occur with the organic ones. Nevertheless, the social and the cultural aspects within the larger sociocultural field can nearly always be distinguished.

The Latin word *socius* denotes a companion or ally, and in their specific sense the words "society" and "social" refer to associations of individuals, to group relations. When we speak of social structure, or the organization of society, it is clear what is meant: the way a mass of people is constituted into families, clans, tribes, states, classes, sets, clubs, communities, and the like. A society is a group of interrelated individuals.

But in a much wider sense the word "social" is also used, loosely, for whatever transcends the biological individual: for what we have so far designated as more-than-organic or sociocultural. Thus popular usage and university curricula recognize the physical, the biological, and the social sciences. The last-named usually comprise history, government, economics, sociology, anthropology, human geography.[3] All these branches of study deal not only with man but with men. In fact they deal primarily with the interrelations of men, or groups of men.

It so happens that man is an essentially unique animal in that he possesses speech faculty and the faculty of symbolizing, abstracting, or generalizing. Through these two associated faculties he is able to communicate his acquired learning, his knowledge and accomplishments, to his fellows and his descendants —in fact, even to his ancestors, if they happen to be still alive and are willing to listen to him. So he transmits much of his ideas, habits, and achievements to succeeding generations of men. This is something that no other animal can do, at least not to any significant degree. This special faculty is what was meant

[3] Psychology is sometimes also partly included, sometimes reckoned rather with the biological sciences.

when someone called man the "time-binding" animal. He "binds" time by transcending it, through influencing other generations by his actions.

Now the mass of learned and transmitted motor reactions, habits, techniques, ideas, and values—and the behavior they induce—is what constitutes *culture*. Culture is the special and exclusive product of men, and is their distinctive quality in the cosmos.

Not only is culture a unique phenomenon, but it can be said to have a large degree of influence. Of course culture can appear and go on only in and through men, men in some kind of societies; without these it could not come into being nor maintain itself. But, given a culture, the human beings that come under its influence behave and operate quite differently from the way they would behave under another culture, and still more differently from the way they would act under no culture. In the latter case they would be merely animals in their behavior. They are human beings precisely because they are animals plus a culture. Somehow human beings began long ago to produce culture and have continued ever since to produce it. In that sense culture derives wholly from men. But the other side of the picture is that every human being is influenced by other men who in turn have been influenced by still others in the direction of maintaining and developing certain ideas, institutions, and standards. And a shorthand way of expressing this is to say that they are all influenced by the culture they grow up in; in fact, in a broad way, they are dependent on it for most of the specific things they do in their lives. Culture is therefore a powerful force in human behavior—in both individual and social behavior. Any given form of culture, whether of the Eskimo or of our contemporary Western civilization, has behind it a long history of other forms of culture by which it was conditioned and from which it derives. And in turn each culture is changing and shaping the forms of culture that will succeed it and which therefore more or less depend on it. Culture thus is a factor that produces enormous effects, and as such we study it.

To be concrete, the reason our Louisiana Negro of a few pages back sings the blues, goes to a Baptist church, and cultivates corn is that these things are parts of American culture. If he had been reared in the Africa of some of his forefathers, his dress, labor, food, religion, government, and amusements would have been quite different, as well as his language. Such is what culture does to men. And, as has been pointed out, the process of transmission, a process of acquisition by learning by which culture is perpetuated and operates on new generations, is quite different from the process by which heredity—another indubitable force—operates on them. Equally distinct are the results. No religion, no tool, no idea was ever produced by heredity.

Culture, then, is all those things about man that are more than just biological or organic, and are also more than merely psychological. It presupposes bodies and personalities, as it presupposes men associated in groups, and it rests upon them; but culture is something more than a sum of psychosomatic qualities and actions. It is more than these in that its phenomena cannot be wholly understood in terms of biology and psychology. Neither of these sciences claims to be able to explain why there are axes and property laws and etiquettes and prayers in the world, why they function and perpetuate as they do, and least of all why these cultural things take the particular and highly variable forms or expressions under which they appear. Culture thus is at one and the same time the totality of products of social men, and a tremendous force affecting all human beings, socially and individually. And in this special but broad sense, culture is universal for man.[4]

This brings us back to the relation of society and culture. Logically, the two are separate, though they also coexist. Many animals are social. Ants and bees and termites are very highly socialized, so much so that they can survive only in societies. But they have no culture. There is no culture on the subhuman level. Ants get along without culture because they are born with many highly specific instincts; but men have only few and general instincts. Society without culture exists on the subhuman level. But culture, which exists only through man, who is also a social animal, presupposes society. The speech faculty makes possible the transmission and perpetuation of culture; and speech could evidently arise only in a somewhat socially inclined species, though the most socialized animals, the social insects, are held together by instinctive drives and do not need speech. In man, however, language helps bind his societies successfully together. And then culture, with its institutions and morals and values, binds each of them together more and helps them to achieve more successful functioning.

Human society and culture are thus perhaps best viewed as two intimately intertwined aspects of a complex of phenomena that regularly occur only in association; whereas on the subhuman level, societies occur but there is no significant culture.

The occurrence of cultureless true societies among the insects makes it clear that, much as living bodies and "minds" underlie societies and cultures, and precede them in evolution, so also, in turn, society precedes and underlies culture, though in man the two always happen to come associated. At any rate, society is a simpler and more obvious concept to grasp than is culture. That is apparently why sociocultural phenomena—the phenomena of man's total history in the broadest sense, which necessarily contain both social facts and cultural facts—usually have their social aspects recognized first. The result has been that

---

[4] Culture as dealt with by the anthropologist is obviously different from what is signified by speaking of "a man of culture," or "a cultured person," in the popular sense, when high culture, or special refinement of it, is meant. Similarly with the word "civilization." When we ordinarily, as laymen, speak of "civilized" and "uncivilized" peoples, we mean, more precisely, peoples of advanced and backward culture, respectively. By many anthropologists, ever since Tylor, the words "civilization" and "culture" are often used to denote the same thing; and always they denote only degrees of the same thing.

the social-plus-cultural combination came at first to be called merely "social," and in popular and general use still carries that ambiguous name.

For those who like their thinking concrete, it may help if they conceive the sociocultural total in man as similar to a sheet of carbon paper, of which the fabric side represents society and the coated side culture. It is obvious that to use carbon paper effectively, we must distinguish the sides. And yet the sheet is also a unit. Moreover, in certain respects, as when we are not concerned with manifolding but only with some operation like sorting, counting, or packing, a sheet of carbon paper is comparable to and is handled like a sheet of uncoated paper—which in turn would correspond to the cultureless animal societies. But if what we are interested in is the use of carbon paper, the impressions made by it, or if we wish to understand how it makes them, then it is the specific carbon coating that we must examine, even though this comes only as a sort of dry-ink film carried by paper of more or less ordinary cellulose fabric and texture. Like all similes, this one has its limitations. But it may be of help in extricating one-self from the confusing difficulty that the word "social" has acquired a precise and limited meaning—society as distinguishable from culture—in anthropology and sociology, while still having a shifting double meaning—society including or excluding culture—in popular usage and in many general contexts.

There is a real difficulty in the confusion that results from the varying usage of the word "society." The difficulty is unfortunate; but it can be met by keeping it constantly in mind. In the present book, the effort is made to be consistent in saying "culture" or "cultural" whenever anything cultural is referred to. "Social" or "society" are used only with specific reference to the organization of individuals into a group and their resulting relations. Culture, on the contrary, whatever else it may also be—such as a tremendous influence on human behavior—is always first of all the *product* of men in groups: a set of ideas, attitudes, and habits—"rules" if one will—evolved by men to help them in their conduct of life.[5]

[5] A further complication arises from the fact that human societies are more than merely innate or instinctual associations like beehives or anthills, but are also culturally shaped and modeled. That is, the forms which human association takes—into nations, tribes, sects, cult groups, classes, castes, clans, and the like—all these forms of social structure are as much the result of varying cultural influences as are the particular forms of economies, technologies, ideologies, arts, manners, and morals at different times and places. In short, specific human societies are more determined by culture than the reverse, even though some kind of social life is a precondition of culture. And therewith social forms become part of culture! This seemingly contradictory situation is intellectually difficult. It touches the heart of the most fundamental social theorizing. A good many anthropologists and sociologists still shrink from facing the problem or admitting the situation to be significant. The beginner is therefore advised not to try to master the difficulty at this stage, but to wait till he has finished the book. He will then presumably understand what the problem is and be in a position either to accept the solution suggested here, or to give his own answer. And if not, he will still be in the company of a lot of professional social scientists of good standing.

7. ANTHROPOLOGY AND THE SOCIAL SCIENCES

All the so-called social sciences deal with cultural as well as social data. Caesar's reform of the calendar was a cultural innovation. His defeat of the senatorial party was a social event, but it led to institutional and therefore cultural changes, just as it affected thousands of individual lives for better or worse. When a historian analyzes Caesar's character and motivation, he has in fact gone beyond both society and culture and is operating in the field of informal, biographical, individual psychology. In economics, a banking system, the gold standard, commerce by credit or barter, are institutions, and hence cultural phenomena.

Of all the social sciences, anthropology is perhaps the most distinctively culture-conscious. It aims to investigate human culture as such: at all times, everywhere, in all its parts and aspects and workings. It looks for generalized findings as to how culture operates—literally, how human beings behave under given cultural conditions—and for the major developments of the history of culture.

To this breadth of aim, one thing contributed. This was the early anthropological preoccupation with the very ancient and primitive and remote, which we have already mentioned as a possible foible or drawback. Unlettered peoples leave no biographies of their great men to distract one with personalities, no written histories of rulers and battles. The one thing we know about them is their customs; and customs are culture. The earliest men in fact have left us evidence of just two things: parts of their organic bodies, as represented by their bones; and, more abundantly, their culture, as represented by those of their tools and implements which happened to be of stone and imperishable, plus such of their customs as may be inferable from these tools.

Now while some of the interest of anthropology in its earlier stages was in the exotic and the out-of-the-way, yet even this antiquarian motivation ultimately contributed to a broader result. Anthropologists became aware of the diversity of culture. They began to see the tremendous range of its variations. From that, they commenced to envisage it as a totality, as no historian of one period or of a single people was ever likely to do, nor any analyst of his own type of civilization alone. They became aware of culture as a "universe," or vast field, in which we of today and our own civilization occupy only one place of many. The result was a widening of a fundamental point of view, a departure from unconscious ethnocentricity toward relativity. This shift from naïve self-centeredness in one's own time and spot to a broader view based on objective comparison is somewhat like the change from the original geocentric assumption of astronomy to the Copernican interpretation of the solar system and the subsequent still greater widening to a universe of galaxies.

A considerable differentiation of anthropology occurred on this point. The other social sciences recognized culture in its specific manifestations as they became aware of this or that fragment or aspect of it—economic or juridical or political or social. Anthropologists became aware of culture as such. From that they went on to try to understand its generic features and processes and their results.

This is one of the few points that sets off from anthropology a science which in the main is almost a twin sister: sociology. Sociologists began mainly with the analysis of our own civilization; they kept the exotic in its place. Therefore as regards culture they tended to remain autocentric somewhat longer. Also, in dealing with ourselves, they dealt mainly with the present, and from that they went on to deal with the future, immediate and ultimate. This inevitably gave to much of early sociology some reformist or ameliorative coloring, and often a program for action. On the contrary, the reproach used to be directed at anthropology that it did not concern itself with practical solutions, or aim at betterment. So far as this was true, it had at least the virtue of helping anthropology to remain a general or fundamental science, undistracted by questions of application from its search for basic findings and meanings. One other distinction is that sociology has been more concerned with strictly social problems: the relations of classes, the organization of family and society, the competitions of individuals within a group. The names are indeed significant here: sociology tends to be concerned with society, anthropology with *anthropos,* man, and his specifically human product, culture.

All in all, however, these are only differences of emphasis. In principle, sociology and anthropology are hard to keep apart. Anthropologists rate Sumner as one of the great names in the history of the study of man; and they feel they stand on common ground with American sociologists like Thomas, Ogburn, Chapin, Sorokin, Wirth, MacIver, Parsons, and Lynd, to name only a few, and with Britons and Frenchmen like Hobhouse, Ginsberg, Durkheim, and Mauss. Sociologists on their side have been if anything even more hospitable. Almost to a man they are culture-conscious, know anthropological literature well, and use it constantly.

The relations of anthropology to psychology are obviously important. The nature of human personality—or let us say simply human nature—must enter vitally into all of man's social and cultural activity. However, the relations of anthropology and psychology are not easy to deal with. Psychologists began by taking their own culture for granted, as if it were uniform and universal, and then studying psychic behavior within it. Reciprocally, anthropologists tend to take human nature for granted, as if it were uniform, and to study the diverse cultures which rest upon it. In technical language, we have two variables, "mind" and culture, and each science assumes that it can go ahead by treating the other variable as if it were constant. All psychologists and anthropologists now know that such constancy is not actual. But to deal with two variables, each highly complex, is difficult; and as for specific findings, only beginnings have as yet been made. This whole set of problems of cultural psychology is taken up in one of the later chapters of this book.

The foregoing will make clear why anthropology is sometimes still regarded as one of the newer subjects of study. As a distinct science, with a program of its own, it is relatively recent, because it could hardly become well organized until the biological and the social sciences had both attained enough development to specialize and become aware of the gap between themselves, and until culture was recognized as a specific and distinctive field of inquiry.

But as an unmethodical body of knowledge, as an interest, anthropology is plainly one of the oldest of the sisterhood of sciences. It could not well be otherwise than that men were at least as much interested in each other as in stars and mountains and plants and animals. Every savage is a bit of an ethnologist about neighboring tribes and knows a legend of the origin of mankind. Herodotus, the "father of history," devoted half of his nine books to pure ethnology. Lucretius, a few centuries later, tried to solve by philosophical deduction and poetical imagination many of the same problems that modern anthropology is more cautiously attacking with concrete methods. Until nearly two thousand years after these ancients, in neither chemistry nor geology nor biology was so serious an interest developed as in anthropology.

CHAPTER SIX

Language

93. LINGUISTIC RELATIONSHIP: THE SPEECH FAMILY

THE QUESTION that the historian and the anthropologist most frequently ask of the philologist is whether this and that language are or are not related. Relationship in such connection means descent from a common source, as two brothers are descended from the same father, or two cousins from a common grandfather. If languages can be demonstrated to possess such common source, it is clear that the peoples who spoke them must at one time have been in close contact, or perhaps have constituted a single people. If, on the other hand, the languages of two peoples prove wholly dissimilar, though their racial types and cultures be virtually identical, as indeed is sometimes found to be the case—witness the Hungarians and their neighbors—it is evident that an element of discontinuous development must somewhere be reckoned with. Perhaps one part of an originally single racial group gradually modified its speech beyond recognition; or under the shock of conquest, migration, or other historical accident it may have entirely discarded its language in favor of a new and foreign tongue. Or the opposite may be true: The two groups were originally wholly separate and distinct in many respects, but, being brought into contact, their cultures interpenetrated, intermarriage followed, and the two physical types became assimilated into one while the languages remained dissimilar. In short, if one wishes full understanding of a people, one must take its language into consideration. This means that the language must be classified. If a classification is to be more than merely logical or theoretical, if it is to be pragmatic and historically significant, it must have reference to relationship, development, origin. In a word, it must be a genetic classification.

The term used to indicate that two or more languages have a common source but are unrelated to certain others, or seem so in the present state of knowledge, is "linguistic family." "Linguistic stock" is frequently used as a synonym. This is the fundamental concept in the historical classification of languages. Without a clear idea of its meaning one involves oneself in confusion on attempting to use philology as an aid to other branches of human history.

There is no abstract reason against referrring to a group of unrelated languages as a "family" because they are all spoken in one area, nor against denominating as "families," as has sometimes been done, the major subdivisions of a group of languages admittedly of common origin. Again, languages that show certain similarities of type or structure, such as inflection, might conceivably be put into one "family." But there is this objection to all such usages: They do not commit themselves on the point of genetic relationship, or they contradict it, or only partially exhaust it. Yet commonness of origin is so important in many connections that it is indispensable to have one term that denotes its ascertainable presence. And for this quality there happens to be no generally understood designation other than "linguistic family," or its synonym, "linguistic stock." This phrase will therefore be used here strictly in the sense of the whole of a group of languages sprung from a single source, and only in that sense. Other groupings will be indicated by phrases like "languages of such and such an area," "subfamily," "division of a family," or "unrelated languages of similar type."

94. CRITERIA OF RELATIONSHIP

The question that first arises in regard to linguistic families is how the relationship of their constituent idioms is determined. In brief, the method is one of comparison. If a considerable proportion of the words and the grammatical forms of two languages are reasonably similar, similar enough to indicate that the resemblances cannot be due to mere accident, these similar words and forms must go back to a common source; and if this source is not borrowing by one language from another, the two tongues are related by descent from a common ancestor. If comparison fails to bring out any such degree of resemblance, the languages are classed in distinct families.

Of course it is possible that the reason two languages seem unrelated is not that they are really so, but that they have in the lapse of ages become so much differentiated that one cannot any longer find resemblance between their forms. In that event true relationship would be obscured by remoteness. Theoretically, there is high probability that many families of languages customarily regarded as totally distinct do go back in the far past to a common origin, and that our ignorance of their history, or inability to analyze them deeply, prevents recognition of their relationship. From time to time it happens that groups of languages which at first seemed unrelated are shown by more intensive study to possess elements enough in common to compel the recognition of their original unity. In that case what were supposed to be several "families" become merged in one. The scope of a particular family may be thus enlarged; but the scope of the generic concept of "family" is not altered.

Whether there is any hope that comparative philology may ultimately be prosecuted with sufficient success to lead all the varied forms of human speech back to a single origin is an interesting speculation. A fair statement is that such a possibility, like any future event, cannot be absolutely denied, but that science is still extremely far from such a realization. Of more immediate concern is an ordering and summarizing of the knowledge in hand with a view to such positive inferences as can be drawn.

In an estimate of the similarity of languages, items that count as evidence must meet two requirements: they must be alike, or traceably similar, or regularly correspondent in sound; and they must be alike or similar or related in meaning. This double requirement holds equally whether full words or separable parts of words, roots, or grammatical forms are compared. The English word *eel* and the French *île,* meaning *island,* are pronounced almost exactly alike, yet their meaning is so different that no sane person would regard them as sprung from the same origin. As a matter of fact *île* is derived from Latin *insula,* and is the source of the English *isle,* whereas *eel* has a cognate in German *aal.* These prototypes *insula* and *aal* being as different in sound as they are in meaning, any possibility that *eel* and *île* might be related is easily disposed of. Yet if the Latin and German cognates were lost, if nothing were known of the history of the English and French languages, and if *île* meant not *island* but, say, *fish* or *water snake,* then it might be reasonable to think of a connection.

Such doubtful cases, of which a certain proportion are likely to be adjudged wrongly, are bound to come up in regard to the less well investigated languages, particularly those of nations without writing, the earlier stages of whose speech have perished without trace. In proportion as more is known of the history of a language, or as careful analysis can reconstruct more of its past stages, the number of such border-line cases obviously becomes fewer.

Before genetic connection between two languages can be thought of, the number of their elements similar in sound and sense must be reasonably large. An isolated handful of resemblances obviously are either importations—loan words— or the result of coincidence. Thus in the native Californian language known as Yuki, *ƙo* means *go,* and *ƙom* means *come.* Yet examination of Yuki reveals no further similarities. It would therefore be absurd to dream of a connection: one swallow does not make a summer. This lone pair of resemblances means nothing except that the mathematical law of probability has operated. Among the thousands of words in one language, a number are likely to be similar in sound to words of another language; and of this number again a small fraction, perhaps one or two or five in all, will happen to bear some resemblance in meaning also. In short, the similarities upon which a verdict of genetic relationship is based must be sufficiently numerous to fall well beyond the possibility of mere coincidence; and it must also be possible to prove with reasonable certainty that they are not the result of one language's borrowing words from another, as, for instance, English has borrowed from French and Latin.

At the same time it is not necessary that the similarities extend to the point of identity. In fact, too close a resemblance between part of the stock of two languages immediately raises a presumption of borrowing. For every language is continually changing, and once a mother tongue has split into several daughters, each of these goes on modifying its sounds, and gradually shifting the meaning of its words, generation after generation. In short, where connection is real, it must be veiled by a certain degree of change or distortion.

Take the English word *foot* and the Latin word of the same meaning, *pes*. To offhand inspection the sounds or forms of the two words do not seem similar. The resemblance becomes more definite in other forms of *pes*, for instance the genitive case *ped-is* or the accusative *ped-em*. Obviously the stem or elementary portion of the Latin word is not *pes* but *ped-;* and the *d* is closer to the English *t* of *foot* than is the *s* of *pes*. The probability of relationship is increased by the Greek word for foot, *pous*, whose stem proves to be *pod-*, with vowel closer to that of English. Meanwhile, it would be recognized that there are English words beginning with *ped-*, such as *pedal, pedestrian, pedestal*, all of which have a clear association with the idea of foot. All these words however possess almost exact equivalents in Latin. One would therefore be justified in concluding from these facts what indeed the history of the languages proves: namely, that *pedal, pedestrian*, and *pedestal* are Latin words taken over into English; whereas *foot* and *pes* and *pous*, and for that matter German *fuss*, are derivatives from a common form that once existed in the now extinct mother tongue from which Greek and Latin and English and German are derived.

95. SOUND EQUIVALENCES AND PHONETIC LAWS

The question next arises whether it is possible to account for the distortions that have modified the original word into *foot, ped-*, and so on. What has caused the initial sound of this ancient word to become *p* in Latin and *f* in English, and its last consonant to be *d* in Latin and Greek, *t* in English, and *ss* in German? To answer this seemingly innocent question with accuracy for this one word alone would involve a treatise on the whole group of languages in question; and even then the causes, as causes, could hardly be set down with certainty. But it has proved possible to assemble a large number of instances of parallel "distortion" in which Latin *p* corresponds to English *f*, or *d* to *t*. Evidently philology has got hold of a generalized phenomenon here. Since *father* corresponds to *pater*, *full* to *pl-enus*, *for* to *pro*, *fish* to *piscis*, and so on in case after case, we are evidently face to face with a happening that has occurred with regularity and to which the name "law" is therefore applicable.

The *f* of *foot* and the *p* of *pes* are both lip sounds. They differ pre-eminently in that *f* can be prolonged indefinitely, whereas *p* is produced by a momentary closure of the lips with stoppage of the breath. It is customary to speak of sounds produced by a process like that for *p* as "stops." *F*, on the other hand, is a "continuant," and more specifically a "fricative" or rubbing sound.

The English word *three* begins with a sound which, although conventionally represented by the two letters *th*, is a simple sound and in a class with *f* in being fricative. *Th* is formed by putting the tongue lightly across the teeth, just as *f* is made by placing the lower lip against the edge of the upper teeth. In both cases the breath is expelled with friction through a narrow passage. Now if the fricative *f* is represented in Latin by the stop *p*, then, if regularity holds good, the English fricative *th* ought to be represented in Latin by the stop sound in the corresponding dental position; namely, *t*. The Latin word for *three* is in fact *tres;* for *thin, ten-uis;* for *mother, mater;* for *thou, tu*, and so on. The regularity therefore extends beyond the limits of the single labial class of sounds, and applies with equal force to the dentals; and, it may be added, to the palatals and gutturals as well.

As one passes from English and Latin to German, one finds the initial sound of the word meaning *three, drei*, to be somewhat different from *th* and *t* but still clearly allied, since it also is made by the tongue against the teeth. *D* is a stop like *t*, but the vocal cords vibrate while it is being pronounced, whereas in *t* the vocal cords are silent. *D* is "voiced" or "sonant," *t* "unvoiced" or "surd." Hence the formulation: Latin, surd stop; German, sonant stop; English, fricative. This triple equivalence can be substantiated in other words. For instance, *ten-uis, dünn, thin; tu, du, thou*.

If it is the English word that contains a surd stop, what will be the equivalent in Latin and German? Compare *ten*, Latin *decem*, German *zehn*, pronounced *tsehn*. Again the three classes of sounds run parallel; but the place of their appearance in the three languages has shifted.

The third possible placing of the three sounds in the three languages is when English has the sonant stop *d*. By exclusion it might be predicted that Latin should then show the fricative *th* and the German the surd stop *t*. The word *daughter* confirms this. The German is *tochter*. Latin in this case fails us, the original corresponding stem having gone out of use and been replaced by the word *filia*. But Greek, whose sounds tend to align with those of Latin as opposed to English and German, provides the *th* as expected: *thygater*.

Let us bring together these results so that the eye may grasp them:

SOUND EQUIVALENCES

Latin, Greek	surd stop	sonant stop	fricative
German	sonant stop	fricative	surd stop
English	fricative	surd stop	sonant stop
Latin, Greek	tres	duo	thygater
German	drei	zwei	tochter
English	three	two	daughter

These relations apply not only to the dentals *d, t, th* (*s, z*), which have been chosen for illustration, but also to the labials *p, b, f,* and to the palatals *k, g, h* (*gh, ch*).

It is evident that most of the sounds occur in all three groups of languages, but not in the same words. The sound *t* is common to English, Latin, and German, but when it appears in a particular word in one of these languages it is replaced by *d* and *th* in the two other languages. This replacing is known as a "sound shift." The sound shifts just enumerated constitute the famous Grimm's Law. This was the first important phonetic law or system of sound substitutions discovered in any family. Yet it is only one of a number of shifts that have been worked out for the Indo-European family of languages to which English, German, and Latin belong. So far, only stopped and fricative consonants have been reviewed here, and no vowels have been considered. Other languages, in the Indo-European family and in other families, also show shifts, but often different ones, as between *l* and *n,* or *s* and *k,* or *p* and *k.*

The significance of a shift lies in the fact that its regularity cannot easily be explained on any other ground than that the words in which the law is operative must originally have been the same. That is, Latin *duo,* German *zwei,* English *two* are all only variants of a word that meant "two" in the mother tongue from which these three languages are descended. This example alone is of course insufficient evidence for the existence of such a common mother tongue. But that each of the shifts discussed is substantiated by hundreds or thousands of words in which it holds true—this fact puts the shift beyond possibility of mere accident: the explanation of coincidence is ruled out. The resemblances therefore are both genuine and genetic. The conclusion becomes inevitable that the languages thus linked are later modifications of a former single speech.

It is in this way that linguistic relationship is determined. Where an ancient sound shift, a law of phonetic change, can be established by a sufficient number of cases, argument ceases. It is true that when most of a language has perished, or when an unwritten language has been but fragmentarily recorded or its analysis not carried far, a strong presumption of genetic unity may crowd in on the investigator who is not yet in a position to present the evidence of laws. The indications may be strong enough to warrant a tentative assumption of relationship. But the final test is always the establishment of laws of sound equivalence that hold good with regularity—part-for-part correspondence, the biologist would say.

96. THE PRINCIPAL SPEECH FAMILIES

The number of linguistic families or stocks [1] is not a matter of much theoretical import. From what has already been said it appears that the number can perhaps never be determined with absolute accuracy. As knowledge accumulates and dissection is carried to greater refinements, new similarities will be uncovered and will serve to unite what now seem to be separate stocks. Yet for the practical purpose of classifying and relating peoples the linguistic family will remain an indispensable historical tool. A rapid survey of the principal families will therefore be given.

In Asia and Europe, which must be considered a unit in this connection, the number of linguistic stocks, according to conservative reckoning, does not exceed twenty-five, and may be fewer. The most important of these, in point of number of speakers, is the Indo-European or Indo-Germanic or Aryan family, whose territory for several thousand years has comprised southwestern Asia and the greater part, but by no means all, of Europe. The most populous branches of the Indo-European family are the Indic, Slavic, Germanic, and Romance or Latin. Others are Persian or Iranic, Armenian, Greek, Albanian, Baltic or Lithuanian, and Keltic. From Europe various Indo-European languages, such as English, Spanish, French, Russian, have in recent centuries been carried to other continents, until in some, such as the Americas and Australia, much the greater area is now inhabited by peoples speaking Indo-European. (As the accompanying maps are intended to depict the historical or native distribution of languages, they omit this recent diffusion, important as it is.) It will be noted that the home distribution of Indo-European has the form of a long belt stretching from western Europe to northeastern India, with an interruption only in Asia Minor (Fig. 14). Turkish peoples displaced Indo-Europeans there about a thousand years ago, thus breaking the territorial continuity. It is probable that another link between the western and eastern Indo-Europeans once stretched around the north and east of the Caspian Sea. Here also there are Turks now.

Almost equaling Indo-European in the number of its speakers is the Sinitic family, which is generally held to include Chinese proper with its dialects; the Tibeto-Burman branch; the T'ai or Shan-Siamese branch; and probably some minor divisions.

[1] "Linguistic family" and "linguistic stock" are used as synonyms in this book. The criterion of both is not the degree of similarity of the included languages, but the fact (or presumptive fact) of relationship through common descent.

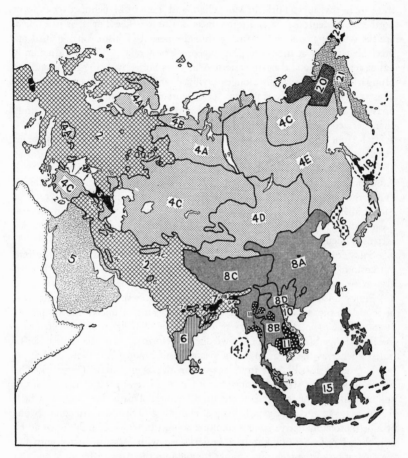

FIG. 14. LINGUISTIC FAMILIES OF ASIA AND EUROPE

1, Basque. 2, Indo-European. 3, Caucasian (perhaps two families). 4, Ural-Altaic (A, Finno-Ugric; B, Samoyed; C, Turkish; D, Mongol; E, Tungus-Manchu). 5, Semitic. 6, Dravidian. 7, Kolarian. 8, Sinitic (A, Chinese; B, Shan-Siamese; C, Tibeto-Burman; D, Miao, Lolo, Moso, etc.). (9, Khasi, belongs to 11.) 10, Annamese. 11, Mon-Khmer. 12, Sakai. 13, Semang. 14, Andaman. 15, Malayo-Polynesian or Austronesian. 16, Korean. 17, Japanese. 18, Ainu. 19, Ket or Yeniseian. 20, Yukaghir. 21, Chukchi-Koryak-Kam-chadal. 22, Eskimo.

In extent of territory occupied the Altaic stock rivals the Indo-European. Its three main divisions, Turkish, Mongolian, and Tungus-Manchu, cover most of northern and central Asia and some tracts in Europe. The Turks, as just noted, are the only linguistic group that within the period of history has gained appreciable territory at Indo-European expense. The Uralic or Finno-Ugric family has eastern Europe and northwestern Asia as its home, with the Finns and the Hungarian Magyars as the longest-civilized and best-known representatives. This is a geographically scattered stock. Most scholars unite the three Altaic divisions with Finno-Ugric and Samoyed into an even larger Ural-Altaic family characterized by certain structural similarities; but some deny the reality of such a Ural-Altaic family on the ground that the similarities are not original or genetic.

Of the Semitic family, Arabic is the chief living representative, with Amharic and Tigré in Ethiopia as little-known African half-sisters. Arabic is one of the most widely diffused of all languages, and as the orthodox vehicle of Mohammedanism has served an important function as a culture-carrier. Several great nations of ancient times also spoke Semitic tongues: Babylonians, Assyrians, Phoenicians, Carthaginians, and Hebrews.

Southern India is Dravidian. While people of this family enter little into our customary thoughts, they number over fifty millions. Japanese and Korean also merit mention as important stock tongues. Annamese, by some regarded as a Sinitic offshoot, may constitute a separate stock. Several minor families will be found on the Asiatic map, most of them consisting of uncivilized peoples or of those limited in their territory or the number of their speakers. Yet, so far as can be judged from present knowledge, they form units of the same order of independence as the great Indo-European, Semitic, and Ural-Altaic stocks.

Language distributions in Africa are in the main simple (Fig. 15). The whole of northern Africa this side of latitude 10° N., and parts of East Africa to and beyond the equator, were at one time Hamitic. This is the family to which the language of ancient Egypt belonged. Hamitic and Semitic, named after sons of Noah, probably derive from a common source, in which case there would be only the Hamitic-Semitic family to be reckoned with. Also, in that eventuality the separation of the common mother tongue into the African Hamitic and the Asiatic Semitic divisions must have occurred in very ancient times. In the past thousand years Hamitic has yielded ground before Semitic, owing to the spread of Arabic in Mohammedan Africa.

Africa south of the equator is the home of the great Bantu family, except in the extreme southwest of the continent. There a tract of considerable area, though of small populational density, was in the possession of the backward Bushmen and Hottentots, distinctive in their physical types as well as their languages.

Between the equator and latitude 10° N., in the belt known as the Sudan, there is much greater speech diversity than elsewhere in Africa. The languages of the Sudan fall into several families, perhaps into a fairly large number. Opinion conflicts or is unsettled as to their classification. They are, at least in the main, non-Hamitic and non-Bantu; but this negative fact does not preclude their having had either a single or a dozen origins. It has usually been easier to throw them all into a vague group designated as non-Hamitic and non-Bantu than to compare them in detail.

In Oceania conditions are similar to those of Africa, in that there are a few great, widely branching stocks and one rather small area, New Guinea, of astounding speech diversity. Indeed, superficially this variety is the outstanding

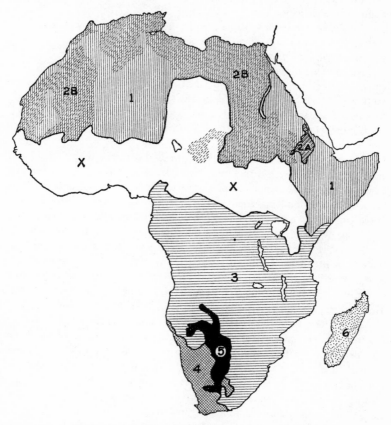

FIG. 15.   LINGUISTIC FAMILIES OF AFRICA

1, Hamitic. 2, Semitic (A, old; B, Arabic, intrusive in former Hamitic territory since Mohammed). 3, Bantu. 4, Hottentot. 5, Bushman, perhaps related to last. 6, Malayo Polynesian. X, The Sudan, not consistently classified.

linguistic feature of New Guinea. The hundreds of Papuan dialects of the island look as if they might require twenty or more families to accommodate them. However, it is inconceivable that so small a population should time and again have evolved totally new forms of speech. It is much more likely that something in the mode of life or the habits of mind of the Papuans has favored the breaking-up of their speech into local dialects and an unusually rapid modification of these into markedly differentiated languages. What the circumstances were that favored this tendency to segregation and change can be only conjectured. At any rate, New Guinea ranks with the Sudan, western North America, and the Amazonian region of South America as one of the areas of greatest linguistic multiplicity.

All the remainder of Oceania is either Australian or Malayo-Polynesian in speech. The Australian idioms have been imperfectly recorded. They were numerous and locally varied, but may derive from a single mother tongue.

All the East Indies, including part of the Malay Peninsula, and all of the island world of the Pacific—Polynesia, Micronesia, and Melanesia, always excepting interior New Guinea—are the habitat of the closely knit Malayo-Polynesian or Austronesian family, whose unity was early recognized by philologists. From Madagascar to Easter Island this speech stretches more than halfway around our planet.

North and South America, according to the usual reckoning, contain more native families of speech than all the remainder of the world. The conventional conservative classification allots forty or more families each to North and South America. These families varied greatly in size at the time of discovery, some being confined to a few hundred souls, whereas others stretched through tribe after tribe over enormous areas. Their distribution is so irregular and their areas so disproportionate as to be impossible of vivid representation except on a large-scale map in colors. The most important in extent of territory, number of speakers, or the cultural importance of the nations adhering to them, in North America are: Eskimo, Athabascan, Algonkin, Iroquoian, Muskogean, Siouan,[2] Uto-Aztecan, Maya; and in South America: Chibcha, Quechua, Aymara, Araucanian, Arawak, Carib, Tupi, Gê. It will be seen on the maps (Figs. 16 and 17) that these sixteen groups held much the greater part of the area of the double continent, the remaining smaller areas being crowded with perhaps four times as many stocks. Obviously, as in New Guinea, such a multiplicity cannot well have been original; in fact, recent studies are tending to consolidate the New World families into fewer and fewer groups. But the evidence for such reductions is necessarily difficult to find and much of it is still incomplete. The large stocks named above have been long determined and are universally accepted.

---

[2] Iroquoian, Siouan, Muskogean (nos. 4, 5, 6 of map 16) are often united with Hokan, Caddoan, and others into a Hokan-Siouan "superfamily"—something like Ural-Altaic—which seems a probable historical unit in origin, but remains unproved as such.

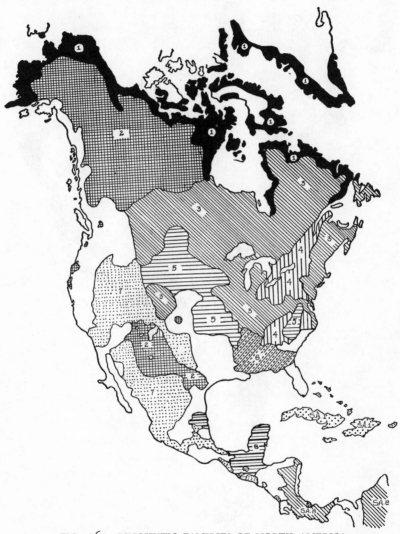

FIG. 16.   LINGUISTIC FAMILIES OF NORTH AMERICA

1, Eskimo. 2, Athabascan. 3, Algonkin. 4, Iroquoian. 5, Siouan. 6, Muskogean. 7, Uto-Aztecan. 8, Mayan. SA1, Arawak = No. 1 and SA8, Chibcha = No. 8 of South American map (Fig. 17). The white areas are occupied by a greater number of smaller families, according to the usual classification.

FIG. 17. LINGUISTIC FAMILIES OF SOUTH AMERICA

1, Arawak. 2, Carib. 3, Gê. 4, Tupi. 5, Araucanian. 6, Aymará. 7, Quechua (Inca).
8, Chibcha. 9, Tucano. 10, Pano. 11, Diaguita. 12, Guaycurú. 13, Puelche. 14, Tehuelche.
Smaller families in unnumbered areas. Nos. 1 and 2 extend into the West Indies, No. 8
into Central America. (After Chamberlain and Jiménez Moreno)

About a third of humanity today speaks some form of Indo-European. Nearly a quarter talks some dialect of Sinitic stock. Semitic, Dravidian, Ural-Altaic, Japanese, Malayo-Polynesian, Bantu have each from about 50 to 100 million speakers. The languages included in these eight families form the speech of approximately 90 per cent of living human beings.

97. CLASSIFICATION OF LANGUAGES BY TYPES

A customary nongenetic classification groups languages or families according to their structure into four main types: inflective, agglutinating, isolating, and polysynthetic or incorporating. These classes are not logically co-ordinate.

An inflecting or fusional language expresses relations or grammatical form by adding prefixes or suffixes that cannot stand alone, or if they stood alone would mean nothing, and which therefore can be considered as fused into the word; or it expresses relations by internal modification of the stem. The *-ing* of *killing* is such an inflection; so are the vowel changes and the ending *-en* in the conjugation *write, wrote, written.*

An isolating language expresses relations by separate words or isolated particles. Words are always unexpanded, unaltered stems or radicals. English *heart of man* is isolating, where *man's heart* and Latin *cor homin-is* are inflective.

An agglutinative language "glues together" into solid words, or juxtaposes, elements for which a definite, exclusive, regular meaning of their own can be traced or felt. English does not use this mechanism for purposes that are ordinarily reckoned as strictly grammatical, but does employ it for the related purpose of derivation. *Under-take, rest-less, fore-go, moon-like,* are examples; *quick-ly,* for *quick-like,* is a border-line case.

Polysynthetic languages are agglutinative ones carried to a high pitch, or those which can unite words into equivalents of fair-sized sentences. *Steam-boat-propeller-blade* might be called a polysynthetic form if we spoke or wrote it in one word as modern German might. Incorporating languages are generally included in polysynthetic ones: they embody the object noun, or the pronoun representing it, into the word that contains the verb stem. This construction is totally foreign to English.[3]

Each of these classes evidently defines one or more distinctive linguistic processes. The mechanisms at work are different. But no one language operates wholly with one process. The instances given show that English employs most of them. Obviously, therefore, it would be arbitrary to classify English as being outright of one type. This is also the situation for most other languages. There

---

[3] Noun incorporation seems mostly to form compounds of nouns with verbs, or verbs with verbs, to form verbs: "to rabbit-kill," "to run-kill," and so on. This construction happens to be so alien to the genius of Indo-European that it has been singled out as notable. Pronominal incorporation is discussed below, in § 108.

are in fact dozens and dozens of mechanisms by which languages operate, and the combinations of these in particular languages are indefinitely numerous. To force these many different actual structures into four classes may be convenient, but is logically roughshod.

There are other difficulties. English, for instance, was mainly inflecting fifteen hundred years ago, but today more largely uses isolating processes. We still say *John's house,* but we use *heart of man* perhaps more often than *man's heart;* and *house's top* would strike a listener as so odd that he might think he had misheard. *Camest thou?* for *Did you come?* would still be intelligible as poetry, but in conversation it would be construed as a stilted attempt at a joke. Which pigeonhole, inflecting or isolating, does modern English go into? And how valid are compartments when languages can wriggle themselves like this from one into another compartment in a fairly short span of their history?

Any classification into types is basically logical; whereas a genetic classification that reflects development and relationship must be empirical. And the only genetic classification yet devised for languages is based on the kind of comparisons described, and yields speech families—certain, probable, or possible families, according as the data are more or less full, exact, and carefully analyzed.

Also, the type classification started with the idea that Latin, Sanskrit, and Hebrew were both inflecting and superior in kind. Chinese, whose literature is also ancient, made the isolating class respectable; but the other types were considered inferior. These implications of better and worse have tended to remain attached to the classification; and it is obvious that such judgments have no place in scientific analysis or description.[4]

98. PERMANENCE OF LANGUAGE AND RACE

It is sometimes thought that because a new speech is readily learned, especially in youth, language is a relatively unstable factor in human history, less permanent than race. It is necessary to guard against two fallacies in this connection. The first is to argue from individuals to societies; the second, to believe that because change is possible, it normally takes place.

As a matter of fact, languages often preserve their existence, and even their territory, with surprising tenacity in the face of conquest, new religions and culture, and the economic disadvantages of unintelligibility. Today, Breton, a Keltic dialect, maintains itself in France as the everyday language of the people in the isolated province of Brittany—a sort of philological fossil. It has withstood the influence of two thousand years of contact with Latin, with Saxon and

---

[4] Sapir has proposed a structural type classification into Pure-relational and Mixed-relational languages, each subdivided into Deriving or Complex and Nonderiving or Simple, and then qualified by the concepts here discussed. But the scheme seems never to have been applied in actual description; perhaps because the scale from concrete to relational values on which the classification is based is sliding, and not easily defined objectively.

Frankish German, with French. Its Welsh sister tongue flourishes in spite of the Anglo-Saxon speech of the remainder of Great Britain. Ancient Egypt was conquered by the Hyksos, the Assyrian, the Persian, the Macedonian, and the Roman, but whatever the official speech of the ruling class, the people continued to speak Egyptian. Finally, the Arab came and brought with him a new religion, which favored use of the Arabic language. After four thousand years, Egypt at last became Arabic-speaking; but until a century or two ago the Coptic language, the daughter of the ancient Egyptian tongue of five thousand years ago, was kept alive by the native Christians along the Nile, and even today it survives in ritual. The boundary between French on the one side and German, Dutch, and Flemish on the other has been accurately known for over six hundred years. With all the wars and conquests back and forth across the speech line, endless political changes and cultural influences, this line has scarcely shifted anywhere more than a few dozen miles, and in places has not moved the distance of a comfortable afternoon's stroll.

While populations can learn and unlearn languages, they tend to do so with reluctance and infinite slowness, especially while they remain in their inherited territories. Speech tends to be one of the most persistent populational characters; and "ethnic" boundaries are most often speech boundaries.

In general, where two populations mingle, the speech of the more numerous most often prevails, even if it be that of the subject nationality. A wide gap in culture may overcome the influence of the majority; yet the speech of even a culturally more active and advanced population ordinarily wrests permanent territory to itself only slowly, except where there is an actual crowding-out or numerical swamping of the natives. This explains the numerous survivals and "islands" of speech: Keltic, Albanian, Basque, Caucasian, in Europe; Dravidian and Kolarian in India; Nahuatl and Maya and many others in modern Mexico; Quechua in Peru; Aymara in Bolivia; Tupi in Brazil. There are cases to the contrary, like the rapid spread of Latin in most of Gaul after Caesar's conquest, but they seem exceptional.

As to the relative permanence of race and speech, everything depends on the side from which the question is approached. From the point of view of hereditary strains, race must be the more conservative, because it can change rapidly only through admixture with another race, whereas a language may be completely exchanged in a short time. From the point of view of history, however, which regards human actions within given territories, speech is often more stable. Wars or trade or migration may bring one racial element after another into an area until the type has become altered or diluted, and yet the original language, or one directly descended from it, remains. The introduction of the Negro from Africa to America illustrates this distinction. From the point of view of biology, the Negro has at least partially preserved his type, although he has taken on a wholly new language. As a matter of history, the reverse is true: pure English continues to be the speech of the southern United States, whereas the population now consists of two races instead of one, and the Negro element has been altered by the infusion of white blood. It is a fallacy to think that because an individual can learn French or become a Christian and yet is powerless to change his eye color or head shape, therefore the language or the culture of large populations is necessarily less stable than race. Speech and culture have an existence and a continuity of their own, whose integrity does not depend on hereditary integrity. The two may move together or separately.

99. THE BIOLOGICAL AND HISTORICAL NATURES OF LANGUAGE

It is a truism, but one important never to forget in the study of man, that the faculty of speech is innate, but that every language is wholly acquired. Moreover, the environment of which languages are the product is not a natural one—that is, geographic or climatic—but social. All words and speech forms that are learned—and they constitute almost the complete mass of language—are imitated directly from other human beings. Those new forms which from time to time come into use rest on existing speech material, and are shaped according to tendencies already operative although perhaps more or less hidden. The new or changed forms cannot generally be attributed, as regards origin, to particular individuals; in short, they present a history similar to that of inventions and new institutions. Language thus is a superorganic product, which fact of course does not contradict—indeed implies—that it rests on an organic basis.

The "speech" of the animals other than man has something in common with human languages. It consists of sounds produced by the body, accompanied by certain mental activities or conditions, and capable of arousing certain definite responses in other individuals of the species (§ 20). It differs from human speech in several fundamental particulars. First of all, the cries and calls and murmurs of the brutes appear to be wholly instinctive. A fowl raised alone in an incubator will peep and crow or cluck as it will scratch and peck. A dog reared by a foster cat will bark, or growl, or whine, or yelp when he has attained the requisite age and on application of the proper stimulus, as he will wag or crouch or hunt or dig, and no differently from the dog brought up in association with other dogs. By contrast, the Japanese infant turned over to American foster parents never utters or knows a single Japanese word, learns only English, and learns that as well as do his Caucasian stepbrothers. Evidently, then, animal speech is to all intents wholly organic and not at all "social" in the sense of being superorganic. If this summary is not absolutely exact, it departs from the truth only infinitesimally.

Further, animal speech has no "meaning," does not serve as a vehicle of "communication." The opposite is often assumed popularly, because we anthropomorphize. If it is said that a dog's growl "means" anger, and that his bark "communicates" suspicion or excitement to his fellows, the words are used in a sense different from their significance when we say that the term *red* "means" the color at one end of the spectrum, or that a message of departure "communicates" information. The animal sounds convey knowledge only of subjective states. They "impart" the fact that the utterer feels anger, excitement, fear, pain, contentment, or some other affect. These are immediate reflex responses to a feeling. They may be "understood" in the sense that a sympathetic feeling is evoked, or at any rate mobilized; and thereby they may lead or tend to lead to action by the hearers. In the same way, any man instinctively "understands" the moan of a fellow human being. But the moan does not tell whether the pain is of a second's or a week's duration, caused by a blow or by gas in the bowel, by an ulcerated tooth or by mental anguish. There is no communication of anything objective, of facts or ideas as distinct from feelings, as when we say *red* or *break* or *up* or *water*. Not one of these simple concepts can be communicated as such by any brute speech.

One consequence is the "arbitrariness" of human speech. Why should the sound cluster *red* denote that particular color rather than green? Why does the same word often designate quite distinct ideas in different languages—the approximate sound combination *lay* meaning "milk" in French; *lass* "a girl" in English, "tired" in French, "allow" in German? Such facts are physiologically arbitrary; just as it is physiologically arbitrary and organically meaningless that Americans live in a republic and Britons under a monarchy, or that they drive respectively to the right and the left on the road. Phenomena like these have other cultural or superorganic phenomena as their immediate antecedents and preconditions. In the light of these antecedents, viewed on the level of history, they are intelligible: we know why the United States is a republic, we can trace the development of words like *lay* and *lass*. It is only from the biological plane that such facts seem nonsignificant or arbitrary.

100. PROBLEMS OF THE RELATION OF LANGUAGE AND CULTURE

This association of language and civilization—or better, let us say the linguistic and nonlinguistic constituents of culture—brings up the problem whether it would be possible for one to exist without the other. Actually, of course, no such case is known. Speculatively, different conclusions might be reached. It is difficult to imagine any generalized thinking taking place without words or symbols derived from words. Religious beliefs and certain phases of social organization also seem dependent on speech: caste ranking, marriage regulations, kinship recognition, law, and the like. On the other hand, it is conceivable that a considerable series of simple inventions might be made, and the applied arts might be developed in a fair measure by imitation, even among a speechless people. Finally there seems no reason why certain elements of culture, such as music, should not flourish as successfully in a society without as with language.

For the converse, a cultureless species of animal might conceivably develop and use a form of true speech. Such communications as "The river is rising," "Bite it off," "What do you find inside?" would be within the range of thought of such a species. But the significant fact in this connection is that no non-human animal possesses even traces of such power of communication. Why? Possibly because such a language would lack survival value for the species, in the absence of accompanying culture.

On the whole, however, it would seem that language and culture rest, in a way that is not yet fully understood, on the same set of faculties, and that these, for some reason that is still more obscure, developed in the ancestors of man while remaining in abeyance in other species. Even the anthropoid apes seem virtually devoid of the impulse to communicate, as we have seen earlier (§ 29), in spite of freely expressing their affective states of mind by voice, facial gesture, and bodily movement. The most responsive to man of all species, the dog, learns to accept a considerable stock of culture in the sense of fitting himself to it: he develops conscience and manners, for example. Yet, however highly bred, he does not hand on his accomplishments to his progeny, who again depend on their human masters for what they acquire. A group of the best-reared dogs left to themselves for a few years would lose all their politeness and revert to the predomestic habits of their species. In short, the culture impulse is lacking in the dog except so far as it is instilled by man and kept instilled by him; and in most animals it can notoriously be instilled only to a very limited degree. In the same way, the impulse toward communication can be said to be wanting. A dog may understand a hundred words of command and express in his behavior fifty shades of emotion; only rarely does he even seem to try to communicate information of objective fact. Very likely we are only attributing to him in these rare cases the impulse we should feel in the same situation. In the event of a member of the family being injured or lost, it is certain that a good dog expresses his agitation, uneasiness, disturbed attachment; but it is much less certain that he *intends* to summon help, as we spontaneously incline to believe because such summoning would be our own reaction to the situation.

The history and the causes of the development in incipient man of the group of traits that may be called the faculties for speech and civilization remain one of the darkest areas in the field of knowledge. It is plain that these faculties lie essentially in the sphere of personality, and therefore of the body. Yet men and the apes are far more similar in their general physiques than they are in the degree of their ability to use their physiques for superphysiological purposes. Or, if the antithesis of physical and mental seems unfortunate, it might be said that the growth of the faculties for speech and culture is connected more with special developments of the central nervous system than with those of the remainder of the body.

101. PERIOD OF THE ORIGIN OF LANGUAGE

Is, then, human language as old as culture? It is difficult to be positive, because words perish like beliefs and institutions, whereas stone tools may endure as direct evidence. On the whole, however, it would appear that the first rudiments of what deserves to be called language are about as ancient as the first culture manifestations, mainly because of the theoretically close association of the two. The skull interiors of fossil men, which conform fairly closely to the brain surface, have been construed by some authorities as indicating that the speech areas of the cortex were sufficiently developed, even in forms as old as Sinanthropus, to suggest that these races talked.

Such findings may be accepted as highly tentative. What is more to the point, however, is that anthropologists are in general agreement that language grew up in correlation with culture, if indeed it was not its necessary antecedent. Cultural activity, even of the simplest kind, inevitably rests on ideas or generalizations; and such or any ideas, in turn, human minds seem to be able to formulate and operate with and transmit only through speech. Nature consists of an endless array of particular phenomena. To combine these particulars into a generalization or an abstraction, such as passing from potential awareness of the thousands of stones along a river bed into the idea of stone as a distinctive material—this synthesis appears to require the production of some kind of a symbol, perhaps as a sort of psychological catalyzing agent or point of crystallization: a symbol such as the sounds that make up the word *stone*. In short, culture can probably function only on the basis of abstractions, and these in turn seem to be possible only through speech, or through a secondary substitute for spoken language such as writing, numeration, mathematical and chemical notation, and the like. Culture, then, began when speech was present; and from then on, the enrichment of either meant the further development of the other.

This view is hardly demonstrable; but it seems pretty much to represent the belief of such anthropologists as have grappled with the problem.

102. SPEECH, CULTURE, AND NATIONALITY

This assumption as to the rise of culture raises the question whether one ought to speak of language and culture or rather of language as a part of culture. So far as the process of their transmission is concerned, and the type of mechanism of their development, it is clear that language and culture are one. For practical purposes it is generally convenient to keep them distinct. There is no doubt that two peoples can share in what is substantially the same culture and yet speak fundamentally different idioms and therefore feel themselves to be separate nationalities; for instance, the Finno-Ugric Magyars or Hungarians among the adjacent Slavs, Germans, and Latins of central Europe, who are all

Indo-Europeans. British and Americans speak the same standard language; they are closely related, in fact derived, in culture; and yet their geographical separation has been followed by enough divergence of institutions and habits to have led to political separation, which in turn induces both populations to feel themselves as distinct nationalities. In fact, nationality is essentially a feeling of distinctness or unity, of sense of demarcation between in-group and out-group. Thus the concept "nationality" is fundamentally subjective, whereas both languages and cultures are objectively alike or unlike, unitary or distinct.

It is therefore logically inadmissible and risky in practice to infer from nationality to language or culture, or vice versa. It is unsound much as it is unsound to assume an identity of race, language, and culture for a given area, or to argue from the prevalence of one to the other (§ 80).

Nevertheless, speech and culture do tend to form something of a unit as opposed to race. It is possible for a population to substitute a wholly new language and type of civilization for the old ones, as the American Negro has done, and yet to remain relatively unmodified racially, or at least to carry on its former physical type unchanged in a large proportion of its members. On the other hand, a decisive change of speech without some change of culture seems impossible. Certainly wherever Sumerian, Greek, Latin, Spanish, English, Arabic, Sanskrit, Pali, and Chinese have penetrated as carriers of a religion, literacy, or an associated culture, there have also been established new forms of civilization (§ 169). In a lower degree, the same principle probably holds true of every gain of one language at the expense of another, even when the spreading idiom is not associated with a great or an active culture.

The linkage of speech and culture is further perceptible in the degree to which they both tend to contribute, ultimately, to the formation of the idea of nationality; and this in turn may contribute to a desire for a politically independent state or nation. What chiefly marks off the French from the Italians, the Dutch from the Germans, the Swedes from the Norwegians—their respective customs and ideals, or the language gap, or their political autonomy? It would be difficult to say. The cultural differences tend to crystallize around language differences, and then in turn are reinforced by language, so that the two factors interact complexly.

It is also important to recognize that nationality and nation are not necessarily the same, although they sometimes coincide. Usually we think of a nation as the population of a wholly autonomous and supreme political unit—what Europeans used to call "the state." Politically, state and nation are one: [5] as when

[5] While a political nation or body politic means a state in its most general and ordinary sense, a special historical accident of our manner of growth has brought it about that in the United States of America we call "national" whatever pertains to the total people and government, and by "state" designate constituted parts thereof. This is an anomaly in Western civilization. In our American term "Department of State," the word still has its original sense of referring to the whole body politic.

we speak of the United Nations. But an essentially single nationality can comprise several states that in modern political terminology are called nations: such as Australians, New Zealanders, Canadians, and British. Or again a century ago Germans formed as definite a nationality as they do now, with distinctive speech, customs, temperament, and ideals, but were broken up into some thirty self-governing units or wholly independent states or, technically in the political sense, nations. On the contrary, most large states, and especially empires, have comprised a variety of nationalities. Thus the mediaeval Holy Roman Empire included French, Dutch, Czechs, Slovenes, and Italians as well as Germans; and the original Roman Empire, particularly in the times of its greatness and peace, included still more nationalities, who became equal before its law in spite of their diversity. The reason for this variability of usage is the ambiguity of the word "nation." Its dictionary definition is double. First, nation denotes a people organized under one government, a "body politic." Second, a nation is a people of common origin, tradition, and language. Now the latter is just what a nationality is, by universal consent; and it would be fine if everyone would always use the word "nationality" when that was the meaning, and if "nation" on the contrary were restricted to denoting politically organized peoples.

Here are some contemporary cases of political nations that include two or more nationalities. Belgium is almost equally divided between Walloons speaking a French dialect in their homes and Flemings speaking a variant of Dutch. Switzerland is 72 per cent German-speaking, 21 per cent French, 6 per cent Italian, 1 per cent Romansh. Canada is one-third French, in origin and in speech. The Union of South Africa has a white population that is part English-speaking and part Afrikaans- or Dutch-speaking, plus the racially distinct Bantu Negro natives. India in 1947 set up housekeeping on its own, as two independent political nations, with dozens of nationalities and languages. Similarly in the Philippines there are seven major and many minor tongues. In the U.S.S.R. there are 78 per cent Russians (Great, White, and Ukrainian), plus forty-six other recognized nationalities. Some of these nationalities, such as Georgians, Armenians, Uzbeks, Kazaks, Moldavians, and Lithuanians, as well as the three Russian groups, have union republics of their own. Formally, therefore, these constitute politically autonomous nations as well as centers of nationality, and three of them have been so recognized in the United Nations organization; whereas the United States is reckoned as a single political nation, with its "states" mere subsidiary divisions.

It is evident from these examples what diverse things "nation" and "nationality" can and do mean. It is certainly clearest always to use the term "nationality" when the reference is ethnic, and to add the epithet "political" to "nation," or to substitute "government," when that is the sense, unless the context leaves no doubt as to meaning. Also it is clear that of the several objective factors which operate to produce nationalities, language is on the whole much the most important. Without the free intercommunication that common speech provides, it is very difficult for the "consciousness of kind" that is the subjective or psychological precondition of nationality to arise. Cultural conditions can either reinforce or thwart the effects of linguistic segregations, or be neutral. Thus the French of Quebec are further set apart by their Catholicism in Protestant Canada. In Switzerland, the Germans of some cantons are Catholics, of others Lutheran Protestants; the French are mainly Calvinist Protestants; the Italians, Catholics. There is a general understanding among the Swiss citizenry that neither religion nor linguistic consideration is to serve as a basis for political crystallization. In India, on the contrary, religious cleavage has proved a strong obstacle to political unity in the formative period. Language diversity was felt to be much less of a bar, perhaps because of the wide availability of English speech on upper educational levels. Should political intransigeance drive out English, the diversity of nationalities kept separate by speech might become a greater threat to the political cohesiveness of India.

All in all, anthropology is more immediately concerned with nationalities than with nations, with ethnic than with political groupings. And in nationalities and ethnic units, language is always a factor, and often the basic one.

103. RELATIVE WORTH OF LANGUAGES

One respect in which languages differ from cultures is that they cannot, like the latter, be rated as higher and lower. Of course, even as regards culture, such rating is often a dubious procedure, meaning little more than that the person making the comparison assumes his own culture to be the highest and estimates other cultures low in proportion as they vary. Although this is a subjective and uncritical procedure, nevertheless certain objective comparisons are possible. Some cultures surpass others in their quantitative content: they possess more different arts, abilities, and items of knowledge. Also, some culture traits may be considered intrinsically superior to others: metal tools against stone ones, for instance, since metal is adopted by all stone-culture peoples who can secure it, whereas the reverse is not true. Further, in most cases a new addition does not wholly obliterate an older element, this retaining a subsidiary place, or perhaps serving some more special function than before. In this way some cultures become richer and more differentiated. The old art may even attain a higher degree of perfection than it had previously, as the finest polish was given to stone implements in northern Europe after bronze was known. In general, accretion is the process typical of culture growth. Older elements come to function in a more limited sphere as new ones are added, but are not extirpated by them. Oars and sails remain as constituent parts of the stock of civilization after it has added steamboats and motorboats. In the senses, then, that a culture has a larger content of elements, that these elements are more differentiated, and that a greater proportion of these elements are of the kind that inherently tend to supersede related elements, the culture may be considered superior.

As regards languages, there are also quantitative differences. Some contain several times as many words as others. But vocabulary is largely a cultural matter. A people that uses more materials, manufactures more objects, possesses knowledge of a larger array of facts, and makes finer discriminations in thought, must inevitably have more words. Yet even notable increases in size of speech content appear not to be accompanied by appreciable changes in form. A larger vocabulary does not mean a different type of structure. Grammar seems to be little influenced by culture status. No clear correspondence has yet been traced between type or degree of civilization and structural type of language. Neither the presence nor the absence of particular features of tense, number, case, reduplication, or the like seems ever to have been of demonstrable advantage toward the attainment of higher culture. The speech of the earlier and the modern nations most active in the propagation of culture has been of quite diverse types. The languages of the Egyptians (Hamitic); Sumerians; Babylonians and Arabs (Semitic); Hindus and Greeks (ancient Indo-European); Anglo-Saxons (modern Indo-European); Chinese; and Mayas are about as different as any that exist. The Sumerian type of civilization was taken over bodily and successfully by the Semitic Babylonians. The bulk of Japanese culture is Chinese; yet Japanese speech is built on wholly different principles.

Then, it is impossible to rate one speech trait or type as inherently or objectively superior to another on any basis like that which justifies the placing of a metal culture above a stone culture. If wealth of grammatical apparatus is a criterion of superiority, Latin is a higher language than French, and Anglo-Saxon than English. But if lack of declensions and conjugations is a virtue, then Chinese surpasses English almost as much as English surpasses Latin. There is no reason favoring one of these possible judgments rather than its opposite. *Amabo* is no better or worse than *I shall or will love* as a means of expressing the same idea. The one is more compact, the other more plastic. There are times when compactness is a virtue, occasions when plasticity has advantages. By the Latin or synthetic standard, the English expression is loose-jointed, lacking in structure; by the English or analytic standard, the Latin form is overcondensed, adhering unnecessarily to form. One cannot similarly balance the merits of a steel and a flint knife, of a medical and a shamanistic phase of society. The one does really cut or cure better than does the other.

So, from the point of view of civilization, language does not matter. Language will always keep up with whatever pace culture sets it. If a new object is invented or a new distinction of thought made, a word is coined or imported or modified in meaning to express the new concept. If a thousand or ten thousand new words are required, they get developed. When it desires to express abstractions like futurity or plurality, any language is capable of doing so, even if it does not habitually express them. If a language is unprovided with formal means for the purpose, such as a grammatical suffix, it falls back on content and uses a word or a circumlocution. If the life of a people changes and comes to be conducted along lines that render it frequently important to express an idea like futurity to which previously little attention has been paid, the appropriate circumlocution soon becomes standardized, conveniently brief, and unambiguous, like *will* in *He will come*. In general, every language is capable of indefinite modification and expansion and thereby is enabled to meet cultural demands almost at once. This is shown by the fact that virtually anything spoken or written can be translated into almost every other language without serious impairment of substance. The aesthetic charm of the original may be lost in the translation; the new forms coined in the receiving language are likely at first to seem awkward; but the meaning, the business of speech, gets expressed.

104. SIZE OF VOCABULARY

The tendency is so instinctive in us to presuppose and therefore to find qualities of inferiority, poverty, or incompleteness in the speech of populations of more backward culture than our own, that a widespread, though unfounded, belief has grown up that the languages of savages and barbarians are extremely limited quantitatively—in the range of their vocabulary. Similar misconceptions are current as to the number of words actually used by single individuals of civilized communities. It is true that no one, not even the most learned and prolific writer, uses all the words of the English language as they are found in an unabridged dictionary. All of us understand many words that we habitually encounter in reading and may even hear frequently spoken, but of which our utterance faculties for some reason have not made us master. In short, a language, being the property and the product of a community, possesses more words than can ever be used by a single individual, the sum total of whose ideas is necessarily less than that of his group. Added to this are a certain mental sluggishness, which restricts most of us to a greater or less degree, and the force of habit. Having spoken a certain word a number of times, our brain becomes accustomed to it and we are likely to employ it to the exclusion of its synonyms or in place of words of related but distinguishable meaning.

The degree to which all this affects the speech of the normal man has, however, been greatly exaggerated. Because there are, all told, including technical terms, some hundred thousands of words in our dictionaries, and because Shakespeare in his writings is said to have used 24,000 different words, Milton in his poems 17,000, and the English Bible contains 7200, it has been concluded that the average man, whose range of thought and power of expression are so much less, must use an enormously smaller vocabulary. It has been stated that many a peasant goes through life without using more than 300 or 400 words, that the vocabulary of Italian grand opera is about 600, and that he is a person above the average who employs more than 3000 to 4000 words. If such were the case it would be natural that uncivilized men, whose life is simpler, and whose knowledge is more confined, should be content with an exceedingly small vocabulary.

But it is certain that the figures just cited are erroneous. If anyone who considers himself an average person will take the trouble to make a list of his speaking vocabulary, he will quickly discover that he knows, and on occasion uses, the names of at least 1000 to 2000 different things. That is, his vocabulary contains so many concrete nouns. To these must be added the abstract nouns, the verbs, adjectives, pronouns, and the other parts of speech, the short and familiar words that are indispensable to communication in any language. It may thus be safely estimated that it is an exceptionally ignorant and stupid person in a civilized country who has not at his command a vocabulary of several thousand words.

Test counts based on dictionaries show, for people of bookish tastes, a knowledge of about 30,000 to 35,000 words. Most of these would perhaps never be spoken by the individuals tested, would not be at their actual command, but it seems that at least 10,000 would be so controlled. The carefully counted vocabulary of a five-and-a-half-year-old American boy comprised 1528 understandingly used words, besides participles and other inflected forms. Two boys between two and three used 642 and 677 different words.

It is therefore likely that statements as to the paucity of the speech of unlettered peoples are equally exaggerated. He who professes to declare on the strength of his observation that a native language consists of only a few hundred terms displays chiefly his ignorance. He has either not taken the trouble to exhaust the vocabulary or has not known how to do so. It is true that the traveler or the settler can usually converse with natives to the satisfaction of his own needs with a few hundred words. Even the missionary can do a great deal with this stock, if it is properly chosen. But it does not follow that because a civilized person has not learned more of a language, there is no more. On this point the testimony of the student is the evidence to be considered.

Dictionaries compiled by missionaries or philologists of languages previously unwritten run to surprising figures. Thus, the number of words recorded in Klamath, the speech of a culturally rude American Indian tribe, is 7000; in Navaho, 11,000; in Zulu, 17,000; in Dakota, 19,000; in Maya, 20,000; in Nahuatl, 27,000. It may safely be estimated that every existing language, no matter how backward its speakers are in their general civilization, possesses a vocabulary of at least 5000 to 10,000 words.[6]

105. QUALITY OF SPEECH SOUNDS

Another mistaken assumption which is frequently made is that the speech of nonliterary peoples is harsh, its pronunciation more difficult than ours. This belief is purely subjective. When one has heard and uttered a language all one's

---

[6] Jespersen, who allows 20,000 words to Shakespeare and 8000 'to Milton, cites 26,000 as the vocabulary of Swedish peasants.

life, its sounds come to one's mouth with a minimum of effort; but unfamiliar vowels and consonants are formed awkwardly and inaccurately. No adult reared in an Anglo-Saxon community finds *th* difficult. Nor does a French or a German child, whose speech habits are still plastic, find long difficulty in mastering the particular tongue control necessary to the production of the *th* sound. But the adult Frenchman or German, whose muscular habits have settled in other lines, tries and tries and falls back on *s* or *t*. A Castilian, however, would agree with the Anglo-Saxon as to the ease and "naturalness" of *th*. Conversely, the "rough" *ch* flows spontaneously out of the mouth of a German or a Scotchman, whereas English, French, and Italians have to struggle long to master it, and are tempted to substitute *k̞*. German *ö* and French *u* trouble us; our "short" *u* is equally resistant to Continental tongues.

Even a novel position can make a familiar sound strange and forbidding. Most Anglo-Saxons fail on the first try to say *ngis;* many give up and declare it beyond their capacity to learn. Yet it is only *sing* pronounced backward. English uses *ng* finally and medially in words, not initially. Any English speaker can quickly acquire its use in the new position if, to keep from being disconcerted, he followings some such sequence as *sing, singing, stinging, ringing, inging, nging, ngis*.

So with surd *l*—Welsh *ll*—which is ordinary *l* minus the accompaniment of vocal-cord vibrations. A little practice makes possible the throwing on or off of these vibrations, the "voicing" and "unvoicing" of speech, for any sound, with as much ease as one would turn a faucet on or off. Surd *l* thereupon flows with the same readiness as sonant *l*. As a matter of fact we often pronounce it unconsciously at the end of words like *little*. When it comes at the beginning, however, as in the tribal name usually written *Tlingit*, Americans tend to substitute something more habitual, such as *kl*, which is familiar from *clip, clean, clear, close, clam*, and many other words. The simple surd *l* has even been repeatedly described quite inappropriately as a "click," which is about as far from picturing it with correctness as calling it a thump or a sigh; all because its "unvoicing" comes in an unaccustomed position.

Combinations of sounds, especially of consonants, are indeed of variable difficulty for anatomical reasons. Some, like *nd* and *ts* and *pf*, have their components telescope or join naturally through being formed in the same part of the mouth. Others, like *k̞w* (*qu*), have the two elements articulated widely apart, but for that reason the elements can easily be formed simultaneously. Still others, like *k̞t* and *ths,* are intrinsically difficult, because the elements differ in place of production but are alike in method, and therefore come under the operation of the generic rule that similar sounds require more effort to join and yet discriminate than dissimilar ones, for much the same reason that it is on the whole easier to acquire the pronunciation of a wholly new type of sound than of one that differs subtly from one already known. Yet in these matters too, habit rather than anatomical functioning determines the reaction. German *pf* comes hard to adult Anglo-Saxons, English *kw* and *ths* to Germans. So far as degree of accumulation of consonants is concerned, English is one of the extremest of all languages. Monosyllables like *tract, stripped (stripd), sixths (siksths)*, must seem irremediably hard to most speakers of other idioms.

Children's speech in all languages shows that certain sounds are, as a rule, learned earlier than others, and are therefore presumably somewhat easier physiologically. Sounds like *p* and *t,* which are formed with the mobile lips and the front of the tongue, normally precede back-tongue sounds like *k*. *B, d, g,* which are voiced like vowels, tend to precede voiceless *p, t, k*. Stops or momentary sounds, such as *b, d, g, p, t, k,* generally come earlier than the fricative continuants *f, v, th, s, z,* which require a delicate adjustment of lip or tongue—close proximity without firm contact—whereas the stops involve only making and breaking a jerky contact. But so slight are the differences of effort or skill in all these cases that as a rule only a few months separate the learning of the easier from that of the more difficult sounds; and adults no longer feel the differences.

106. RAPIDITY OF LINGUISTIC CHANGE

The rate of change in language remains a somewhat obscure subject. The opinion often held that unwritten languages necessarily alter faster than written ones, or that those of savages are less stable than the tongues of civilized men, is mainly a naïve reflection of our sense of superiority. It contravenes the principles just referred to and is not supported by evidence. Occasional stories that a primitive tribe after a generation or two was found speaking an almost made-over language are unconscious fabrications due to preconception and supported by hasty acquaintance, faulty records, misunderstanding, or perhaps change of inhabitants. Nahuatl, the language of the Aztecs, has probably changed less in four hundred years than Spanish; Quechua, that of the Incas, no more. English has apparently altered more than any of the three in the same period. Dozens of native tongues, some of them from wholly rude peoples, were written down in the sixteenth and seventeenth centuries by Spanish and other priests, and in most instances the grammars and dictionaries are usable today.

Cultural alteration would appear to work toward speech change chiefly in the following way: New things need new names; new acts mean new thoughts and new ideas require new words. These may be imported; or they may be made out of elements already in the language; or old words may undergo a shift of meaning. In any event, the change is mainly on the side of vocabulary. The sounds of a language are generally much less affected, its plan of structure least of all. The introduction of a new religion or the development of a new form of government among a people need not be accompanied by changes in the grammar of their speech, and usually are not, as abundant historical examples prove.

While the causes of grammatical innovation are far from clear, contact with alien tongues is certainly a factor in some degree. An isolated offshoot of a linguistic group is generally more specialized, and therefore presumably more altered, than the main body of dialects of the family. The reason is that the latter, maintaining abundant reciprocal contact, tend to steady one another, or if they swerve, to do so in the same direction. The speakers of the branch that is geographically detached, however, come to know quite different grammars so far as they learn languages other than their native one, and such knowledge seems to act as an unconscious stimulus toward the growth of new forms and uses. It is not that grammatical concepts are often imitated outright or grammatical elements borrowed. Acquaintance with a language of different type seems rather to act as a ferment that sets new processes going.

It is in the nature of the case that direct specific evidence of changes of this character is hard to secure. But comparison of related languages or dialects with reference to their location frequently shows that the dialects which are geographically situated among strange languages are the most differentiated. This holds of Amharic in the Semitic family, of Singhalese in the Indic branch of Indo-European, of Hopi in Shoshonean, of Arapaho in Algonkin, of Huastec in Mayan.

But it is also likely that languages differ among each other in their susceptibility to change, and that the same language differs in successive periods of its history. It is rather to be anticipated that a language may be in a phase now of rapid and then of retarded metabolism, so to speak; that at one stage its tendency may be toward breaking-down and absorption, at another toward a more rigid setting of its forms. Similarly, there is reason to believe that languages of certain types of structure are inherently more plastic than others. At any rate, actual differences in rate of change are known. The Indo-European languages, for instance, have perhaps without exception altered more in the three thousand years of historical record than the Semitic ones. And so in native America, while contemporary documentary record is of course wanting, the degree of differentiation within the two stocks suggests strongly that Athabascan is more tenaciously conservative than Siouan.

There are also notable differences in the readiness to borrow words ready-made. English is distinctly more hospitable in this regard than German, which tends rather to express a new concept by a new formation of old elements. Certain South American languages appear to have borrowed more words from one another than have any of those of North America. In this matter the type of language is probably of some influence, yet on the whole cultural factors perhaps predominate. The direction and degree of cultural absorption seem to determine the absorption of words to a considerable measure. Here writing is certainly potent. The Latin and French elements in English, the Sanskrit and Arabic elements in the Malaysian languages, were brought in to a large extent by writing, and were fixed by being written. They would probably have remained smaller if the historical contacts had been wholly oral. This is perhaps an important way in which writing exerts influence on the development of spoken language, an influence that in other respects is often overestimated.

107. SPEAKING AND WRITING

Learning our mother tongue is a largely unconscious process which goes on until control has become automatic. The process or act of acquisition is imitative, and it fades quickly from our memories. Learning to read and write, on the contrary, is at least started by teaching, comes later in life, and is a conscious process. Writing of course is a secondary symbol system serving as a surrogate for the primary symbol system of spoken language; it has certain special purposes such as distant or anonymous communication, permanent record, and the like. By one method or another, and more or less accurately, the visible symbols stand for the audible ones. Their reconversion into audible symbols, or into actually silent but potentially audible ones, is what we call reading. This writing-reading process comes so much later than speech-learning in the life histories of each of us—as well as in the history of the species—that it remains much less automatic and much more in our awareness. Consequently we tend often to think and express ourselves in terms of writing-reading when we mean speaking. The common term "word" is ambiguous: it denotes both an element of audible utterance that we feel as having a certain isolable identity, and an element of writing or printing to which we give a formal identity by spacing it apart from others. But a "letter" is merely a visible silent sign for an audible sound. It belongs to a writing system, as sounds belong to a speech system. To say therefore that such and such a language lacks the letter *f* is undiscriminating nonsense, especially if the language is an unwritten one. Such a language does lack the *sound* which in writing English we *represent* by the character *f*. It is not so long ago that even writers of grammars made this confusion. Some educated and intelligent people who have never given much thought to linguistics still make it. If we are not on intellectual guard, this prevalent nondiscrimination tends to color all our thinking on linguistic matters. Popularly, we "speak" English spontaneously, but "language" is something foreign we are taught after we can read and write. Most language instructors still misplace the emphasis on writing and reading of, for example, French, instead of on hearing and pronouncing it and remembering it kinaesthetically with ear and tongue.

That the basic component always is the actually spoken or "living" speech is shown by the fact that spoken languages change in essentially the same way and at about the same rate, apparently, whether they are also written or unwritten. Speech alters; writing may or may not conform for a while. If the writing, through blind habit persistence or prestige of the past, refuses to change, the actual speech may alter and alter until it has become really a new and distinct language before an adjustment is made.

After Caesar's conquest, the Gauls of France rapidly gave up their Keltic speech and learned Latin instead. This was not the highbrow Latin that Cicero wrote and perhaps actually spoke in his orations, but the "vulgar Latin" which legionaries and nonliterary people spoke in their daily life. With the centuries this Latin progressively changed. In part it altered provincially, with the growth of Gallic peculiarities; in part, through the development of new features common to all late local Latins, in Italy and Spain as well as in France, such as the well-attested growth of articles alongside the shrinkage of inflections (§ 108). Also, with the centuries sliding into the Dark Ages, fewer and fewer people learned to write; but those who did spelled words as they used to be spelled in literary Latin, not as rewritten to conform to the contemporary pronunciation. Gradually the spoken language changed so much that it, and the Latin used to represent it in writing, had only very partial similarity. People probably still thought that they were dealing with only one language when they were really already speaking French but still writing Latin. Then suddenly the two pulled apart with a jerk. In the Strasbourg Oaths of the grandsons of Charlemagne in 842, we have the actual spoken French of the time written as French—very Old French, to be sure, but indubitable French, and no longer spelled at all as the Latin originals of the words were spelled. The document marks the birth of the French daughter of the Latin mother—as a written language. But for spoken French, who can set a birthday? It had been changing continuously through the nine hundred years since Caesar. This typical continuity of change is what characterizes spoken languages as being natural, spontaneous, underlying growths, in contrast with their superimposed and more "artificial" writing systems, which quickly tend to crystallize. The difficulty with any *spoken* language is to keep it the same; with its *written* expression, it is to keep it plastic. The writing will set and finally break in a sort of revolution, but it has great difficulty in conforming and adapting. Written languages that have survived for millennia, like Latin and Sanskrit, are dead as spoken languages.[7]

This relation results in revivals of dead or dying languages, such as the attempted revival of Gaelic and Hebrew (§ 181), which seem somewhat uncertain as regards successful outcome, though of extraordinary theoretical interest. These present revivals are highly original and conscious experiments, if sentimental ones, being made in the laboratory of history. Whatever the final results, they will illuminate our understanding of the nature of language, by establishing new principles or confirming old ones.

It would be going too far to say that writing is unable to react on speech and to influence it. For instance, we have taken from French the word *niche,*

[7] Classical Arabic is a thousand years younger than Latin and Sanskrit, but the relation to it of its living provincial dialects is beginning to approach the relation of French and Spanish to Latin around 800.

and pronounce it either "neesh" if we follow the original sound or "nich" if we follow spelling. Those who know French, and that the word is French, are likely to say the former; those who do not, the latter. That dictionaries "allow" us choice in such cases means only that there is not yet a decisive majority of quantity or quality lined up on either side. More recent but probably more often used in English is the French *chic,* which those who know French, or who associate with those that have heard how the magic word is pronounced in France, pronounce as "shick" (or "sheek," if very ultra), while the unilinguals, who perhaps learned the word from reading clothing advertisements in the newspapers, say "chick." Here the issue is between the socially more and less advantaged; between prestige and numbers. *Silo* comes to us from Spanish, where of course it is spoken "seelo," just as our pronunciation of it would be "sailo" in Mexican or Spanish. Interlanguage transfers are perhaps the most common cause of changes of this type. The written form of a word penetrates farther, is learned first by the majority, and its pronunciation is then adapted to the spelling as if this were native. The slightly varying pronunciations current for the names Illinois, Chicago, St. Louis, Des Moines, reflect greater or smaller degrees of attempted adhesion to the original French pronunciation, though they all deviate from it.

These examples suggest minutiae, or special points. And that is what on the whole the influence of writing on speech is: a very partial reaction. This we might expect from the fact that speech comes first, is spontaneous and automatic, and has less of the conventional about it, less of the arbitrarily agreed upon (§ 204), than writing.

The strength and independence of writing are at their maximum where the system is primarily ideographic by word units—"logographic"—and is phonetic only in supplementary degree. Chinese is the important living example. Here writing is essentially a self-sufficient code rather than a script of spoken and heard sounds. In consequence, North and South Chinese will read off the same passage of writing with so much dialect difference of utterance as to be mutually unintelligible. In fact, an old-fashioned Chinese scholar wants to read his classic poetry by himself. If he listens to it read aloud, even by a fellow scholar, he is disturbed by the possible ambiguities in the many homonyms. This is because in the historical development of the Chinese language many words that were once spoken differently are now spoken alike, so that there remain far fewer distinct sound words than there are distinct word characters. The apparatus of the written language has remained rich, though the spoken language has shrunk.

Still more different are the pronunciations of Chinese [8] taken over along with the system of written characters centuries ago by Koreans, Japanese, and Annamese. These were somewhat mispronounced by the foreign learners to

[8] Called Sino-Japanese. Sino-Annamese, etc.

begin with, and are more so now. In fact, wholly different-sounding words of pure Japanese origin, often polysyllabic, can be spoken for some of the written characters, which also have their imported imitation-Chinese "pronunciation." This is as if we used both the English word *five* and the French word *cinq* as alternative-choice words expressing the number and visible symbol 5.

All this development in the Sinitic sphere is obviously an illustration of the degree to which writing *can* become autonomous of spoken language—rather than being an example of its normal reflex action on speech. Indeed, as has been said, the actual pronunciations of all the East Asiatic languages have altered through the centuries while the script system maintained its crystallized identity or even grew. For that matter, it would be theoretically possible to divorce the Chinese writing from Chinese speech, marry it to a new set of English words, and have it function with reasonable adequacy. Or, going still farther, it could be successfully used, with certain extensions, as the ready-made core of an international or universal code "translatable" into any spoken language.

108. DIFFUSION AND PARALLELISM IN LANGUAGE AND CULTURE

A phenomenon that language shows more conspicuously than culture, or which is more readily demonstrated in it, is parallel or convergent development, the repeated, independent growth of a trait (§ 223).

Thus sex gender is an old part of Indo-European structure. In English, by the way, it has wholly disappeared, so far as formal expression goes, from noun, adjective, and demonstrative and interrogative pronoun. It lingers only in the personal pronoun of the third person singular—*he, she, it*. A grammar of living English that was genuinely practical and unbound by tradition would never mention gender except in discussing these three little words. That our grammars specify *man* as a masculine and *woman* as a feminine noun is due merely to the fact that in Latin the corresponding words *vir* and *femina* possess endings that are recognized as generally masculine and feminine, and that an adjective associated with ends respectively in masculine *-us* and feminine *-a*. These are distinctions of form for which English possesses no equivalents. The survival of distinction between *he, she,* and *it,* while *this* and *that* and *which* have become alike irrespective of the sex of the person or thing they denote, is therefore historically significant. It points back to the past and to surviving Indo-European languages.

Besides, Indo-European, Semitic and Hamitic also express sex by grammatical forms, although like French and Spanish and Italian, they know only two genders, the neuter being unrepresented. These three are the only large language stocks in which sex gender finds expression. Ural-Altaic, Chinese, Japanese, Dravidian, Malayo-Polynesian, Bantu, and in general the language families of Asia, Africa, and the Americas do without, although a number of languages make other "gender" classifications, as of animate and inanimate, personal and impersonal, superior and inferior, intelligent and unintelligent. Sex gender however reappears in Hottentot of South Africa and in the Chinook and Coast Salish and Pomo languages of the Pacific coast of North America.

How is this distribution to be accounted for? Indo-European, Semitic, and Hamitic occupy contiguous territory, in fact surround the Mediterranean over a tract largely coextensive with the Caucasian area. Could they in the remote past have influenced one another? That is, could grammatical sex gender have been invented, so to speak, by one of them, and borrowed by the others, as we know that cultural inventions are constantly diffused? Not many philologists would grant this to be likely: there are relatively few authenticated cases of formal elements or concepts having been disseminated between unrelated languages (though see § 109). Is it then possible that our three stocks are at bottom related and one? Sex gender in that case would be part of their common inheritance. For Semitic and Hamitic, a number of specialists have accepted a common origin on other grounds. But for Semitic and Indo-European, many linguists remain dubious: positive evidence is still scant. Nevertheless, the territorial continuity of the three speech groups possessing the trait is difficult to accept as mere coincidence. In a parallel case in the realm of culture history a common source would be accepted as probable. Even Hottentot has been considered a remote Semitic-Hamitic offshoot, largely, it is true, because of the very fact that it expresses gender. Linguists, accordingly, may consider the case still open; but it is at least conceivable that the phenomenon goes back to a single origin in these four Old World stocks.

Yet no stretch will account for sex gender in the three native American languages as due to contact influence or diffusion, nor relate these tongues to the Old World ones. Clearly, here is a case of independent origin or parallel "invention." Chinook and Coast Salish, indeed, are in contiguity, and one may therefore have taken up the trait in imitation of the other. But Pomo lies well to the south and its affiliations run still farther south. Here sex gender is obviously an independent, secondary, and presumably rather recent growth in the grammar. The application of the category in Pomo is limited as narrowly as possible: to human beings; whereas in Chinook, as in older Indo-European, all nouns are given a gender, usually "artificial."

In short, it remains doubtful whether sex gender originated three or four or five or six times among these seven language stocks; but it evidently did originate repeatedly.

Other traits crop out the world over in much the same manner. A dual number, for instance, is found in Indo-European, Malayo-Polynesian, Eskimo, and several American languages. The distinction between inclusive and exclusive *we*—between *you-and-I* and *he-and-I*—is made in Malayo-Polynesian, Hottentot, Iroquois, Uto-Aztecan.

A true nominative case-ending, such as Latin and other early varieties of Indo-European evince, is an exceedingly specialized and rare formation; yet is found in the Maidu language of California. Articles, in regard to which Indo-European varies, Latin for instance being without while its Romance daughter tongues have developed them, recur in Semitic, in Polynesian, and in several groups of American languages, such as Siouan and Hokan. The growth in Romance is significant because of its historicity. That is, French developed its articles independently and secondarily, a fact which makes it probable that many languages in other parts of the world, whose history we do not know, also developed theirs instead of inheriting them—"invented" them, in short, although unconsciously.

A trait found in a considerable proportion of the American languages is the so-called incorporation of the object pronoun (§ 97). The objective pronoun, or an element representing it, is prefixed or suffixed to the verb, is made a part of it. The process is familiar enough to us from Indo-European so far as the subject is concerned: in the Latin *ama-s, ama-t, ama-nt*, the suffixes express "you, he, they," and independent pronouns comparable to the English ones are usually omitted. The *-s* in *he love-s* is the sole survival of this same process in modern English. None of the older Indo-European tongues however showed an inclination to affix similar elements to the verb for its object, although there are some approaches in a few recent languages of the family: Spanish *diga-me*, "tell me," and *mata-le*, "kill him," for instance; or French *je le vois*, "I see him," pronounced as one word, "zhlvwa." Semitic, on the other hand, and Basque, do "incorporate" objective elements, whereas most Asiatic and some American languages do not. Many other instances of parallel or convergent traits could be cited.

That frequency of parallel developments is greater in language than in culture is perhaps in part due to easier demonstrability in the field of speech. But in the main the high frequency seems real. Two reasons for the higher frequency of parallel developments in language suggest themselves.

First, the number of possibilities is small in language, so far as form or structure is concerned. The categories or concepts used for classifying and for the indication of relations are limited, and so are the means of expression. The distinctions expressed by gender, for instance, may refer to sex, animateness, personality, worth, shape, position, or possibly two or three other qualities; but there they end. If a language recognizes gender at all, it must have gender of one of these few types. Consequently there is some probability of several unconnected languages sooner or later happening upon the same type of gender. Similarly for the kinds of number (singular, dual, trial, plural, collective, distributive), or of case, or of person expressed. And these categories, such as gender and number and case, are themselves not numerous. Then too, the means of expressing the categories are limited. Of such mechanisms there are: position or relative order of words; compounding of them; accretions of elements to stems—namely, prefixes, infixes, and suffixes; reduplication, the repetition of part or the whole of words; internal changes by shift of vowel or accent within words; and therewith the types of grammatical means are about exhausted. Again the number of possible choices is so small that accidental probability must cause some languages to hit upon the same devices.

A second reason for the greater frequency of parallelism or independent reinvention in language is that structural traits—that is, grammars—appear to resist diffusion by imitation to a considerable degree. Words are borrowed, sometimes freely, almost always to some degree, between contiguous languages; sounds considerably less so; grammar least of all. That is, linguistic content lends itself to diffusion readily, linguistic pattern with more difficulty.

At bottom, it is true, the same holds of culture in some degree. Specific elements of culture, or groups of such elements, diffuse very widely at times and may be said to be always tending to diffuse: the wheel, for instance, smelting of metals, the crown as a symbol of royalty, battleships, Buddhism. The relations of elements among themselves, on the other hand, tend to change by internal growth rather than by external imitation. Of this sort are the relations of the classes and members of societies, the fervor with which religion is felt, the esteem accorded to learning or wealth or tradition, the inclination toward this or that avenue of subsistence or economic development. By conquest or peaceful pressure or penetration one people may shatter the political structure or social fabric of another, may undermine its conservatism, may swerve its economic habits. But it is more difficult to find cases of one people voluntarily adopting such tendencies or schemes of cultural organization in mere imitation of the example of another than of its adopting specific culture content—the wheel or the crown or Buddhism—from outside. The result is that culture relations or patterns develop spontaneously or from within probably more frequently than as a result of direct taking-over. Also, the types of culture forms being limited in number, the same type is frequently evolved independently. Thus monarchical and democratic societies, feudal or caste-divided ones, priest-ridden and relatively irreligious ones, expansive and mercantile or self-sufficient and agricultural nations, evolve over and over again. On the whole, therefore, actual comparative culture history more often deals with the specific contents of civilization. In part, also, this is true because events like the spread of an invention can usually be traced more exactly than the complex evolutions of, say, two feudal systems can be compared. The result, at any rate, is that specific diffusions seem to outnumber precise and sure parallels in culture, as is set forth in several of the chapters that follow (Twelve to Fourteen).

In general linguistics, on the contrary, interest inclines to the side of pattern rather than content; hence it is the parallelisms or convergences, the independent similarities, that stand out conspicuously. If as much attention were generally given to words and their meanings as to grammar, and if they could be traced in their prehistoric or unrecorded wanderings as reliably as many culture traits have been, it is probable that diffusion would loom larger than it now does as a principle shaping human speech. There are words that have traveled almost as far as the objects they denote: *tobacco* and *maize,* for example. And the absorption of words of Latin origin into English was as extensive as the absorption for over a thousand years of Latin, Christian, and Mediterranean culture by the English people—in fact, went on as its accompaniment and result.

109. CONVERGENT LANGUAGES

Parallel development in speech is not restricted to special traits like sex gender and object incorporation. It may affect whole languages in their types. Chinese a long time ago became an extremely analytical or "isolating" language. That is, it lost all affixes and internal change. Each word element or item became an unalterable unit. Sentences are built up by putting together these atoms. Grammatical relations are expressed by the order of words: the subject precedes the predicate, for instance. Other ideas that in many languages are treated formally, such as the plural or person, are expressed by content elements; that is, by other words: *many* for the plural, separate pronouns instead of affixes for person, and so on. The now uniformly monosyllabic stems of Chinese accentuate this isolating character, which however does not depend intrinsically upon monosyllabism. In the Indo-European family, as already mentioned, for over two thousand years there has been a drift toward something of the Chinese type of structure. This drift toward loss of formal mechanisms and toward the expression of grammar by material elements, or by their position only, has been evident in all branches of Indo-European, but has been most marked in English. The chief remnants of the older inflectional processes in spoken English today are four verb endings, *-s, -ed, -ing, -en;* three noun endings, the possessive *-'s* and the plurals *-s* and *-en,* the latter rare; the case ending *-m* in *whom, them;* a few vowel changes for plurals, as in *man—men, goose—geese;* and perhaps two hundred vowel changes in verbs, such as *sing, sang, sung.* Compared with Latin, Sanskrit, or even primitive Germanic, this brief list represents a survival of possibly a tenth of the original synthetic inflectional apparatus. That is, English has gone approximately nine-tenths of the way toward attaining a grammar of the Chinese type. A third language of independent origin, Polynesian, has traveled about the same distance in the same direction. Superficially it is less like Chinese in that it remains prevailingly polysyllabic, but more like it in having undergone heavy phonetic attrition. This then is a clear case of entire languages converging toward a similar type.

It is further remarkable that this change, from a complex, close-knit, "synthetic" type of structure to a simple, loose-jointed, "analytic" one, occurs throughout Indo-European, though it has been carried somewhat the farthest in English. The same kind of form reduction took place in Latin as it transformed into

French or Spanish; between classical and contemporary Greek; between ancient and modern Persian; between Sanskrit and Hindi: it can be traced in every Indo-European branch language of which our historical record is long enough. Most of these languages have not been in contact with each other for the one to three thousand years that the change has been going on. Change by influence of one on the other, leading to imitation, is therefore excluded. In the first edition of this book, the phenomenon was called "secondary parallelism"; that is, parallelism of change of type in the same direction, persisting subsequent to and during the increasing diversification of the languages in content and specific form. Sapir has made the situation famous by citing it as "linguistic drift," a sort of "slope" or long-range secular trend; but he has not been able to put his finger on a cause. Possibly the change toward looser structure got under way early, in original Indo-European, before this stock had branched out into its daughter languages, and the impulse persisted in the latter in greater or less strength. That would make the process carry on by momentum from the past. Whatever the cause, the breadth of the continuous drift or trend over thousands of miles and thousands of years makes the phenomenon impressive.

Another instance of convergence or superficial secondary assimilation of form in originally wholly separate and diverse languages is found in the remarkable resemblances in plan of structure of Indo-European, especially in its older forms, and the Penutian group of languages in native California. Common to these two families are an apparatus of similar cases, including accusative, genitive, locative, ablative, instrumental, sometimes even a true nominative; plural by suffix; vowel changes in the verb according to tense and mode; a passive and several participles and modal forms expressed by suffixes; and pronouns either separate or expressed by endings fused with the tense-modal suffixes. Thus, the processes that make English *sing, sang, sung, song,* or *bind, bound, band, bond,* are formally similar to those which have produced in Penutian Yokuts such forms as *shokud,* pierce, *shukid-ji,* pierced, *shokod,* perforation or hole, *shikid,* piercer or arrow. In short, many of the traits usually thought to characterize Indo-European as typically inflectional reappear in Penutian; and of course they appear there quite independently as regards their origin and history.

These are linguistic phenomena comparable in kind to the growth of feudalism in China more than a thousand years earlier than in Europe, or the appearance of a great centrally governed empire in Peru similar to the ancient monarchies of the Orient.

We have seen that while words can diffuse freely from one language to another when social pressures are set in that direction, grammars have much greater difficulty in diffusing. Forms and relations as such are not easily taken over by the stranger. Either he keeps his own, or he accepts the whole of the impinging other language, word content along with grammar. There are innumerable cases of one language replacing another in a given society; but there is very little evidence of a population accepting any considerable part of the grammar of another language to embody in their own. That is why we can speak so confidently of linguistic parallels, convergences, and joint drifts. If there were free imitation, borrowing, and diffusion of structural form, the cases we have discussed might just as well be attributable to that process.

Yet to a limited extent, alien influence on structural form can now and then be established, as distinct from word-borrowing. There is a Balkan instance where several Slavic, Albanian, and Latin languages have taken over a series of grammatical and idiomatic traits from Greek, which as the old language of religion and higher civilization long enjoyed a prestige priority. Some of these features due to Greek influence are: articles, which the Slavic and Latin tongues did not originally have; disuse of the infinitive: *give me that I drink* instead of *give me to drink;* genitive case including the dative; suffixion of an unaccented pronoun, like *daughter-mine;* double pronoun on the plan of *me-seems to me;* similar tautology of pronoun and clause, as *she believed him that he was her brother;* substitution of co-ordinate for subordinate conjunction: *hardly I escape and I meet another;* and idioms like *he was of twenty years* (that is, old), and *he saw how fifty* (for about fifty). These Greek idioms and structure features recur in Latin-derived Rumanian and with equal frequency in Slavic Bulgarian; Serbian, which is also Slavic but more distant, has adopted about half of them. Most of the same features have been accepted also in Albanian, but more in the nearer southern dialect than in remoter North Albanian.

Herewith the principle is established that structural form can be taken over by one language from another. However, the dozen formal traits involved here constitute only a minute fraction of the total grammar and idiom of the Balkan languages. The amount or degree of grammatical imitation or diffusion in fluence is therefore small. This limitation seems to hold in other instances also. A general "wave theory" evolved by certain Indo-Europeanists maintains that a trait—even a new sound—which originates in one dialect, language, or group of languages tends to be propagated to other related ones, or at least to be diffusible. In proportion as this wave theory holds true, it tends logically to vitiate the evidence of phonetic law and comparability on which linguists have built their family trees and classifications of relationship during the past century and a half of study. This is because genetic descent is intrinsically a process of diversification, whereas wave influence leads to assimilation. The wave theory must unquestionably be accepted as true to some extent; but the extent is minor. Internal change of related languages away from one another appears to be much the more prevalent process. Assimilation by imitation in waves, convergent resemblances developing independent of relationship, are occasional secondary crosscutting influences. The wave principle has a certain theoretical interest because it establishes to some extent for language a factor or force which as diffusion by imitation is extremely influential in the development of culture.

110. UNCONSCIOUS FACTORS IN LANGUAGE AND CULTURE CHANGE

The unceasing processes of change in language are mainly unconscious or covert, or at least implicit. The results of the change may come to be recognized by speakers of the changing language; the gradual act of change, and especially the causes, mostly happen without the speakers' being aware of them. This principle holds for all departments of language: the sounds, the structural form, even the meaning of words. When a change has begun to creep in, it may be tacitly accepted or it may be observed and consciously resisted on the ground of being incorrect or vulgar or foreign. But the underlying motives of the objectors and the impulses of the innovator are likely to be equally unknown to themselves.

If this view seem extreme, it can easily be shown that the great bulk of any language as it is, apart from any question of change, is employed unconsciously. An illiterate person will use such forms as *child, child's, children, children's* with the same "correctness" as a philologist, yet without being able to give an explanation of the involved grammatical ideas of singularity and plurality, absoluteness and possession, or to lay down rules as to the manner of expression of these ideas in English. Grammar, in short, exists before grammarians, whose legitimate business is to uncover such rules as are already there. It is an obviously hasty thought that because grammar happens to be taught in schools, speech can be grammatical only through schooling. The Sanskrit and Greek and Latin languages had their declensions and conjugations before Hindu and Greek and Roman scholars first analyzed and described them. The languages of primitive peoples frequently abound with complicated forms and mechanisms that are used consistently and are applied without suspicion of their existence. It is much as the blood went round in our bodies quite healthily before Harvey's discovery of its circulation.

The quality of unconsciousness seems to be a trait not specifically limited to linguistic causes and processes, but to hold in principle of culture generally. It is only that the unconsciousness pervades speech farther. A custom, a belief, an art, however deep down its springs, sooner or later rises into social consciousness. It then seems deliberate, planned, willed, and is construed as arising from conscious motives and developing through conscious channels. But many social phenomena can be led back only to nonrational and obscure motives: the wearing of silk hats, for instance. The whole class of changes in dress styles springs from unconscious causes. Sleeves and skirts lengthen or shorten, trousers flare or tighten, and who can say why? It is perhaps possible to trace a new fashion to Paris or London, and to a particular stratum of society there. But what is it that in the winter of a particular year makes every woman—or man—of a certain social group wear, let us say, a high-collared coat, or a shoe that does not come above the ankle, and the next year, or the tenth after, the reverse? It is insufficient to say that this is imitation of a leader of fashion, of a professional creator of style. Why does the group follow him, and think the innovation attractive and correct? A decade earlier the same innovation would have appeared senseless or extravagant to the same group. A decade after, it appeals as belated and ridiculous, and everyone wonders that style was so tasteless so short a time ago.

Evidently the aesthetic emotions evoked by fashions are largely beyond the control of both individuals and groups. It is difficult to say where the creative and imitative impulses of fashion come from—which, inasmuch as the impulses obviously reside somewhere in human minds, means that they spring from the unconscious portions of the mind. Evidently, then, our justification of the dress styles we happen at any time to be following, our pronouncing them artistic or comfortable or sensible or what not, is secondary. A low shoe may be more convenient—or inconvenient—than a high one, a brown one more or less practical than a black or a white one. That that is not the reason which determines the wearing of low brown shoes when they are customarily worn is shown by the fact that at other times high black ones are put on by everyone. The reasons that can be and are given are so changeable and inconsistent that they evidently are not the real reasons, but are the false secondary reasons which are best distinguished as rationalizations. Excuses, we should call them with reference to individual conduct.

What applies to fashion holds also of manners, of morals, and of many religious observances. Why we defer to women by rising in their presence and passing through a door behind them; why we refrain from eating fish with a knife or drinking soup out of a two-handled cup, though drinking it from a single-handled one is legitimate; why we do not marry close kin; why we remove our hats in the presence of the deity or his emblems but would feel it impious to pull off our shoes—all the thousands of prescriptions and taboos of which these are examples possess an unconscious motivation.

Such cases are also illustrations of what is known as the relativity of morals (§ 116). The Jew sets his hat on to worship, the Oriental punctiliously slips out of his shoes. Some people forbid the marriage of the most remote relatives, others encourage that of first cousins, still others permit the union of uncle and niece. It would seem that all sociocultural phenomena which can be brought under this principle of relativity of standard are unconsciously grounded. This in turn implies the unconscious causation of the mores, those products of the social environment in which one is reared and which one accepts as the ultimate authority of conduct. As mores are those folkways or customs to which an emotional coloring has become attached, so that adherence to the custom or departure from it arouses a feeling respectively of approval of disapproval, it is evident that the origin of folkways generally is also unconscious, since there seems no reason why the emotions or the ethical affect enveloping a customary action should incline more than the custom itself to spring up unconsciously.

It has long since been recognized that the average man's convictions on social matters remote from him are not developed through examination of evidence and exercise of reason, but are taken over, by means of what used to be denominated the herd instinct and is now called social suggestion, from the society or period in which he happens to have been born and nurtured. His belief in democracy, in monotheism, in his right to charge profit and his freedom to change residence or occupation, have such origin. In many instances it is easy to render striking proof of the proposition—as in the problems of high tariff, or the Athanasian creed, or vitamin deficiencies, which are so technical as to their evidence or so intricate in their argument as to be impossible of independent solution by the majority of men. Time alone would forbid; we should starve while making the necessary research. And the difference between the average man's attitude on such difficult points and the highly gifted individual's attitude toward them, or even toward simpler problems, would seem to be one of degree only.

Even on the material sides of culture, undesigned motivation plays a part. In the propulsion of ships, oars and sails fluctuate as the prevalent means down almost to the period of steam vessels. It would be impossible to say that one method was logically superior to the other, that it was recognized as such and then rationally adhered to. The history of warfare shows similar changes between throwing and thrusting spears, stabbing and hewing swords, light and heavy armor. The Greeks and the Macedonians in the days of their military superiority lengthened their lances and held them. It no doubt seemed for a time that a definitive superiority had been proved for this type of weapon over the shorter, hurled javelin. Then the Romans, as part of their legionary tactics, reverted to the javelin and broke the Macedonian phalanx with their pilum. By the end of the Roman Empire, the infantry legion had yielded to heavy cavalry as the most effective military arm. After about nine centuries, around 1300, infantry began once more to come into its own, and then to dominate. Armor reached its perfection after gunpowder had begun to come into use; but firearms finally crowded armor out altogether. Yet the last few decades have brought the rebirth of the helmet.

These fashions in tools and practical appliances do not alter as fast as modern dress styles, and some of their causes can often be recognized. Yet as regards consciousness or intent there seems no essential difference between the fluctuation of fashions in weapons—or in navigation or cooking or travel or house-building—and, let us say, the fluctuation of mode between soft and stiff hats or high and low shoes. It may have been the open array of the legion that led to the pilum, ever more rapidly fired bullets that induced the abandonment of the breastplate, shrapnel and the machine gun that caused the reintroduction of the helmet. But these initiating factors were not deliberate as regards the effects that came in their train; and in their turn they themselves were the effects of more remote causes, such as improvements in general metallurgical arts. The whole chain of development in such cases is intricate and branching, unforeseen, mainly unforeseeable. At most there is recognition of what is happening; in general the recognition seems to become full only after the change in tool or weapon or industrial process has become complete and is perhaps already being undermined once more.

Of course purely stylistic alterations—and linguistic innovations—also possess their causes. When the derby hat or the pronoun *thou* becomes obsolete, there is a reason; only, we generally cannot cite a really convincing specific cause.

The common causal element in all these changes may be called a shift in social values, in attitudes, or in the configuration of the total culture; often perhaps a change in some other and remote part of the culture—or language. Perhaps practical chemical experience has grown, and gunpowder explodes more satisfactorily; or an economic readjustment has made it possible to equip more soldiers with guns. The first result is a greater frequency of bullet penetrations in battle; the next, the abandonment of the breastplate as hampering and useless. Increasing wealth or schooling or city residence or class differentiation makes indiscriminate familiarity of manners seem less desirable than at an earlier period: brusque *thou* begins to yield to indirect plural *you*. Or again, new verbs, all of regular conjugation like *love, loved,* are formed in English, or imported from French, until their number outweighs that of the ancient irregular ones like *sing, sang.* A standardizing tendency is thereby set going—"analogizing" is the technical term of the philologist—which begins to turn irregular verbs into regular ones: *shaped* replaces *shopen,* just as *lenger* becomes *longer* and *toon* becomes *toes.* Or, conversely, the analogy of *write-wrote, drive-drove, ride-rode,* causes *dived* to tend to be replaced by "colloquial" *dove.* There is much the same sort of causality in one of these phenomena as in another. The individual or community that leaves off the breastplate or the stiff hat may more likely be aware that it is making the change than the one that leaves off saying *toon* or *thou.* But there does not seem to be an essential difference of process. Linguistic and aesthetic changes may be most fully unconscious, social ones next, material and economic ones perhaps least so. But normally, change or innovation is accompanied by a shift of values that are broader than the single phenomenon in question, and that are held to impulsively far more often than they are deliberately planned. That is why all social creations—institutions, beliefs, codes, styles, grammars—prove on impartial analysis to be full of inconsistencies and irrationalities. They have sprung not from a premeditated system of weighed or reasoned choices but from impulsive desires, from emotionally colored habits, or from "accidents" happening in some other part of the culture.

The foregoing discussion may be summarized as follows. Linguistic phenomena and processes are on the whole less conscious than cultural ones, without however differing in principle. In both language and culture, content is more readily imparted and assimilated than form, and it enters farther into consciousness. Organization or structure in both cases takes place according to unconscious or covert or implicit patterns, such as grammatical categories, social standards, political or economic points of view, religious or intellectual assumptions. These patterns tend to attain recognition only in a last or sophisticated stage of their development, and even then continue to alter further even without the exercise of conscious control. The number of such linguistic and social patterns or forms being limited, there is some tendency for them to repeat in different cultures with a degree of similarity, though without historical connection or without attaining actual identity. Partially similar combinations of such patterns sometimes recur, producing languages or cultures of roughly similar type. But established patterns of form, and still more their combinations, replace each other with difficulty. Their spread therefore takes place mostly though the integral substitution of one language or culture for another, rather than by piecemeal absorption. This is in contrast to the specific content elements of which language and culture consist—individual words, mechanical devices, institutional symbols, particular religious ideas or actions, and the like. These elements absorb and diffuse readily. They are therefore imitated and imported more often than they are reinvented. But, as if in compensation, linguistic and cultural patterns or structures growing up spontaneously may acquire, through the accidents of convergence, considerable resemblance of general form that is not dependent on historical connection or spread.

III. LINGUISTIC AND CULTURAL STANDARDS

It does not follow that because social usages largely fail to spring out of purposive and deliberate reasoning, they are therefore unworthy of being followed, or that standards of conduct need be renounced because they are relative—that is, unconsciously founded and changing. The natural inclination of men being to regard their standards of taste, behavior, and social arrangement as reasonable, perfect, and fixed, there follows a first inclination to regard these standards as devalued as soon as their emotionality and variability have been recognized. Such a negative reaction is disappointing: it is a further result of the illusion. Once the fundamental and automatic assumption of fixity and inherent value of social patterns has been given up, and it is recognized that the chief motive power of behavior in man as in the other animals is affective and unconscious, there is nothing in institutions and codes to quarrel with. They are neither despicable nor glorious; no more deserving, in virtue of their existence, to be uprooted and demolished than to be defended as absolute and eternal. In some form or other, they are inevitable; and the particular form they take at this time or that place is always tolerably well founded, in the sense of being adapted with fair success, or having been but recently well adapted, to the conditions of the natural and social environment of the group which holds the institution, code, or standard.

That this is a sane attitude is sometimes more easily shown in the field of language than of culture. This is because language is primarily a mechanism or means, whereas in culture ends or purposes obtrude more. It is thus easier to view linguistic phenomena dispassionately. Grammars and dictionaries, for instance, are evidently the result of self-consciousness arising about speech which has previously been mainly unconscious. They may be roughly compared to social formulations like law codes or written constitutions or philosophical systems or religious dogmas, which typically begin also as representations of usages or beliefs already in existence. When moralists about language stigmatize expressions like *ain't* or *them cows* or *he don't* as "wrong," they are judging an innovation, or one of several established but conflicting usages, by a standard of correctness that seems to them absolute and permanent, but which is really only the hallmark of a class or a locality to which they choose to give priority. As a matter of actuality, the condemned form may or may not succeed in becoming established. *He don't,* for example, might in time attain to "correctness" —meaning social reputability—although *ain't* is perhaps less likely to become legitimized, and *them cows,* though old, to have still smaller prospect of ultimate general recognition. That a form departs from the canon of today of course no more proves that it will be accepted in future than that it will not. What is certain is that if it wins sufficient usage by the right people, it will also win sanction, and will become part of the standard of its time.

Linguistic instances like these differ little if at all in principle, in their involved psychology, from the finding of the Supreme Court that a certain legislative enactment is unconstitutional and therefore void, or from the decision of a religious sect that Sunday baseball is wicked. The chief point of divergence would seem to be that a court is a constituted body endowed with an authority that is not paralleled on the linguistic side, at any rate in Anglo-Saxon countries; although the Latin nations possess Academies whose dicta on correctness of speech enjoy a moral authority—though a sanctionless one—approximating the verdicts of a high court. And it is notorious that courts and religious denominations, like speech purists, may begin by condemning and yet end by tolerating or even accepting innovations, after actual usage of the times has drifted far enough. Witness the fates of the American income tax, Methodist dancing, and the rule that prepositions are not words to end sentences with!

It is also of interest to remember that the power of nullifying legislation was not specifically granted the Supreme Court by the Constitution of the United States, but that the practice grew up gradually, quite like a speech innovation that becomes established. Certain elements in the American population look upon this power as undesirable and therefore take satisfaction in pointing out its unsanctioned origin. The majority, on the other hand, feel that the situation on the whole works out well, and that a Supreme Court with its present powers is better than the risk of a Supreme Court without power. Still, it remains curiously illogical that the preservation of the Constitution should take place partly through the extraconstitutional functioning of a constitutional body. In principle such a case is similar to that of grammarians who at the same time lay down a "rule" and exceptions to the rule, because the contradictory usages happen to be actually established.

Codes, dogmas, and grammars are thus normally reflections, secondary rather than primary causes. Such influence as they have is mainly in outward crystallization. They produce an appearance of permanence. In the field of speech, it is easy to recognize that it is not grammarians that make languages, but languages that make grammarians. The analogous process evidently holds for culture. Lawgivers, statesmen, religious leaders, discoverers, inventors seem to shape civilization when actually they much more express it. The complex and often obscure forces that shape culture also mold the so-called creative leaders of society as essentially as they mold the mass of humanity. Progress, so far as it exists objectively, can be construed as something that happens rather than as something we make as we set out to make it. Our frequent assumption to the contrary is probably the result of a reluctance to realize our individual near-impotence as regards remodeling the culture we live in, as contrasted with the overpowering molding we receive from it. But how much does any one of us create or shape or alter his language? Culture no doubt is a bit more malleable; but the comparison with speech should make us cautious not to overrate our capacity for initiative.

Undoubtedly we do have social influence as individuals. It is an influence on the fortune and the careers of other individuals, sometimes on larger segments of society, and it is concerned largely with aims of personal security, relative dominance, or affection among ourselves. We also have many choices among the alternatives contained in our culture and in our speech. To some extent we can manipulate certain alternatives and ambiguities of the culture in our personal favor, or in the direction of our ideals. Now and then, perhaps, we succeed in establishing, with the support of others, some altered behavior or idea or idiom, some novel twist of custom or phrase. That seems to describe the range of our exertion of influence on the form or content of those mass products and mass influences which we call civilization and language.

CHAPTER SEVEN

The Nature of Culture

112. WHAT CULTURE IS

WHAT CULTURE is can be better understood from knowledge of what forms it takes and how it works than by a definition. Culture is in this respect like life or matter: it is the total of their varied phenomena that is more significant than a concentrated phrase about them. And again as with life and with matter, it is true that when we are dealing with the actual manifestations we are less often in doubt as to whether a phenomenon is or is not cultural than we are in deciding on what is includable in the concept of culture when we reason abstractly about it. Nevertheless, it will be worth while to consider some definitions briefly.

Tylor says that "culture or civilization is that complex whole which includes knowledge, belief, art, morals, law, customs, and any other capabilities and habits acquired by man as a member of society." Linton equates culture with "social heredity." Lowie calls it "the whole of social tradition." All three statements use the term "social" or "society," but in an attributive or qualifying sense. We can accept this: society and culture, social and cultural, are closely related concepts. There can obviously be no culture without a society—much as there can be no society without individuals. The converse—no society without culture—holds for man: no cultureless human society is known; it would even be hard to imagine. But it does not hold on the subhuman level. As we have seen (§ 6, 20), ants and bees do have genuine societies without culture, as well as without speech. Less integrated and simpler associations are frequent among animals. Even a pair of nesting birds rearing their young constitute a society, though a small and temporary one. Accordingly, so far as man is concerned, culture always has society as a counterpart; it rests on, and is carried by, society. Beyond the range of man there are societies, but no cultures. Cultural phenomena thus characterize man more specifically than his social manifestations characterize him, for these latter he shares with vertebrate and invertebrate animals.

Roughly, then, we can approximate what culture is by saying it is that which the human species has and other social species lack. This would include speech, knowledge, beliefs, customs, arts and technologies, ideals and rules. That, in short, is what we learn from other men, from our elders or the past, plus what we may add to it. That is why Tylor speaks of "capabilities and habits acquired by man," and what Lowie means when he says "the whole of social tradition," or Linton by "social heredity." The last term is unfortunate because heredity now denotes in biology precisely what is received organically or genetically to the exclusion of what is acquired socially or culturally. But if we substitute for "heredity" the more noncommittal near-synonym "inheritance," the phrase then conveys much the same meaning as Lowie's "social tradition."

The terms "social inheritance" or "tradition" put the emphasis on how culture is acquired rather than on what it consists of. Yet a naming of all the kinds of things that we receive by tradition—speech, knowledges, activities, rules, and the rest—runs into quite an enumeration. We have already seen in § 2 that things so diverse as hoeing corn, singing the blues, wearing a shirt, speaking English, and being a Baptist are involved. Perhaps a shorter way of designating the content of culture is the negative way of telling what is excluded from it. Put this way around, culture might be defined as all the activities and non-physiological products of human personalities that are not automatically reflex or instinctive. That in turn means, in biological and psychological parlance, that culture consists of conditioned or learned activities (plus the manufactured results of these); and the idea of learning brings us back again to what is socially transmitted, what is received from tradition, what "is acquired by man as a member of societies." So perhaps *how it comes to be* is really more distinctive of culture than what it *is*. It certainly is more easily expressed specifically.

In one sense culture is both superindividual and superorganic. But it is necessary to know what is meant by these terms so as not to misunderstand their implications. "Superorganic" does not mean nonorganic, or free of organic influence and causation; nor does it mean that culture is an entity independent of organic life in the sense that some theologians might assert that there is a soul which is or can become independent of the living body. "Superorganic" means simply that when we consider culture we are dealing with something that is organic but which must also be viewed as something more than organic if it is to be fully intelligible to us. In the same way when we say that plants and animals are "organic" we do not thereby try to place them outside the laws of matter and energy in general. We only affirm that fully to understand organic beings and how they behave, we have to recognize certain kinds of phenomena or properties—such as the powers of reproduction, assimilation, irritability—as added to those which we encounter in inorganic substances. Just so, there are certain properties of culture—such as transmissibility, high variability, cumulativeness, value standards, influence on individuals—which it is difficult to explain, or to see much significance in, strictly in terms of the organic composition of personalities or individuals. These properties or qualities of culture evidently attach not to the organic individual man as such, but to the actions and the behavior products of societies of men—that is, to culture.

In short, culture is superorganic and superindividual in that, although carried, participated in, and produced by organic individuals, it is acquired; and it is acquired by learning. What is learned is the existent culture. The content of this is transmitted between individuals without becoming a part of their inherent endowment. The mass or body of culture, the institutions and practices and ideas constituting it, have a persistence and can be conceived as going on their slowly changing way "above" or outside the societies that support them. They are "above" them in that a particular culture, a particular set of institutions, can pass to other societies; also in that the culture continuously influences or conditions the members of the underlying society or societies—indeed, largely determines the content of their lives. Further, particular manifestations of cultures find their primary significance in other cultural manifestations, and can be most fully understood in terms of these manifestations; whereas they cannot be specifically explained from the generic organic endowment of the human personality, even though cultural phenomena must always conform to the frame of this endowment.

An illustration may make this superorganic quality more vivid. A religion, say Roman Catholicism or Mohammedanism, is of course a piece of culture, and a typical piece or sample. Obviously Catholicism exists only in so far as there are Catholics; that is, when and where there are human individuals who have acquired the faith. Once established, however, the Catholic hierarchy, beliefs, rituals, habits, and attitudes can also be viewed as going on century after century. Popes, bishops, communicants succeed one another; the church persists. It certainly possesses a continuity and an influence of its own: it affects not only its adherents but the course of history. On a smaller scale, or for shorter periods, the same thing holds for smaller segments of culture—institutions, beliefs, or customs down to short-lived trivialities of fashion and etiquette. On a larger and more general scale, the same holds for the totality of human culture since it first began to develop. Big or little, then, culture affects human action. It is the accident of what culture happens to be in Occidental countries toward the middle of the twentieth century which determines that when I get up in the morning I put on a shirt and pants and not a chlamys or a toga or just a breech-clout. Can we call this contemporary Western culture the cause of my shirt-wearing? In ordinary parlance, we might; the specific custom can certainly not be derived from anything in human hereditary constitution. Dialectically, the cultural causation might be challenged; it depends on logical definitions. But everyone will agree at least that the concrete cultural fact of habitual shirt-wearing is specifically related to or conditioned by other cultural facts, such as antecedent dress styles, manners, laws, or religion.

Again, the English language is a piece of culture. The faculty of speaking and understanding some or any language is organic: it is a faculty of the human species. The sounds of words are of course made by individual men and women, and are understood and reacted to by individuals, not by the species. But the total aggregation of words, forms, grammar, and meanings which constitute the English language are the cumulative and joint product of millions of individuals for many centuries past. No one of us creates or invents for himself the English he speaks. He talks it as it comes to him, ready-made, from his millions of predecessors and from his elders and age mates. English is obviously super-individual in the sense that it is something enormously bigger and more significant than the speech of any individual man, and in that it influences his speaking infinitely more than his speaking can hope to contribute to or influence the English language. And English is superorganic in that its words and meanings are not direct outflows or consequences of men's being human organisms—else all men would spontaneously talk as much alike as they walk alike. Instead, how they talk depends overwhelmingly on how the societies in which they were raised talked before.

A piece of culture such as the English language is therefore a historical phenomenon. This means that its specific features cannot be adequately explained by the organic features of our species—nor of a race—but are most intelligible in the light of the long, complex, and locally varied history of the institution we call English speech. In short, a cultural fact is always a historical fact; and its most immediate understanding, and usually the fullest understanding of it to which we can attain, is a historical one. To a large degree calling culture superorganic or superindividual means that it yields more readily to historical interpretation than to organic or psychosomatic explanations.

A simile that may further help the realization of what culture is and how it works is that of a coral reef. Such a reef may be miles long and inhabited by billions of tiny polyp animals. The firm, solid part of the reef consists of calcium carbonate produced by the secretions of these animals over thousands of years—a product at once cumulative and communal and therefore social. What is alive and organic in the reef is these innumerable little animals on its ocean-fronting surface. Without their ancestors, there would have been no reef. But the reef now exists independently of the living polyps, and would long continue to endure even if every polyp were killed by, say, a change in ocean temperature or salinity. It would still break the surf, would now and then wreck ships, and would bar off quiet water behind. While a coral reef is the accumulated precipitate of dead polyps, it is also a phenomenon affording to millions of living polyps a base and a foothold, and a place to thrive.

This parallel is incomplete. It breaks down in that a reef is actual physical matter, whereas only the artifacts and the manufactures of culture are material or physical, most of culture consisting of ideas and behaviors. Also, a reef determines that and where new polyps are to live, but not how they will live, not the specific way of many possible ways in which they will function, which on the contrary is just what culture does largely determine for men. Yet the simile is valid and suggestive on one point: the minute role played by the individual polyp or human being in proportion, respectively, to the mass of reef or of culture. Each of us undoubtedly contributes something to the slowly but ever changing culture in which we live, as each coral contributes his gram or two of lime to the Great Barrier Reef. In the main, though, it is our culture that directs and outlines the kind of life we can lead. There is left to our individual gifts and temperaments the relative success and happiness we attain in life; and to our own volition, the alternative choices provided by our culture—the choice, perhaps, between being doctor, lawyer, or merchant chief; or whether our next drink shall be water, beer, tea, or milk. Even this last set of choices would not be wholly free to the individual if he were a participant in strict Methodist or Mohammedan culture; and in old China the beer would not be available and the milk considered too nasty to want.

At any rate, the comparison may be of aid toward seeing things in perspective; with a consequence, perhaps, of somewhat deepened personal humility in the face of the larger world and human history.

113. COMPOSITENESS OF CULTURE

One general characteristic of culture is what may be called its openness, its receptivity. The culture of today is always largely received from yesterday: that is what tradition or transmission means; it is a passing or sending along, a "handing-through" from one generation to another. Even in times of the most radical change and innovation there are probably several times as many items of culture being transmitted from the past as there are being newly devised. Historians would be unanimous, for instance, that with all the important changes produced by the great French Revolution, France of 1780 and France of 1820 nevertheless still were far more alike than different. It would take a series of revolutions, or a quite long series of generations, before the changes equaled the persistences. Even French culture of 1520 would almost certainly be rated as more like than unlike that of 1820. We might have to go back to A.D. 820, or even to A.D. 220, before the alterations could safely be estimated as surpassing the transmissions. This does not mean merely that mankind is generally hidebound and unimaginative, and that its cultures are therefore inclined to be persistent. It means also, put in terms of process or dynamics, that on the whole the passive or receptive faculties of culture tend to be considerably stronger than its active or innovating faculties. This is something that seems to be pretty deeply ingrained in the nature of culture because it is deeply ingrained in the nature of man, something without which it would lose its continuity, and therewith its stability. And most participants in most cultures—most human beings, in short—seem to want a pretty high degree of social stability on account of the security and repose it gives them. A culture that was so unstable and novelty-mongering that it could continually reverse its religion, government, social classification, property, food habits, manners, and ethics, or could basically alter them within each lifetime—such a culture can be imagined. But it would scarcely seem attractive to live under, to most men and women; and it would presumably not survive very long in comparison or competition with more stable cultures, through lacking the necessary continuity. If what was on today were mostly off tomorrow, there would be little chance for institutions or sets of habit to be carried on long enough to develop to their most successful fruition. There would be conflicting ideas, ideals, and aims, in place of the at least partly coherent ideology which characterizes most actual cultures; and along with them, confusion, indecision, and a constant starting all over again. In short, we can see that it is profitable for cultures to carry a considerable degree of ballast in the shape of consistency and continuity, and that those which have fallen markedly short in these qualities have soon disintegrated and perished; quite likely that is why they are so inconspicuous in history. But to maintain a real continuity, a culture must put a genuine value on what each generation hands on to its children; it must, in short, be receptive to its own past, or at least largely acquiescent to it.

Now allied to this receptivity of its own past is a receptivity that every culture shows toward cultural material worked out by other cultures. Such acceptance of foreign elements and systems of course constitutes a geographical spread; and the designation most in use for it is "diffusion" (§ 171). Such spreads occasionally are rapid, but often they require a considerable time interval. Accordingly, much of what is acquired by diffusion from outside also has its origin in the past, much as what a culture receives by internal handing-on of traditions; but the characteristic of diffusion, the emphasis of the process, is on transmission in *space*. The amount of diffusion which is constantly going on between cultures that have contacts is impressive, and the amount of cultural material or content of foreign origin which gradually accumulates within any one culture may fairly be said to be normally greater than what is originated within it. Also, an integrating process, discussed again in § 122 and 171, brings it about that as soon as a culture has accepted a new item, it tends to lose interest in the foreignness of origin of this item, as against the fact that the item is now functioning within the culture. One might say that once acceptance is made, the source is played down and forgotten as soon as possible. So it comes about that a large proportion of every culture was not spontaneously developed by it, but was introduced from outside and fitted into it, after which the people of the culture were no longer much concerned about the fact of introduction. Probably the greater part of every culture has percolated into it.

We do not think of our American civilization as something that is particularly discordant or ill-assembled. Yet we speak an Anglo-Saxon form of a Germanic language that contains more original Latin than English words. Our religion is Palestinian, with its specific formulations into denominations made chiefly in Rome, Germany, England, Scotland, and Holland. Our Bible is translated partly from Hebrew, partly from Greek. We drink coffee first grown in Ethiopia and adopted in Arabia, tea discovered in China, beer first brewed in ancient Mesopotamia or Egypt, hard liquor invented in mediaeval Europe. Our bread, beef, and other meats are from plants and animals first domesticated in Asia; our potatoes, corn, tomatoes, and beans were first used by the American Indians; likewise tobacco. We write an Etruscan-Roman variant of a Greek form of an alphabet invented in or near Phoenicia by a Semitic people on the basis of nonalphabetic writing in still more ancient cultures; its first printing took place in Germany, on paper devised in China. It is needless to extend the catalogue. We no longer feel these things of foreign origin as being foreign; they have become an integral part of our culture. It is only when we pause for scientific analysis, for historical retrospect, that we become aware of their alien or remote source. They *are* a part of our culture, and are used as such.

This is not because modern American civilization is particularly polyglot, but because so far as we can tell such a condition is typical of all cultures. If ancient Egypt, Sumer, India, or China seems less flooded with import and more original, it is only because historical record fails, and we get no more than occasional indications of the alien and still more ancient sources of their culture content.

This is not to say that there are no resistances, strains, and dislocations when particular culture import takes place. They may or may not occur; they frequently do. We shall consider some of these resistances later (§ 172, 176). But in spite of them, in the long pull, absorptions and assimilations continue to take place. How far such assimilation is also an integration, or how far it may be simply a collocation of things that are treated as if they were functionally fitted together even though they are not—this is a complicating problem whose consideration we must also defer. But it is a fair question: Why is cultural receptivity so high, and the amount of diffusion and absorption so great?

There are several reasons. A steel knife or ax just is physically more effective than a stone one; a motortruck more so than a freight wagon. In other words, in the sphere of practical, mechanical things, there are objective superiorities, and the invention of a superior artifact in one culture anywhere tends to start the process of its adoption by other cultures as soon as they learn about it. Then, whatever comes from a society that is stronger, wealthier, cleverer, or has greater prestige comes with a favorable recommendation. Missionization may accentuate this process; and there often is conscious missionization for products and brands, for political and social ideas, as well as for religions. Finally, man is an animal who has a great faculty for getting bored, and many things are taken up just because they are new and different. Some of these will be dropped again for the same reason; but others will stick. There probably are still other factors at work; but those mentioned may suffice to make it reasonable that there should be so much cultural receptivity, diffusion, assimilation, and compositeness.

114. ORGANIC DIVERSITY, CULTURAL HYBRIDITY

It is a striking fact that on the organic level there is nothing parallel to this cultural assimilativeness. Animals and plants absorb and assimilate their food—note the identity of the words, but with the metaphorical connotation quite different—but they do so by breaking it down. It is no longer grass or seed or flesh; it has become muscle or blood or bone in a new organism. But Christianity and the Roman alphabet are still Christianity and the alphabet after our culture, or that of our ancestors or successors, has taken them in, has "absorbed" them. The counterpart of course is that no part of Christianity is destroyed or made over into something radically different on being taken into a new culture, as food is in the body. There simply is more Christianity in the world than there was before, instead of less. This is one way in which culture may be said to work cumulatively, in comparison with organisms.

Another comparison, or rather contrast, with the organic may be made. A cow and a bison can, with some difficulty, be crossed or hybridized, so that an intermediate form results. This is because they are both of the family *Bovidae;* that is, sprung from common ancestors from whom they have not yet diverged very far. A horse and a donkey will hybridize, but the offspring is sterile. It seems impossible to produce a self-perpetuating species of mules. If the divergence is a little greater, there will not even be offspring. Cows and horses simply cannot be amalgamated. In other words, the organic process, while it allows enormous persistences, is also, so far as its general or longer course is concerned, both diversifying and irretraceable. Once the genetic diversification or "evolution" has gone beyond a certain quite narrow degree, there is no more possibility of reversal and assimilation.

By contrast, cultures can blend to almost any degree and not only thrive but perpetuate themselves. Classic Greek civilization was a mixture of primitive Greek, Minoan, Egyptian, and Asiatic elements. Of the Asiatic elements, the alphabet, the zodiac, and the system of weights (§ 191, 208, 229) are only a few examples. Japanese civilization is partly autochthonous, whence its god-descended Emperor and Shinto ritual; partly Chinese, such as its writing and philosophy; Indian in its prevalent Buddhism; Western in its factories, export trade, telephones, and movies. It is needless to pile up examples: as has already been said, the greater part of the content of every culture is probably of foreign origin, although assimilated into a whole that works more or less coherently and is felt as a unit. However diversified or specialized a culture grows in its development, it can therefore always largely retrace its course; and it does normally do so, by absorbing more generalized content from other cultures, and thereby assimilating not only to them but to the totality or the average of human cultures. Cultures are always tending to equate themselves by imparting their characteristics to one another, even while another set of impulses pushes each of them toward particularistic peculiarity.

It is as if, let us say, a rabbit could graft into itself the ruminant digestive system of a sheep, the breathing gills of a fish, the claws and teeth of a cat, some of the tentacles of an octopus, and an assortment of other odd organs from elsewhere in the animal kingdom; and then not only survive, but perpetuate its new type and flourish. Organically, this is of course sheer nonsense; but in culture, it is a near-enough figure of what happens.

A result of this difference is that the course of organic evolution can be portrayed properly as a tree of life, as Darwin has called it, with trunk, limbs, branches, and twigs. The course of development of human culture in history cannot be so described, even metaphorically. There is a constant branching-out, but the branches also grow together again, wholly or partially, all the time. Culture diverges, but it syncretizes and anastomoses too. Life really does nothing but diverge: its occasional convergences are superficial resemblances, not a joining or a reabsorption. A branch on the tree of life may approach another branch;

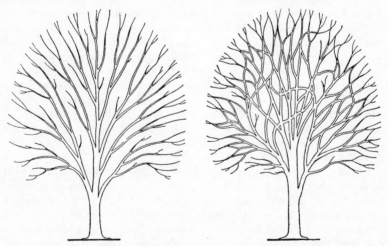

FIG. 18.   THE TREE OF LIFE AND THE TREE OF THE KNOWLEDGE OF
GOOD AND EVIL—THAT IS, OF HUMAN CULTURE

it will not normally coalesce with it. The tree of culture, on the contrary, is a ramification of such coalescences, assimilations, or acculturations. The schematic diagram in Figure 18 visualizes this contrast.

It is true that no figure of speech or of drawing will really prove a point like this. Nevertheless the illustration, both in words and in diagram, does validly represent something significant: that the specific processes of life and the specific processes of culture are drastically different.

115. THE CONTINUITY OF CULTURE

This unlimited receptivity and assimilativeness of culture make the totality of culture a continuum: the parts merge into each other without definite breaks. It is generally assumed that all life is also a continuum; but the continuity of life is traceable only by going back in its history and then reascending other branches. One moral of our diagram is precisely that culture is a far more closely and frequently interconnected continuum, in space and time as well as in developmental relations.

Perhaps this is why we have only the one word "culture," or its equivalent, "civilization," for its broadest as well as its narrowest exemplifications. We use the same term for the totality of human culture considered philosophically, and for the specific and distinctive culture of a little tribe of a hundred souls. This is because the English language, like other modern languages, has not yet evolved distinct terms for the big and the little, the general and the special aspects of culture. Nor have anthropologists and other social students managed to agree on any technical terms to help out the distinction—which is perhaps just as well, since sharper terms might help, but once the process of free coining starts, everyone prefers his own words and there are endless quarrels about them. But it is interesting to note how different this condition is from what we have in biology—even in popular biology. Everyone knows that life falls into two primary divisions, animals and plants, which can nearly always be distinguished without difficulty. The animals fall into phyla, of which the vertebrates are one,[1] among which the mammals constitute a class, and so on down the line to orders, families, genera, and species, like *Homo sapiens* or *Equus caballus;* and the species may have subspecies, and within these we get the near-repetitive individuals with only their individual or personal peculiarities. To all these different ranks of manifestation of life we have scarcely a counterpart in the terminology for culture. Such distinctions as are made are expressed in terms of societies or areas, such as tribal versus national, or local, provincial, national, and continental; and even these concepts intergrade somewhat in actual practice, precisely because their cultures intergrade.

[1] Popularly speaking; technically, of course, the vertebrates are only the largest and most important subphylum of the chordates (§ 9).

Let us run down an example. It needs no proof that total human culture shows a number of well-marked varieties, such as contemporary Western or Occidental or Eur-American civilization; the East Asiatic, the Indian, and the Islamic civilizations; and a number of cultures that are possessed by smaller societies and are often labeled "primitive" or "savage." Within each of these, subvarieties are recognizable without difficulty, such as Chinese and Japanese within East Asiatic. From the point of view of the outsider, Japanese culture is still very similar to Chinese culture, because so much of it has been derived from the Chinese or through the Chinese. Yet recent Japanese culture contained a native cult religion, Shinto, that was without counterpart in China; but Japan lacked any Taoist establishment. It provided for a ruler who was also a god—an institution lacking in Chinese culture; but it never accepted the women's foot-binding or men's queues which so long characterized the latter. And so on. Deviations of a roughly similar degree separate the main areas or nations within Occidental civilization: Italian from German, German from French, French from British, American from British, in ways that are familiar. Somewhat lesser are the differentiations we generally call regional: as of Bavaria within Germany, the Midi in France, Scotland in Great Britain. To the foreigner, these regional peculiarities may be a bit elusive, but a native is likely to be oriented about them. He will know roughly how New England and the South or the Middle West diverge in denominational and party affiliation, in degree of industrialization or agrarianism, in manners, temperament, and dialect. A step lower, and we come to what is usually called provincial distinctiveness, as of Normandy from Brittany. To this there might correspond the differentiation between North and South Carolina. Beyond this, there is the cantonal or local—Swiss Geneva being Calvinist, watchmaking, and international-minded; but Swiss Schwyz, Catholic, agricultural, home-centered. It was on this level that until recently peasant costumes and folk dances varied from valley to valley, or even from village to village, in much of Europe. At present in Europe, and almost from the first in historically shallow-rooted America and Australia, differences of the scope of these cantonal cultures are more likely to be expressed between economic classes or professions than locally; as between, say, doctors, barbers, printers, railroad men, and ministers, rather than between counties. There is no doubt that, quite apart from their vocational skills, the average culture of these professional groups differs slightly in dress, manners, standards, tastes, knowledge, habits, and amusements. We might call them professional subcultures or sub-subcultures.

This example shows how the same term is actually applied to the important cultures of great societies spread over large areas and to their more transient local or divisional phases. There even seems to be a degree of good reason for applying the same term. Occidental civilization no doubt represents something more generic and more important than the subculture of Midwestern clergymen. But it cannot possibly be defined as rigorously as the latter, because it is itself only a composite, a common denominator, of innumerable such phases, which have the greater definiteness. That is to say, it is the subcultures of clerical, sporting, transportational, and other such groups, and the Southern, New England, Midwest, Pacific-coast variants of these, which possess the sharper characterization, as against which total "American" culture is a slightly blurred composite or average. On the other hand, these local and divisional phases die out, merge, or get absorbed, like the cantonal cultures characterized by costume and dance. They are being obliterated by the spread of communications, by the rise of syndicated newspapers, by radio and films, and by ready-made-clothing factories. While the larger cultures are therefore less easily definable in terms of precise combinations of the traits characterizing them, they tend to be more durable in their main aggregations. There is thus a continuous transition from the greater to the minutest manifestations of cultures, with corresponding variation from more permanence to more precision; but all of them are significant.

Similarly, where sessile primitive populations live in small groups, it has been found that their local cultures vary almost exactly in proportion to distance. Thus the Pomo Indians of California lived in independent groups or tribelets of perhaps two hundred, each owning a tract of land and a main settlement. These settlements averaged possibly ten miles apart. A careful estimate, based on count of culture traits found present and absent, has shown that adjacent communities shared about 95 per cent of their culture, and that each was likely to have evolved perhaps 1 per cent of innovations or specific originalities. The other 4 per cent of their cultures consisted of a border zone of traits known to both communities but used by one only, or practiced by one for the other. In this cultural transition there might fall a ritual performed only by tribelet A but attended by B; a fishing harpoon known to all communities in the area and used by B but not used by A because the streams in A's territory were too small for fish of harpoonable size; and so on. Tribelet C—say twenty miles from A, beyond B—would differ from A more than B differed from A, but by the same ratio; D still more; and so on; the process continuing in all directions until perhaps a mountain range or an uninhabited tract, a radical change of speech, or some not too ancient movement of people or other accident of history, produced a slightly greater jump in the continuity. Where the situation of the tribelets or communities was linear, as along the coast from California to Alaska, the gradualness of the change is particularly striking, and renders it quite difficult to decide, except on the basis of speech, where one culture type ended and another began. Surprisingly, it seems to have made little difference whether adjacent communities were prevailingly friendly or hostile. All this seems very much like the locally variant forms of culture in Europe, especially rural Europe, of only a century or two ago.

A moment's reflection will show that a well-known historical phenomenon, the continuity of history, parallels in time this continuity of culture in space.

The fall of Rome did not mean that a former culture was completely obliterated in A.D. 476, or that a new kind of history first began then; it is just a convenient landmark. Culture in Western Europe, even in the city of Rome itself, almost certainly changed less in the decade enclosing 476—say from 470 to 480—than in the two decades before or the two after—say from 450 to 470, and from 480 to 500. At any rate historians would say that this is a fair example of normal historical change. The same thing is involved in what we have already seen in regard to cultural changeability (§ 113): while cultures practically cannot stand wholly still and do always alter, their prevailing behavior is one of inclination toward dominant stability, so that their normal change is gradual.

It is just that we are more familiar with the principle of continuity in historical time than we are with that in geographic space. Country L is red on the map, country M blue. Their speech, at least the standard or official language, changes abruptly at the frontier. The inhabitants pay taxes, in different currencies, to a nominal King directed by a prime minister in one capital, to a republican President in the other. The two states are sometimes at war, and in between times erect tariff barriers and require passports. The whole setup is calculated to emphasize the thoroughness of the break at a political frontier. Contemporary governments usually do their best to emphasize it; national prejudices often reinforce it; and finally the colors on the maps rub in an equally false visual image of it. There is never as great a uniformity within a national frontier as is aimed at or pretended, nor as deep a change across it.

The upshot of all of which is that human culture is a continuum or continuity, but a continuity gradually changing, and changing equally as it is followed through space and through time. We recognize, and for convenience label, culture periods like the Periclean age, the Renaissance, the Enlightenment or the Rococo in Europe, the Colonial period in America. We recognize also culture areas, such as the Occident, the Far East, India, the Nearer or Mohammedan East. Ethnologists recognize a good many more for illiterate native peoples outside the scope of documentary history; such as the Southwest of the United States, the United States Plains, the Arctic coast of America (again included in a larger Circumpolar Zone), Andean South America, western Polynesia, Congo-West African coast. An accidental difference is that culture periods are often named after something cultural that happened within them, such as reformation, enlightenment, exploration, colonization, increase of ignorance and rudeness; whereas culture areas are mostly named geographically. Nevertheless, they also really denote a particular culture rather than its mere geographical frame. "Southwestern" culture primarily refers to peaceful, maize-farming, heavily ritualistic Indians living in storied stone communal houses, only incidentally to the area this type of culture covered in New Mexico and Arizona.

Context alone, then, decides whether the word "culture" refers to *a* culture, a particular larger form or manifestation of it, such as Southwest Indian or

Korean; or to a subdivision thereof, such as Zuni; or to all culture seen as a whole, as a generalization, as when we say that culture is carried by society, or that it tends to change gradually.

116. FOLKWAYS AND THE RELATIVITY OF MORALS

In the eighteenth century of the "Enlightenment" in Europe it began to be widely recognized that the variety of national and tribal customs the world over was not merely a lot of strange oddities, but had certain significances. If Huron "savages" took their family line from their mothers, and if "Esquimaux" felt it their duty to dispatch their aged parents, this might well have some bearing on original man, as contrasted with members of the highly "polished" societies of western Europe. This original or "natural" man proved to be an effective club with which to pound contemporary civilization for its departure or corruption from an imagined condition of primeval purity. The motivation was variously anticlerical, antireligious, nostalgically daydreaming, or idealistically imaginative.

The nineteenth century came to adhere more and more passionately to the idea of progress. This idea forbade any looking backward and up to the "noble savage," but it was favorable to attitudes of relativity, instead of fixity or a perfection already achieved. There was accordingly a growing realization among intellectuals, during the latter part of that century, of what came to be called the relativity of morals. The Eskimo custom which obligated killing off one's old father was part of an ethical code as genuine as ours. If, in reverse of our way, the Jew put on his hat and the Moslem took off his shoes on entering a house of worship, that did not prove them "wrong," but did prove that there were many and even opposite ways of showing respect. The diversity in fact suggested that probably there was no absolute right or wrong in such matters: it was clear that the Arab and the Jew were as convinced as the Christian that they were doing right by doing the opposite from him.

Moreover, as soon as people were opposed, pressed, or cross-questioned on customs of this sort, they manifested resentment: it was evident that they held to their rules of conduct with emotion. When asked as to the reason for the observance, they either had none beyond the allegation that that was the way it had always been done (which belief could often be proved erroneous); or they gave a mythological justification that was obvious fantasy. All in all, comparative studies not only revealed great diversity, but showed that moral codes were essentially mere group habits or customs. They were nonrational, though often falsely rationalized; and they were emotionally charged. Moreover, the customs were "blind": those who followed them might be unconscious of them until the customs suffered infraction; and the followers were usually unconscious of any larger system of principles uniting the customs, or of partial contradictions of logic between customs.

The general effect of these nineteenth-century recognitions of course was in favor of tolerance and in diminution of ethnocentrism—that tendency to assume the universe as pivoted around one's particular people and to see one's in-group as always right and all out-groups as wrong wherever they differ. The realization that every culture is more or less right in its ways when judged in terms of its own premises, and that no culture is provably more right than others in the abstract, was achieved by a much wider circle of minds than the scattering anthropologists of the later nineteenth century. But anthropologists, being in most continuous contact with a wide series of highly divergent cultures, were perhaps most consistently impressed, and they came to take the principle for granted as underlying their work.

The most eloquent exposition in English of the point of view is Sumner's *Folkways* of 1906. A somewhat heterodox sociologist and economist freely using ethnographic and historical data, Sumner wrote brilliantly and exemplified vividly and abundantly. To him, folkways are ways of the folk, of the unsophisticated, unanalytic mass of mankind. They are, in short, customs, held to with much momentum but with incomplete rationality; and crossing them may cause a flare-up of fear or anger. They grow unconsciously; they are not creations of purpose; but they are basic societal forces. Mores,[2] Latin for customs and the origin of our word "morals," is a somewhat more special concept that Sumner helped to establish in nontechnical English usage. Mores are folkways which include a belief that they are desirable for social welfare and which people insist that their fellows conform to, though the mores are not derived from politically constituted authority. They are not laws, though they may produce laws, just as they result in taboos. "Folkways whose ethical sanctions have risen into consciousness" might be a fair definition of mores.

Similar ideas as to the nonrational and unconscious elements in culture were widely diffused throughout the field of later nineteenth-century social thought and studies. Marx, for instance, was certainly convinced that he knew the right understanding of past history as well as the solution of the problems of the future. Yet his economic determinism is tempered by considerable realization of the unconsciousness of social forces. He holds that it is not consciousness or purpose but methods of material production which determine the social, political, and spiritual processes of life—in other words, the noneconomic culture; and then, in turn, this socio-politico-spiritual culture "determines" or produces consciousness or recognition of itself.

Psychology has arrived at much the same basic concepts, largely by a route of its own—a route of reaction in some ways. Formally, psychology began as a branch of philosophy after this had become preoccupied with the problem of how we know things and what knowledge is valid. The early psychology was introspective, self-conscious, and rational. As it drifted, in the later nineteenth

[2] The little-used singular is mos.

century, from philosophical and deductive affiliations into inductive and exploratory aims, it worked on the one hand into objective experiment and test; on the other, into the fields of the nonrational, the emotions and the subconscious, where direct introspection pretty much breaks down. Psychoanalysis is one special manifestation of this general psychological trend. The realm of the nonrational is also the realm of custom and morals, analytically viewed; and cultural, social, and psychological thinking have more and more approached and reinforced one another. The element of relativity, of a new culture making a new environment for the individual, came into psychology latest, because there was nothing in the antecedents of psychology to suggest that differences of culture had much significance. Introspection in its nature emphasizes the ego and underemphasizes environment, social or other. Also, the philosophy in which psychology had its root was so completely concerned with universals and constants that it gave little notice to relativities and differences. Recent decades however have seen a thorough swing-over of psychology; and while as a science directed at the individual it must operate quite differently from anthropology, whose central concern is the superindividual aspect called culture, the two approaches now make essentially the same basic assumptions as to the relations of individual and culture. They may therefore be said to be attacking the same set of problems each from its own side—each in its own proper way, but with cooperative understanding.

117. CULTURE AND SOCIETY

Cultures are products of human societies operating under the influence of cultures handed down to them from earlier societies. This description illustrates the close relation of culture and society: they are counterparts, like the two faces of a sheet of paper. To each distinctive culture there corresponds, necessarily and automatically, a particular society: to Hottentot culture, the Hottentot nationality, to Chinese civilization, the Chinese people. It is rather futile to discuss which of the two phases or aspects is primary. It is obvious that if there were no people and therefore no societies, there could be no cultures. But equally, if there were no cultures, humanity would be merely another species of brute animals. We should in fact in that event probably not even be organized in tight societies like the ants, bees, and termites, because of lack of the highly specific instinctual faculties of these animals, and of their altruistic devotion to the hive.

Occasionally someone or other still attempts to assert that culture is secondary to society and therefore relatively negligible; or that within culture the domain of social relations is primary over the fields of economics, technology, knowledge, and belief. We have already seen (§ 6) that the first of these opinions is arbitrary. The second is equally so. It is true that social structure of some sort cannot be dispensed with in any culture. But neither can a subsistence economy be dispensed with. And it is clear that the threats as well as the final victories of nations and cultures in the two World Wars depended on their technological capacities, which in turn are parts of their bodies of knowledge. And as to beliefs—ideologies and standards—how can these be relegated to a humble secondary place when they permeate and express all of human living? It is fair enough to select one aspect of this human living as a personal interest or for special study; but it is unwarranted to insist on its superior importance.

As a matter of fact, culture and society are so interwoven as actual phenomena that they are often quite difficult to disentangle. An upper class is certainly a significant feature of the structure of any society in which it occurs. Yet it is also a feature of the culture—an overt feature if the aristocracy has privileges in its own name; an implicit but perhaps no less important trait if the de-facto class is unavowed. There is a social and there is a cultural aspect to a situation like this, undoubtedly; but the phenomena actually constitute but a single cluster or nexus of facts.

When the philosopher Comte, "the father of sociology," coined its name more than a century ago, he appeared to be emphasizing the function of society. But as soon as he classified societies according to the "stage" they had attained, he rated them as mythological, metaphysical, and positive—in other words, according to their beliefs or type of thought; which is certainly first of all a cultural criterion, and not a societal one.

Conversely, it is impossible to give an adequate picture of any culture without including an account of its social structure, which almost inevitably ramifies into economics, government, law, religion, art—in fact touches almost every department of the culture.

It is customary to speak of social solidarity but cultural integration. The two are related, but not quite the same thing. A society can lack solidarity yet retain a fairly integrated culture. France during the Great Revolution is an example. England is socially a more class-conscious and class-observing country than the United States, but most non-Anglo-Saxons would probably agree that its culture is somewhat more stable and better-integrated. American culture is perhaps less differentiated, but the British differentiations seem more tied together and adjusted, probably because England has had longer to shake itself down.

Nevertheless, social solidarity and cultural integration tend to go together; and there is nothing against turning the terminology around, and speaking of social integration or even cultural solidarity.

It is obvious that each class in a society will possess a slightly different phase of the same culture, just as each regional section or district will have one (§ 115). The speech may differ a little, manners and dress are even more likely to, incomes and occupations almost inevitably will. Mediaeval Europe and East Asia had sumptuary laws to enforce class distinctions of dress. We do not usually consider class cultures as actual cultures, because they are parts of "one society" and this tends to correspond in modern life with the larger political unit of the nation, and it is to this that we are wont to consider a type of civilization as attaching. But if there is any need for it, it is just as legitimate intellectually to speak of "lower-middle-class English culture" as of French culture: the one is part of all-class English culture and shades off into it; the other, of western-European culture. For that matter, a class has as much right to be considered "a society," at any rate within one locality, as has the total population of a country. It is more homogeneous, can function more easily as a unit, may or may not have more solidarity. But it is also a lesser thing, and normally of less significance. In short, what has already been said about the range of inclusiveness of the word "culture," of its being determined by the context, holds equally for society.

In the United States, classes theoretically differ less than in most Occidental national societies. People do differ in income, but that is not supposed to put them into separate classes. In part this condition is actual, having been initiated by the newness of the country and the once nearly equal opportunities of start for everyone. But in part it is an unreal condition: social classes exist in America, yet our basic national ideology disapproves of them. Hence we disavow them as much as we can, or fail to be frank in admitting their existence. Our formal institutions have certainly long been geared against class segregation: for instance, the franchise and the public school—state-provided education for all. As if in conformity with the institutions and the ideals, a rather unusual degree of outward class uniformity has been achieved in America. This means relative cultural uniformity between the classes, or relatively similar participation of all strata and occupations in the benefits and pleasures held out by the culture. Owning cars, eating steaks, seeing films, and reading the funnies are more widely shared than in other countries, except perhaps New Zealand and Australia. Actually, the American standard of living certainly has a lot to do with this: the standard is high enough to enable more of the population to participate regularly in these desirables. Nevertheless, the range of American culture does get narrowed by the uniformizing, and the spread between our actual social classes is obscured by our approval of uniformity.

An interesting result of the American inclination to ignore or deny such social stratification as exists is that social anthropology took a particular turn in the United States under Warner. He set out to show that classes exist among us, how they are characterized, and how people operate in staying in their class or getting out of it into a higher or a lower one. The classification is basically in terms of the old common-knowledge recognition of upper, middle, and lower classes, more or less corresponding to the aristocracy, bourgeoisie, and proletariat of Marxian ideology. Following the suggestion given by the familiar British phrase "lower middle class" with its very definite connotations, each of the three levels is further subdivided, in the Warner scheme, into upper and lower. Individuals are put into the subclass to which the community assigns them: mostly, anyone in the community that knows a given individual agrees pretty well with everyone else as to his place in the scale. In an old but smallish New England town thinly disguised as "Yankee City," the percentage strength of the six classes from Upper Upper to Lower Lower is: 1.5, 1.5, 10, 28, 33, 25, with 1 per cent unknown. In this New England community the classes are also very well characterized culturally, by what clubs or organizations their members belong to, denominational affiliation, type of magazines read, and so forth; and social mobility—social climbing—is low and slow.

It remains to be seen how far this scheme is of general utility, even in other American situations. It is of course possible to slice any population into three or six levels; the question is: How far will these levels represent natural segregations, distinctions, existing de facto in the society and culture? It seems doubtful how far the seven million people of New York City could be easily allocated to the same six levels; or for that matter the members of a prosperous rural community in Iowa; and if it turned out that they could somehow be allocated, it is certain that the cultural criterion of each class would be very different. For instance, "Cottonville" in the Deep South proved no longer to contain any Upper Upper old aristocracy, though it was still definitely under the influence of the ideals and standards of that class. This recognition of a class existing outside the community would indicate that Cottonville was not a society complete in itself; that its culture is only part of a larger culture (§ 119). At the other end of the scale, its "poor whites" are set off as an essentially unitary Lower class; and everything in between them and the nonpresent aristocracy, from Lower Upper to Lower Middle, also seems remarkably homogeneous. All this is for Caucasians in Cottonville: the Negroes form a separate "caste"—really therefore a separate though interlocked society—with its own social classes. Of these the Upper, containing 5 per cent of the Negroes, is determined by sex morality, education, and professional occupation rather than by income.

"Plainville," as described by West, is an agricultural Missouri community with a small-town center. Just about half the population tends to describe itself as "good, self-respecting, average people," less frequently as "better," "middle class," "all right," or occasionally even as "upper class." This half would seem to correspond objectively more or less to Warner's Middle Class, probably Lower Middle. A few families among them are somewhat more prosperous and influential than the rest, and are occasionally referred to as "upper crust," "rich," or "think they're better." However, they do not differ in manners or in professed social claims, and West refrains from designating them as a distinct group. The whole upper half of Plainville lives overwhelmingly on prairie land, the lower half, on hill land. Of this lower half, somewhat more than the majority—say around 30 per cent of the total population—is described by the upper half as "good lower class." The remaining 20 per cent or so segregate in a ratio of about two to one respectively into "the lower element" and "people who live like animals"—these last not only poor but without pride, ignorant, and apparently often subnormal in intelligence. Both the groups above these two lowest groups are in full agreement as to which families are to be assigned there. The two lowest subgroups together would correspond roughly to Warner's Lower Lower; the 30 per cent above them, to his Upper Lower. Here we have another example of a community without an upper class within itself: if it has a top, that exists elsewhere, in the larger national society. In other words, the community is not self-sufficient, nor is the culture wholly intelligible in terms of community structure as such. This condition is probably true in some degree even of fairly large communities, but is increasingly conspicuous as their size is smaller.

Plainville also agrees with our previous American examples in that the bottom stratum is less numerous than those above it. The social classes do not form a broad-based pyramid, as social theorists have often proclaimed or assumed—and as may have been true until recently in countries of mediaeval retardation like China, Czarist Russia, and parts of Latin America. The better diagrammatic representation of social stratification in the United States is evidently by the figure of a lozenge or diamond stood on end, as West employs it for Plainville.

Religion was still socially significant in Plainville as of 1941. Nonchurch people easily outnumbered any one sect, but the five denominations together had perhaps twice as many adherents as there were nonchurch people. These denominations would probably have been somewhat different in the next town, but in Plainville they happened to be, in order of their strength: Baptist, next Holiness, then Christian and Methodist about even, and Dunkard last. The distribution in terms of social rank is however quite uneven. Membership in the Holiness Church is a full 95 per cent Lower Class. Dunkards are about half and half, and Baptist somewhat more Middle. Neither of these sects includes persons from the very apex of the local social structure; but Christians and Methodists do. Both these denominations, and especially the Christian, also penetrate only very slightly into the lower half of the society. By contrast, the nonchurch contingent reaches all the way up and down the Plainville social scale. It includes nearly half of the Middle Class apex, but a decreasing proportion as one descends the Middle ranks. Then it increases again toward the Middle border line and throughout the Lower half, finally taking in most of "the lower element" and nearly all of the "live-like-animals" segment. It is evident that the church denominations serve as symbols and instruments of social hierarchy, but that the distribution of the nonchurch population is due to other and less obvious factors.

In "Small Town," of less than 1000 souls in eastern New York, Hicks found only two classes, the upper one nearly twice as large as the lower. There is considerable difficulty in defining criteria of distinction between the classes, but no difficulty in assigning any resident to his class. Public opinion seems spontane-

ously unanimous on that. In fact, the largest factor in determining class affiliation in Small Town seems to be subjective admission of belonging. Some
accept lower-class affiliation with a dour sense of frustration, but more do so
with a sense of relief at being able to let themselves go instead of having to live
up to responsibilities and standards.

Obviously there is no one class pattern that can be applied everywhere.
Conversely, some class segregation can be expected in practically all societies
except the smallest and poorest in culture. The most important effect of the
Yankee City school of social anthropology is probably to prove to us that we
Americans too are socially stratified in spite of wanting to believe that we are
not. If the stratification proves to be locally variable, that only makes it so much
the more interesting.

The trick of professing one thing and doing another is no doubt common
to all societies. They vary chiefly in what they are inconsistent about. The habit
of rationalization has been discussed (§ 81) and will be referred to again (§ 216).
One need not feel too harsh about it. Professions after all mean standards and
ideals; and it may be better for societies to have standards and fall short of them
than not to have them. Obviously, the important thing intellectually is to recognize whatever discrepancy there is, instead of covering up to produce a sensitive
blind spot.

118. INFLUENCE OF SIZE OF SOCIETY

It has long been recognized that the size of a society can be expected to exert
certain effects on its culture. This influence appears to be most marked in the
periods when higher civilizations first take shape. While reasoning on this
matter is somewhat a priori, the drift of history and archaeology confirms it.

Assume a given population in a given area, but divided into a hundred
tribes, each owning a territory yielding it subsistence, each independent, each
jealous and suspicious of its neighbors. With a million people in the area, the
tribes would average 10,000 souls. There might be a council or a chief or a
kinglet to govern each of these tribes. There might be in each tribe some sort
of a central settlement or market or town, but nothing like a real city, nor any
serious accumulation of wealth. Most of the tribal members would be scattered
over the land getting their subsistence. As in our wholly rural sections until
quite lately, every man would be something of a jack-of-all-trades, able to farm,
clear, build, fell, repair, or fight; his women would know how to cook, spin,
weave, sew, milk, and thresh, or the equivalents of these in the local form of
culture. There would be little need for writing or records, hence limited learning. Arts would most likely be home crafts. The priest and the doctor might
function as such mainly in their spare time after making a living; a smith or
two perhaps would work full time and professionally—if iron and tools were
abundant enough to keep him busy. In short, the smallness of the social group

would tend to keep it undifferentiated in its activities, and therefore culturally undeveloped.

Now let our hundred little tribes be united into one society acknowledging its unity—whether by voluntary conglomeration or by the conquests of one leader. The hundred councils or chiefs are replaced by a central government. The seat of this would tend to become a city; its house, the largest in the country, would now be a palace of sorts; its shrine, a national temple. To tend the shrine there might follow full-time priests, who would leave their offices to their descendants or to trained successors. Revenues and trade would flow into the capital; craftsmen could now expect steady custom and could become skilled. The ruler's resources and inclination toward show might lead to patronage which in turn would encourage the arts; the lifelong priests might pile up observations leading to the devising of a regulated calendar. All in all, the mere size of the society, now a hundredfold greater and with its parts in closer intercommunication than before—at least toward its center—would trend toward professional differentiation, accumulation of skills, new inventions, and an upsurge of cultural content.

To a greater or less degree this is what appears actually to have happened in ancient Egypt and Mesopotamia, China and Japan, Mexico and Peru, and again, with intensification, in Western civilization since 1650. The period was by or before 3000 B.C. in Egypt and Mesopotamia (§ 286); perhaps a thousand years later in China (§ 299); during the Christian era in the other countries. In each case there was more political unity than there had previously been, rulers of greater authority and sometimes with attribution of divinity, the beginnings of cities, development of metallurgical and other arts, and usually the formulation or the introduction of systems of writing and calendars. Any one of these advances tended to bring advancement in others. For instance, city life meant that there were classes no longer working the soil themselves: rulers, or craftsmen, or merchants, or priests. Wealth could accumulate; and temples or palaces called for new architectural endeavors. Similarly, writing opened a variety of new avenues: bookkeeping for taxes, history on behalf of the reigning dynasty, more exactly transmitted rituals, records for the calendar-framers. The entire complex process of forward movement may have been actually initiated by any one of its interwoven components, for all we know—by urbanization, or by metallurgy, writing, the divinity ascribed to rulers, or by some other factor. But the distinctive accompaniment in any one of these cases was the political unification.

That meant there was a much larger society, which could now diversify into a variety of classes and professions instead of being broken up quantitatively into a series of nearly uniform tribal units. And of course a society diversified qualitatively means a richer culture instead of a repetitively narrow one.

This summary of what actually happened in the protohistoric period in several parts of the world should not be construed as a universal "must." The successful development of Greek culture in a period of autonomous tiny city-states is enough to show that. Emphatically, the richness of civilizations cannot be measured in the abstract by the size of their societies. All that can be maintained is that, other things being equal, an integrated society large enough to be socially diversified has a better chance to produce a richly diversified culture than an equally large population broken up into many small units each with less diversification. This seems especially true at a certain level or stage; namely, after agriculture has made concentration of numbers possible, and when tribal, oral, folk culture is about to begin to convert into urban and literate culture. The Greek states remained minute in the period of their cultural efflorescence; but they were urban, and they had recently become literate.

Also, it is possible for a society to attain new peaks in its culture while many of its members are worse off than before through not sharing in the new attainments. This is a price that tends to be paid for the gains of specialization; and it can become fatal. This counterpart is discussed below under Participation in § 124.

119. SUBCULTURES AND PART-CULTURES

We have seen how each class in a society exhibits a more or less distinct phase, a subculture, of the total culture carried by the society; just as geographical segments of the society manifest regional aspects of the culture. This principle extends farther: to age levels and the sexes. Men do not practice the specific habits of the women in their culture, and vice versa. And though both sexes are generically oriented about these habits—they always know that certain peculiarly feminine (or masculine) activities exist—they may be so hazily informed about them that they could not adequately practice them or transmit them in their entirety if they would. At the same time these sex phases are never felt as constituting more than a side or an aspect of the culture—nor, indeed, do they constitute more. A unisexual society could no more exist among human beings than could a unisexual race; and neither are there unisexual cultures. The feminine component is always a complement of the masculine: the culture is not felt as complete, and is not complete, without both components. The same things holds, incidentally, for the class phases, and often for the regional phases, of well-integrated cultures. Scavengers and bankers will be recognized in such cultures as quite properly following diverse strains of life and making diverse contributions, but their coherence within the body politic of culture and society is felt to outweigh the separateness. They are both organs within the same body, like the patricians and the plebeians in the old Roman fable about the stomach and the limbs.

The cultural differences between age levels within a society follow a somewhat different pattern. The ages are inevitably continuous and overlapping, as sexes and many classes are not. Culture phases associated with age may be assumed to correspond to changes taking place in the culture, rather than to reflect chronic or static lines of segregation like those between social classes. Individuals above fifty will largely be trying to practice and maintain their established habits and status, and therewith a phase of culture some of which is just beginning to pass; those under thirty will be interested in the phase that is trying to arrive.

It is now well recognized that in contemporary civilization adolescents in the larger sense—the individuals between dependent childhood and full maturity with social responsibility—learn more about many things from age mates or near-age mates than from their elders. At any rate, they learn more willingly, often eagerly, from age mates, and are more conditioned socially by them. As for the effect of this fact on culture, that is an intriguing and little-explored problem. However, it seems that the constant change which is normal in every culture is chiefly initiated not by its adolescents, but by its mature individuals, especially by the younger half of these mature individuals.

What then do adolescents teach each other? It appears to be little in the way of substantial cultural content. This substantial content, if well established in the culture, would come of itself from the parental generation; if new, from the younger or more progressive section of the adult population as a whole. What adolescents impart to one another seems chiefly to be accepted cultural content stylistically modified as to its manner or form. This means fashions, mannerisms, ways of speaking, sitting, dancing, or reacting, and the like: special brands of slang, for instance, or of slouches and other postures; modifications of existing traits, in short, rather than brand-new elements of culture. The subadult age class goes in for certain choices among existing types of clothes, such as low flat shoes and sweaters for coeds, or even only a certain way of pushing the sleeves back; they do not ordinarily invent a new garment. This example seems typical of adolescent culture. Its quality is a special twist given to the standard culture; a conscious departure from some elements of it, or a sort of deliberately distorted reflection. Ordinarily there is no real revolt, no seeking a reform, but a basic conformity with the existing order, accentuated by an assertion of age-class independence at points of no great moment. By the time full social maturity is entered, most of the twists are abandoned by each individual. The whole phenomenon may be compared to the slight wave or bulge of water that the bow of a moving ship keeps pushing just ahead of it.

It must also be remembered that this kind of adolescent-culture phase is specially characteristic of modern city life and the leisure of prolonged education. In cultures or classes where economic responsibility is assumed early, the more usual adolescent urge seems to be toward acquisition of adult status and privilege in normal form.

It also seems possible that in our contemporary society the urge of each adolescent generation to set itself off as an age class is an unconscious compensation for the relative lack of sharp demarcation of overt social levels.

A particular kind of class is caste. Castes are closed classes. Individual mobility from one into another class is forbidden by the larger society. Naturally, each caste reflects one particular facet of a larger culture. This is true even where, as in most of the United States, the basic doctrine of democratic equality sets limits to the functioning of caste. American Negro culture may aim at being an integration into white culture or a repetition of it, but actually it is a variant and not a duplication. In a country like India, differentiations are so intensive, and so firmly entrenched, that the more extreme castes might almost be accredited as following distinct cultures, so much do they differ—not only in occupation and rank, but in food, manners, internal laws, education, amusements, worship, and standards. Essentially it is the less extreme intervening castes, plus intercaste community of regional speech, which succeed in holding the top and bottom levels within the frame of one society and one culture in India.

India is almost perversely unique in the degree to which it is caste-ridden, and the American color situation carries a high-voltage charge of emotion, so it may be well to examine a case that does not involve either race or a wholesale caste system. Through much of North Africa and Arabia smiths form an in-marrying profession. They may be respected, despised, or feared, but are set apart. Among the camel-breeding Beduin of northern Arabia, such as the Ruwala, smiths and the Negro slaves form the only separate castes not marrying with the main population. The smiths alone know how to shoe horses, repair guns, and the like, and get paid for their work, with which income they purchase their food and living, instead of raising camels as do the rest of the Beduin. They are uninvolved in the touchy honor system, vendettas, and raids of their tribes. If by oversight a smith is pillaged, the smiths in the raiding group arrange for his property to be returned to him. On the other hand, though they do not fight, smiths receive what may be described as a small fixed percentage of the spoils taken in battle. It is evident that the social and prestige system as well as the occupational and economic activities of the smiths is wholly distinct from those of the main body of the Ruwala Beduin. Yet the two form parts of one society. The Ruwala would be paralyzed without their smiths, and the latter of course could not exist at all without the Ruwala.

120. NOMADIC, CASTE, AND PARASITIC CULTURES

Much the same sort of relation holds, on a larger scale, between the Beduin and the neighboring settled Arabs. The livelihood of the nomads is in their camels, whose milk is their main food, whose herds are their wealth and their only salable produce (§ 165). Each midsummer when the water holes of the steppe and the desert go dry, it is with their camels that they buy, in the settled country, all their clothing and black tents, their carpets, their weapons and iron pans, barley to feed their prized brood mares, and virtually all their own non-milk food—wheat, rice, dates, and coffee. The very poor may have to do without this bought food; but the reasonably prosperous consume close to a pound of it a day per capita. Meat is too valuable to eat, ordinarily; a butchered camel is so much capital eaten up. It is clear that without what they secure from the towns and traders of the farming country, the Beduin would have so one-sided a culture that they could not survive by it: no clothing, shelter, weapons, few utensils, limited diet. In one sense, accordingly, their own culture is no more than a half-culture. At least they can produce only half of it, and are dependent on the Hadhar, the "dwellers in brick," for the other half. Yet the Beduin are not a mere occupational subgroup, nor a caste like the smiths. They are a full-fledged society, or series of tribal societies, independent, autonomous, each owning territory, waging war.

To some extent, this condition of possessing a "half-culture" holds for most nomads. Their range is from Arabia westward across Africa through and south of the Sahara; and eastward through Iran, Soviet Turkestan, Chinese Turkestan and Tibet, North China and Mongolia, to Manchuria—the great transcontinental arid belt of Africa-Asia. With insignificant exceptions it is only in this belt that true pastoral nomads occur: peoples making their living wholly off their flocks without settling down to plant. Alongside them, however, in rainier tracts and oases or on irrigated land within the belt, there normally are farmers, and often towns or cities. These agricultural populations are frequently the more numerous, though the herders loom large on the map because they need and have more of the low-grade land. In some areas the herding people are politically dominant, like the Masai and Bahima and Banyankole in East Africa, and the Fulah in West Africa. Elsewhere, the settled people are more often on top, though it may be difficult, or not very worth while, for them to control the roamers in the steppe. Jenghis Khan was a pastoral nomad Mongol when he and his sons and grandsons in the 1200's conquered out from Central Asia as far as to include Russia and China. But by 1600 Mongolia was again dominated by China. Nomads in general feel free, are proud, and look down on the sedentary groups, though they are fewer, poorer, and envious of the latters' luxury and wealth. The roaming life in the desert largely colored early Arabic poetry; but Mohammed, who launched the Arabs and their culture to greatness, was a townsman and a trader. Lattimore has even advanced a theory that East Asiatic nomadism developed secondarily out of the mixed farming and stockbreeding of China when increase of population began to push this mixed method of livelihood northward and inland into marginal steppe and then into submarginal desert. After a certain point was reached, it proved more profitable to renounce planting altogether in favor of wide herd range and human mobility. This is suggested as having begun to happen on the North China frontier only shortly before the Christian era; whereupon the power of the Hiung-Nu arose as the first of a succession of transient pastoral-nomadic states of which the Mongol finally became the greatest. This interpretation still remains hypothetical; but it is interesting because it does recognize pure pastoralism as a specialty secondarily segregated out of a more balanced economy by accentuation of one part.

In passing, it may be mentioned that the view of a succession of stages of human-culture evolution from hunting to herding to farming is now considered a completely antiquated theory. It was a pseudo-philosophical guess aiming to supersede actual history, and there are masses of scholarly and scientific evidence to the contrary. In fact, the theory has been traced back in its germs to speculations made by the Sumerians of lower Mesopotamia five thousand years ago.

All in all, while it would be an exaggeration to say that all pastoral nomad cultures would perish if they tried to become wholly self-sufficient in isolation, yet it is clear that they are particularly one-sided and limited, and tend to stand in a relation of complement to the richer and more varied cultures of adjacent or interspersed sedentary societies. This is what is meant here by calling them half-cultures or part-cultures. They would not have been able to specialize to the same degree if they were wholly isolated and independent. They exist in some degree of cultural and social symbiosis.

Our cowboy world of Western fiction and films is much the same sort of thing on a fantasy level. On that level, attention is directed toward romance, and away from the fact that this appealing world of the Bar-X ranch would collapse, or at least squalidly deteriorate, if it were really cut off from the rest of the United States. Riding range in actual life is just one occupation of many in our economy, and in everything else the cowpuncher is a participant in American culture and only in that. If he lived in the pastoral belt of Africa-Asia, the cowpuncher would often be set apart from the nonpastoral population in race or speech or religion also, and perhaps he would be politically independent. But his complementary integration with the nonnomadic culture would remain fairly similar to the cowpuncher's with ours. It is in his social consciousness that the nomad is free, separate, and proud. His specific culture may be almost as largely a part of a greater culture as the facet cultures of classes or castes elsewhere are only such parts.

There are several other populations, ranging from castes to small races, to whom something like half-cultures might be attributed—and disputed.

There are the Jews, whose culture differs from that of coterritorial Gentiles primarily in religion and ritual practices. When this religion loses its hold, Jews come to approximate Gentiles very closely, and generally tend to merge socially, or at least are willing to lose their group identity. Where the culture of Jews is distinctive in nonreligious matters, as in their occupations, it is most often because they are confined to these through being shut out from other callings; or through having been shut out legally from them until so recently that enforced habits still persist. The degree to which Jews are separate in their bodily heredity has been discussed in § 68. It can be at best only a quite minor factor in their culture determination. Their speech too is usually that of the country in which they live. If it differs, it is through recency of immigration, as in New

York. Or it is because of enforced migration, as of the Spanish-speaking Jews of Salonika, or the corrupt German called Yiddish which the Jews of much of eastern Europe spoke because they were driven there from Germany. Compulsory ghetto segregation, as in Czarist Russia, has kept dialects like Yiddish alive through the centuries. Biblical Hebrew was a dead language to about the same degree as Latin until it was resuscitated as a living national speech by some hundreds of thousands of Zionists in Palestine; but whether with historical success, only the future can tell (§ 107, 181).

All in all, the Jews seem to constitute a social quasi-caste based originally and mainly on a religion that of course is voluntary, not enforced. Their social segregation is markedly stronger than their cultural distinctness, though the latter is not absolutely lacking.

The Gypsy situation is a little different. Fundamentally, the Gypsies are an endogamous caste. They originated in India; and they show definite evidence of that fact in their blood type (§ 72) and in the Romany speech of which they retain remnants in addition to the language of whatever country they inhabit. In religion they are more or less professing Christians; and they specialize in certain occupations like horse-trading and tinkering. But what sets them off from the rest of the population is not so much positive cultural peculiarities as the inclination toward an unrooted and vagrant life. Their distinctness lies above all in an attitude, or orientation, which leads them to select a certain group of activities in Western civilization and to discard most of the others. They want a horse or an automobile, but not a house; silver jewelry, but not a bank account; music, but no education; and so on. In many of their attitudes they are like hobos: both elect to follow one particular vein of the many that make up our culture—the vein or line of freedom, irresponsibility, and instability. But of course hobos have no separateness of race or speech, nor are they strictly a caste, because without women and families they lack hereditary continuity and are merely an association group constantly rerecruited by adversity or temperament. Gypsies evince definite cultural distinctness; only, as they neither constitute a full society nor possess a complete culture, they serve as another example of half-cultures. They certainly have an ethos (§ 125) all their own.

At the extreme edge of this concept, we have peoples like the Seri Indians or the Negritos, whose attitudes are in part like those of Gypsies. Here we have indubitably distinct and autonomous social groups, each with its specific culture. The Negritos are even markedly distinct in their miniature racial type (§ 64), though they speak the languages of their neighbors.[3] The mode of life of both peoples is unsettled, and, in line with that propensity, the culture of both may be described as kept simple. It contains nothing specific that is not known in the surrounding richer cultures. The specializations consist of makeshifts like the

[3] The Negritos of the Andaman Islands are the only ones who have no immediate neighbors and who do have a language of their own.

single shaft that the Seri use interchangeably as harpoon, mast, or raft-poler; or like the Negrito bow, which the non-Negrito Filipinos have discarded as useless to them. Historically at any rate, cultures such as these are parasitic. They have contributed little or nothing, so far as we can judge, to the stock of human culture, while they have taken from other cultures what they do possess, and that with heavy reduction. The Seri, so far back as we know them, have also been outrightly parasitic on other groups, so far as they could, by force, cajolery, or sufferance, much like Gypsies. On the contrary, the Negritos are sturdily independent; so that the cases are not quite parallel. Moreover, the historical dependence or parasitism of one culture on another is by no means the same thing as the social parasitism of one group on another. Nevertheless, if all non-Gypsies were suddenly blotted out of Europe and North America and those continents left wholly to the Gypsies, it is reasonable to believe that the culture of the Gypsies in a few generations would fairly resemble that of Seris or Negritos in orientation, and perhaps ultimately in simplicity of substance or content also.

This matter of partial cultures or half-cultures needs more defining and exploring. It is evident that the relations between the larger or "enclosing" cultures and the special smaller ones vary a great deal—as much so as the relations between "whole" societies and their castes or classes or regional segments. Unconsciously we tend to think in terms of large ethnic units, such as the French, whose geographic boundaries are within a single color block on the map, and whose society, nation, language, and culture pretty well coincide. Actually of course France includes not only "Frenchmen" but Gypsies, Jews, Bretons, Walloons, Basques, hobos, and apache criminals, each of which groups has its variant form of French civilization, just as French officials and French dirt farmers have. And of course French civilization itself is only one phase or form of Western culture. Also we tend to think of the units as static, whereas they are constantly flowing, changing, and influencing one another. If we knew better the history of peoples like Negritos, Seris, or even Gypsies, or if we kept more in mind the total composite history of peoples like the French and the Bretons, we would realize more clearly the continuity of the material of culture, and how its segregations are never complete. In their origin and their history even the greatest and richest cultures are only parts of the great nexus of human culture as a whole.

121. RURAL AND URBAN—FOLK AND SOPHISTICATE FACETS

It is customary to distinguish rural and urban components in modern populations. There are of course corresponding rural and urban facets or aspects in the culture of such societies. Moreover, whole societies and cultures can be classified into those predominantly rural or predominantly urban. India, China, and Czarist Russia will serve as examples of the one; England or Massachusetts of the other—or even Australia, recent as it is, with the majority of its inhabitants living in its capital cities. In this familiar form, the rural-urban distinction is well enough known to need no detailed analysis—except for one comment on a fundamental though obvious fact. The rural condition is the underlying one, logically and historically: there must be a country area producing more food than it consumes before other people can live in cities.

On the widest consideration, the rural-urban differentiation is a somewhat special and modern form of a more general distinction of societies and cultures into those which are more folklike and those which are more sophisticated or "civilized." This is not an either-or segregation. Rather we must conceive of a line or an axis along which societies and cultures, or the part-cultures of segments of societies, can be ranged from the one extreme or pole of greatest folklike or tribal backwardness to the opposite pole of greatest sophistication. The concept is of some importance because it gathers in and subsumes a series of diverse but related recognitions that have gradually become established in social science.

A characteristic folk culture or tribal culture belongs to a small, isolated, close-knit society, in which person-to-person relations are prevalent, kinship is a dominant factor, and organization, both societal and cultural, is therefore largely on a basis of kinship—sometimes including fictitious kinship, as in many clans and moieties. By contrast, political institutions are weakly developed: "primitive democracy" is the characteristic form; but this denotes only a maximum of equality coexisting with a minimum of authority or control. Such a way of doing works because of the strong integration within the small group involved. Everyone knows everyone else, and many of them are blood or affinal relatives.[4] It has long been noted that there seems to be a spontaneous upper limit of tribal size: probably around five thousand souls, in many areas less than that. When this limit is transcended, the society breaks into two, often painlessly. Where "tribes" of fifty or a hundred thousand or a million persons are spoken of, they are either organized into a supertribal state, or they are really no longer tribes, but nationalities. Nationalities possess a culture and a speech that they recognize as common in essentials, but they may constitute many societies. This means that, in the case of a nationality, ethnically and culturally we are dealing with a single people, but politically often with multiple independent societies, each one autonomous and owning its own distinct tract of land. Such would be populations like the Lolo, the Ifugao, the Maya, all of whom are sometimes inaccurately called "tribes" when they really are multiple-society nationalities of nearly uniform culture. The mere fact of the narrowness of range of their social integration holds them near the folk end of the polar axis.[5]

[4] Related to the folk-sophisticate polarity are the distinctions made by Durkheim between "organic" and "mechanical" solidarity, and by Tönnies between "community" and 'society," as his *Gemeinschaft* and *Gesellschaft* are approximately translated.

[5] The subject of nationality is discussed also in § 80, 102, 180-81.

It is also the smallness of the maximal social unit which keeps folk populations homogeneous and uniform, with only slight division-of-labor specialization, beginnings of class divisions, or slender concentrations of residence in permanent towns. Folk societies are attached to their soil emotionally by ties of habit, and economically by experience. Consequently they belong to that group of societies which identify themselves with their locality, in contrast to the sophisticated city dwellers who float without roots but take pride in living in their era and day and are therefore constantly subject to the play of fashion (§ 121, 164, 253).

Finally, it is folk societies that are specially dominated in their culture and their behavior by the folkways discussed in § 116. Their moral and religious sense is therefore strong. They believe in the sacred things; their sense of right and wrong springs from unconscious roots of social feeling, and is therefore unreasoned, compulsive, and strong.

Folk cultures afford their individual members full participation in their functioning—they invite and encourage such participation; their functioning, however limited and inadequate, is therefore personalized and saturated. The relatively small range of their culture content, the close-knitness of the participation in it, the very limitation of scope, all make for a sharpness of patterns in the culture, which are well characterized, consistent, and interrelated. Narrowness, depth, and intensity are the qualities of folk cultures.

Maturely civilized societies are inevitably large. A population that has become great, whether by its own growth, by absorption, or by the welding together of originally independent groups, inevitably becomes depersonalized on the one hand, individualized on the other. The kin group, of lifelong close associates bound by affective ties, has lost its force, except for the immediate or biological family, and often partly even within that. In consequence, each individual's relations with others take on an impersonal character. There are now numerous such relations, but most of them are special, limited, shallow, without emotional implications. We do not know our milkman, who in fact probably represents a corporation none of whose members we have ever set eyes on. And as for the actual delivery driver, if we do now and then see him, it is to extend a greeting or a comment on the weather: we do not invite him to dinner or seriously exchange views on religion or social problems with him. If we have real business with him, such as ordering an extra quart, we usually make sure of it by leaving him a note in an empty bottle—about as impersonal and unemotional a method as there is. In fact, most writing and all printing are inevitably indirect, remote, and "denatured" as regards feeling, compared with face-to-face contact. Writing, then, greatly reinforces population size as a joint cause of the growing impersonalization of higher civilization. So do large-scale urbanization and mechanical industrialization. The four constitute a set of interdependent causes, and of intercorrelated effects as well.

At the same time, kin and associative groups, which were dominant under tribal culture, have lost most of their strength and influence, and the large total society being only remotely and mechanically interested in persons, the individual has become relatively free. He is free to try to develop as he wishes, free to choose his own contacts and to change them. There is nothing to hold him in the course of his forefathers, nor even in his own original course. Individuals therefore become highly differentiated—not indeed in their inner personality, which the immense society and great culture have difficulty in reaching intimately—but in their behavior, their actions. This differentiation corresponds to the differentiation of labor and profession. With it also there tends to go a certain instability. This shows in the fluctuating careers of individuals: they may live here today, there tomorrow, with ever new associates but perhaps never close friends. On the sociocultural side it shows in the fluctuations of fashion, not only of dress but of fads, novelties, amusements, and the fleeting popularity of persons as well as things (§ 164, 253). The influence of the total sociocultural mass on the individual is probably as great as in the small folk society; but it is indirect, remote, "mechanical," because it is impersonal, extensive instead of intensive, and directed toward time co-ordination rather than toward association based on spatial contiguity.

With this diluting and spreading of the fervid intensities of attachment, it is inevitable that religiosity, piety, regard for the sacred things, should tend to evaporate with civilization. Shrines become show places rather than spots of worship. Criticism and rationalism grow. As beliefs fade that have rested largely on the social dictation of a homogeneous small group, empirical and actual knowledge comes to seem more desirable, and accumulates. Faith in the supernatural and the magical gives way to faith in science. The culture and the life are secularized. Here again dilution of the affective social group into impersonality goes hand in hand with rationalization, secularization, and urbanization: each tends to produce the others and to be further produced by them.

It is evident that our present-day Western civilization is near one polar end—the most urbanized, lay, depersonalized, sophisticatedly civilized end—of an axis that can be traced through all societies and cultures. Basically this classification or ranging on a scale is perhaps social in character, concerned with size and integration of the group. It is however expressed also in culture, and apparently more emphatically so; namely, as secularization, ceaselessness of the swings of fashion, and cultural instability. Even the rural-urban and tribal-state distinctions deal with forms that are cultural as well as social. And finally, there is a psychological expression of the polarity, manifest in affectiveness, depersonalization of relations, and the like.

Of course, intergradations occur all along the axis. China, for instance, and India are markedly less sophisticate-urban-depersonalized than Western countries, but much more so than most tribal nationalities.

An intermediate place is occupied also by peasantry. Peasants are definitely rural—yet live in relation to market towns; they form a class segment of a larger population which usually contains also urban centers, sometimes metropolitan capitals. They constitute part-societies with part-cultures. They lack the isolation, the political autonomy, and the self-sufficiency of tribal populations; but their local units retain much of their old identity, integration, and attachment to soil and cults. Peasantries persisted in probably every European country alongside growing urbanization and industrialization all through the nineteenth century, and they had been modified but were by no means extinct when the crash of World War II overwhelmed the Continent. In Russia, four-fifths of the population in 1917 consisted of ex-serf peasants. New countries rapidly settled by large-scale immigration, such as the United States and Australia, leave small room for peasant conditions or attitudes. There is too little rooting in the soil, too little stability or knitting together by kinship, for local particularity as expressed in folk custom or peasant art to develop. However, a close approximation to a true peasantry did develop in those Latin American countries like Mexico, Guatemala, Peru, and Bolivia where the Spanish conquest froze the bulk of the native population resident on the land into a depressed class living under its own partial or folk culture. In later prehistory, after food production had become established, a number of societies exhibit rather conspicuous peasantlike qualities: the Neolithic Europeans, for instance, including the Swiss lake dwellers (§ 283); also the Indian, Greek, and other early Indo-Europeans (§ 305). These are all peoples who had become settled but, either from newness or from remoteness, had made little progress toward urbanization. The Near East may have gone through a similar phase on which we are less well informed because it happened two to three thousand years earlier. And there were some interesting national differences in this regard; as between Mesopotamia and Egypt, for instance. In these two lands amorphous folk cultures grew simultaneously into early civilizations, with writing, towns, political organization, metallic industry. But during the last millennium before Christ, Mesopotamia had become sophisticatedly civilized, with a conquered empire, great cities of metropolitan character like Babylon, and prosecution of true science; whereas Egypt had stood nearly still for a thousand years. This difference was perhaps partly due to the fact that the population of Egypt consisted overwhelmingly of a rural peasantry, capped by little else than a governing bureaucracy.

The question fairly arises whether the trend from the rural to the urban, from folk to sophisticate culture, involves the gradual extinction of religion and morality, as might seem inferable from the strength that the mores and beliefs in the *sacra* retain in localized folk cultures, but tend to lose in civilization. In short, can we project this tendency, so apparent at the present day, and perhaps most strongly so in Western civilization, forward into the future to a vanishing point? In line with such a trend is the fact that as time has gone on, states or empires have been growing larger; and that "universal" states and churches—

universal in the Toynbee sense of aiming at totality—are regular and expectable phases in the growth of major civilizations.

However, any prophecy resting on the extrapolation or projection of a trend assumes that the trend is constant. There is no proof that such constancy holds throughout for the change from folk culture to sophisticate civilization. We know of pieces of history that show the change; our own American contemporary history is impressively so oriented; and over the total range of human culture the net drift is perhaps to the same effect. But the trend is not universal and is not irreversible. For instance, following Alexander the Great's conquest and the fusion of mature Greek and mature western-Asiatic civilizations, there first occurred a conspicuous development of many of the symptoms that characterize modern life: withering of the closer social ties, along with decay of beliefs and piety, democratization, growth of population, cities and larger states, industrialization, marked accumulation of knowledge, general sophistication. This culture period is known as Hellenistic; in the early Roman Empire its character was both accentuated and spread to the western Mediterranean. However, from the beginning of the breakdown of the Roman Empire in the third century, the drift was reversed in most respects. The international state fell apart; the fragments had little intercommunication; loyalties became ethnic, often tribal; outlooks were parochial, at best provincial, instead of metropolitan. Cities shrank tremendously; the self-sufficient economic unit now was the rural *villa*. Knowledge and education decreased; religious convictions under Christianity were far firmer and more influential than they had been in late paganism. The outcome was the western-European "Dark Ages" of rural custom, ignorance, piety, and folkway dominance, from which our own civilization made its first step of gradual emergence when it attained to mediaevalism. In the East, Constantinople and in a measure Alexandria indeed remained great cities of wealth and sophistication for some centuries longer. But they finally fell before the expansion of Islamic society, whose culture must in some ways be regarded as recessive also; it certainly aimed at simplification.

There have presumably been other reversals in history. The overturn from the Indus Valley civilization to that of the Vedic Aryans certainly signified the partial triumph of rural folkway living (§ 105). And even primitives vary considerably in the strength of their piety and animistic beliefs (§ 250). It may therefore be fairly concluded that movement along the rural-urban, folk-sophisticate axis is not necessarily one-way or predestined.

It is of interest in this connection that Soviet doctrine aims at bringing about a condition closely resembling one of the polar extremes we are discussing. The program includes a single world state with only one class of citizens, speaking a single language; what remains of other idioms and of regional customs will be harmless nostalgic remembrances of the order of folk songs and dances (§ 182). Life will be fully industrialized, according to the Soviet program; it will be lived urbanly even on the farm. Knowledge and enlightenment will be universal; religion will be defunct, rationalism in full control, the individual a willing, depersonalized cog serving the ends of the universal community. It is really rather curious how closely the goal of Communism approximates an anticipatory projection or sensing from the drift of the last two or three centuries: it is like a Lindberghian "wave of the future."

Finally, the folk-sophisticate polarity, especially when it is viewed not so much as a scale but as a one-way drift, definitely overlaps with the emotionally tinged idea of "progress" that is discussed farther on in this chapter, in § 127-128.

122. INTEGRATION—INHERENT OR INDUCED

The double proposition can hardly be overaffirmed that most of what is in any one culture was produced outside of it, but that the highly composite product nevertheless is regularly felt as something coherent and integrated, and normally is accepted as "right." It is so accepted because the average individual is so thoroughly under the influence of his culture, has been so molded by it in growing up and adjusting to it, that even its incoherences and contradictions tend to be taken for granted as if they were logically sound and a-priori evident. It must be remembered also that any "average" individual knows little or nothing through convincing personal experience of other cultures, so that his own must appear to him as being natural and inevitable. He accepts his culture, his social inheritance, as he accepts the surrounding atmosphere he breathes, or as a fish accepts water. What is fifty years old in this culture and what is three thousand years old touch him alike and affect him alike. So do elements that the culture originated, and elements which were introduced into it. Thus it is no wonder that his immediate reaction to it is as to a homogeneous unit. It is only dissective analysis and knowledge of history that reveal the compositeness of any culture.

As regards the historical origin of its contents, accordingly, every civilization is what Lowie has called it: a "thing of shreds and patches," a "planless hodge-podge"; but it does not ordinarily seem so to the people living under it, nor does it function as such. Every culture is an accretion to a far greater degree than any living organism. It is the end product of a long series of events occurring mostly in other cultures, accidents from its own point of view, but ultimately of influence upon it. Plan or pattern there always is—and in some ways its pattern is the most important thing about any culture—see the whole next chapter: nevertheless, as regards origin, plan or pattern is secondary. The plan modifies the cultural material that flows in, sometimes rejects it, fits it all, native and foreign, into something that is not too discordant, something that the majority of the society can get along under tolerably and some of them successfully and pleasantly. It is patternings that produce the internal consistency. But it is important to recognize that cultures do not start with a pattern or predetermined plan and then fill it in. That is what inveterate reformers and dreamers of

Utopias do. Actual societies tend to evolve the plan of their cultures as the content of these grows. And the plan changes as introduced content changes, although traits of internal origin—innovations—are likely to develop in accord with the way the pattern-plan stands at the moment.

In short, cultures are constantly and automatically acquiring or reacquiring a sort of integration. But this is a very different thing from the organic integration that holds together, say, a grasshopper or a rabbit. This organic integration involves a pattern of finished animal that is essentially predetermined when two germ cells unite to start a new individual. Cultural integration—or for that matter human social integration—is invariably of a much looser sort. It is an accommodation of discrete parts, largely inflowing parts, into a more or less workable fit. It is not a growth of parts unfolding from a germ in accord with a pre-existing harmonious master plan. Such an unfolding has often been assumed, insinuated, or asserted by writers as diverse as Frazer, Spengler, and Malinowski. But it remains wholly undemonstrated, and history shows it to be at least partly untrue.

The point sometimes made, as by Radcliffe-Brown, that every society is confronted by the constant problem of how it is to preserve or maintain itself, seems a false analogy with the organic world, where the struggle for existence mostly is indeed keen. But when one society incorporates another, it does not ordinarily destroy it, except perhaps as a conceptually separate entity. Its members go on living under somewhat altered conditions; the frame of the society has been enlarged; whereas if a society splits, there merely are two instead of one. Culture we have seen to be even more plastic than societies in merging, partly merging, or dividing.

Moreover, while animals make every effort to maintain themselves, they are evidently not aware of a constant need of self-preservation; nor indeed are men, who are the most conscious of organisms. Food is necessary to life, and animals get hungry and set about satisfying their hunger, with pleasure if successful; but they do not feel it as an unremitting *problem* of self-preservation. That is rather the intellectual attitude of philosophers, or emotionally of neurotics. When it comes to societies and cultures, the problem of preservation seems even more philosophical and remote. The normal attitude of the normal man probably is that his society and culture were, are, and will be. If anything, he is likely to assume more perpetuity for them than they possess. And not without reason. Most cultures do continue for quite a while. Sooner or later they may be superseded, or altered out of recognition; but ordinarily there is no immediate prospect whatever of that.

In fact, what has impressed most observers is the power of persistence of cultures. They always change, but they change slowly—too gradually to suit the reformer. Every nation or tribe has its conservative party, whether it is so labeled or not. There is nothing mystical in this faculty of cultures to maintain themselves and to resist overrapid alteration. Any culture, even the lowly one of a small society, is a pretty big thing, a complex of thousands of items and activities, each interconnected with many others. It just is a large mass to dent, or roll along, or do away with. And this holds even more for the great civilizations of great nations. There is so much to them that it is almost a wonder that they alter as much as they do. Even pieces of them are enormous. Take the government of the State of Pennsylvania, or the Presbyterian Church, or the educational system of Switzerland, or the commerce of England, and think of all they comprise, plus all that they touch or interlock with in addition. How can they be destroyed quickly, except by rare world catastrophes or revolutions? Big things at rest have great inertia, and if in motion they have great momentum. Such seems the way to look at the enormous superindividual aggregations that we call our greater civilizations. They change; they are always changing; but at any given moment the expectation is that they will go on, mainly as they are, though never wholly so. To fail to realize this is to disregard the total trend of history.

123. MOLDING THE INDIVIDUAL

Through being born into a society, every individual is also born into a culture. This culture molds him, and he participates in it.

The degree to which every individual is molded by his culture is enormous. We do not ordinarily recognize the full strength of this shaping process, because it happens to everyone, it happens gradually, it is satisfying at least as often as it is painful, and usually there is no obvious alternative open anyway. Hence the molding is taken for granted and is accepted, like the culture itself— perhaps not quite unconsciously, but uncritically. The formal or deliberate part of the process we call education: education through schools, in religion, and in manners and morals primarily at home. These agencies convey the mores and some of the folkways (§ 116). But perhaps a larger fraction of the cultural tradition is acquired by each individual at his own initiative. He is left to "pick it up," to grow into it. In this class are his speech, bodily postures and gestures, mental and social attitudes, which he imitates from his elders or from near-age mates, and a thousand and one activities, such as putting on shoes, splitting firewood, or driving a car, which a child "learns," often without any formal instruction, because he has seen others do these things and wants to do them too.

How much of all that a person knows how to do, and does do, comes to him from outside, from the cultural environment that surrounds him, and how much from within, from his independent personality? The former is surely much the larger mass. That he speaks, say, English and not Chinese is the result of "where he is born" or raised; that is, of which language forms part of the culture in which he grows up. Similarly with his being a Christian instead of a Buddhist, casting his vote in November, observing Sunday, celebrating New Year on January 1 instead of in February, eating with a fork and not with chopsticks, and bread and butter in place of rice, tucking his shirt in and not out (in Kipling's day at least), saying hello to his parents instead of using honorifics, steering a tractor and not a lightly shod wooden plow, writing with letters instead of a thousand logograms, and so on endlessly. In fact, the mass of what any person receives from his culture is so great as to make it look at first glance as if he were nothing but an individual exemplar of his culture, a reduction of it abbreviated to the scope of what one personality can contain. All there remains of him that is not induced by his culture consists of two sets of things. First are his innate general human capacities, and second, his individual peculiarities.

The capacities—already discussed in § 30-35, 87-89, 103-105, and again in 241—merely ensure, just because they are generic, that our normal person has the faculty of learning to speak, to read, to operate tools, to practice a religion of some kind or other. What the kind of speech, tools, religion is depends absolutely on the culture, not on him. In other words, his birth as a normal man gives him certain potentialities, but his birth in a culture determines how these potentialities will be expressed and realized.

Individual peculiarities comprise such traits as speaking with a lisp or a drawl, having a bass or a tenor voice, worshiping piously or perfunctorily, being naturally tidy or hasty or bright or the opposite. These are individual variations from the average intelligence, energy, or temperament. They range all the way from genius to imbecility, from superexcitability to ultrasluggishness; but of course the great majority of individuals depart only slightly from the mean in any one trait. These "individualisms" or idiosyncrasies do have a physiological and hereditary basis, in the main. Yet in part their qualities too can be culturally induced, as when a drawl is a Southerner's or a cowboy's, or the tidiness and phlegm are those of Hollanders. In such instances it is the occasional Southerner who doesn't drawl, or drawls infernally, the Dutchman who is precipitate and disorderly, who represents the individual variation from the norm that is characteristic of the culture or the subculture of his society.

This brings us to a second class of features in which individuals differ: roughly, those areas which are alternatives within one's culture. Shall I be a farmer or a storekeeper or a dentist, go in for tennis or baseball or golf, join the Army or the Navy, be a Methodist or a Presbyterian or a Quaker? Here the culture leaves several choices more or less open to the individual members, though it is well to remember that each culture has a different array of choices. In unwesternized China, for instance, there would be no choice of dentistry or baseball or Navy, and the religious denominations available would be altered to Confucian, Buddhist, and Taoist. Even among ourselves, not all choices would be open to everyone everywhere: golf might be only a theoretical possibility to a farm laborer or a sheepshearer on the Great Plains. In fact in rigidly segregated India only a few of all occupations, worships, amusements, and foods known to Hindu civilization would be open to the members of any one caste.

In summary, heredity gives us at birth certain generic human faculties. How we shall use these, and therefore how we shall mainly live, the culture in which we are launched thereupon decides. But it leaves us, theoretically at least, certain choices between alternatives in its total scheme; and it leaves us also a degree of freedom of departure from its norms in personal mannerisms, innovations, and successes.

This enormous influence of culture in molding the individual has a bearing on psychology. This science is set up to study particular individuals in order to reach understanding of human beings in general; that is, of what might be called the abstracted human person. But since all individuals as they actually occur in life are patterned by culture, and their behavior is full of culture, the task of psychology is made difficult. This was not clear at first. But then psychologists began to realize how great was the effect on individuals of their happening to be exposed to different influences, as these exist within our civilization; how the children of articulate parents generally come to be above-average in verbal facility; how the children of unhappy or broken marriages are more likely than the average to be emotionally unstable in their adjustments to other persons; and so on. So "conditioning" came to be one of the slogans of modern psychology where innateness of behavior had been assumed before. Then, as psychologists gradually came to be culture-conscious also, the variety of cultures was seen to increase enormously the range of the conditioning people are subject to. The abstract man, or what the psychologist felt he could properly say about him, shrank in proportion. This is why there is such great difficulty, as we have seen (§ 86-90), in deciding how alike or different the heredity equipment of races or descent groups is. It is not that psychological tests are unsound. The tests are valid enough, within limits, within the culture for which they were constructed. They show at any rate how much culture an individual has absorbed in comparison with other individuals. They are less good at showing, per se, whether greater absorption is due to greater exposure or to greater inborn capacity. And the tests break down, or become dubious, when they are applied interculturally. Hence it is that we do not yet know how different the races are in their endowment, while we do know that cultures differ enormously in content and orientation. And of course individuals differ both in their heredity and in what their conditioning has made them.

124. PARTICIPATION

Besides differing in heredity and conditioning, individuals also differ in degree of participation in their culture. How large a share does a given person hold in the stock company of his society, and what dividends of satisfaction does it pay him? It is evident that the complex culture carried by a large society is just too big for one individual to take an active part in, in all its many departments. It is only the exceptionally gifted or favored member of a large society who can hope to operate successfully in a number of its more important activities. The run-of-the-mill man is likely to be equipped to follow only one or two occupations out of hundreds or thousands of existing ones, and to have a run-of-the-mill income, wife, home, a run-of-the-mill seat in the church or at the game, run-of-the-mill tastes, thoughts, and habits. With a little bad luck, he may even come out below-average in all or most of these things. In a culture full of books he may not read a newspaper; in a land of wealth he may be ragged and half-famished.

This is the counterpart, the seamy side, of what has already been discussed in § 118: that large societies make for division of labor and specialization of function, therefore for professional training, advances in the arts, and inventions or at least improvements in the ways of living. But as the total culture is thereby varied and enriched, it also becomes more difficult for each member of the society really to participate in most of its activities. He begins to be an onlooker at most of it, then a bystander, and may end up with indifference to the welfare of his society and the values of his culture. He falls back upon the immediate problems of his livelihood and the narrowing range of enjoyments still open to him, because he senses that his society and his culture have become indifferent to him. If the society and the culture retain a degree of integration, the lower classes may participate vicariously: in imagination, by symbols or through pageantry. The British lower classes participate thus in the life of the aristocracy, which is so much richer than theirs, and even more in the doings of the royal court. No doubt Egyptian peasant-serfs of five thousand years ago got some similar satisfactions out of what went on in the god-king's entourage at Memphis, or even when they contemplated his pyramid tomb over which they sweated for years in a labor draft. In fact, one of the uses or values of kings and costly courts is precisely to serve as symbols increasing the integration of large societies. But vicarious participation at best is partial, and it may be lacking. Wherever there exists a true urban proletariat, or where the mass of country people are outright serfs, a large part of the population is participating very incompletely in their culture and being denied many of its satisfactions. This in turn means that those who are most largely supporting the culture economically are getting the least of its rewards; and, reciprocally, that the values of the culture are being continued in their development by only a fraction of the society.

Most revolutions, successful and unsuccessful, seem to be preceded by such a condition of imperfect participation. Only we must remember that there is no absolute scale of measurement. A sufficient discrepancy in one country between actual participation and what is considered possible participation will bring on efforts at remedy; whereas elsewhere there may be even less participation by most of the society in most of the culture, but the ideal of participation being also low, the condition is endured fatalistically. Thus the French Revolution was precipitated not because the oppression and the nonparticipation of the lower classes were extreme: as a matter of fact, their situation was better than in some other European countries which did not revolt, and on the whole it had probably improved in the generation before 1789. But just because France was the home of enlightenment and considered itself the most highly civilized country in the world, the gap between top and bottom was felt keenly and engendered the revolution.

The Russian muzhik had probably achieved even less participation by the early twentieth century. Nor is it probable that Russia left to itself would have achieved a deep-going social revolution at one stroke. But conscious Westernization, initiated by Peter the Great two centuries before, finally brought in its train also the Marxian ideology, which was organized to operate by revolution on the gap of nonparticipation, and had as its ultimate aim the abolition of the gap. Marxism completely missed its own prediction of first succeeding in the most highly industrialized countries of Europe. It did succeed in a marginal area of low industrialization, because the standard of living and cultural participation of the population in Russia had remained unduly low for twentieth-century-conscious Europe—and for twentieth-century-Europe-conscious Russian intellectuals.

The contrast of all this of course is with primitive cultures. Here societal units are small; skills, differentiations, and privileges are limited; and participations are reasonably equal. No one is evicted for nonpayment of rent, or left on the sidewalk to watch the prosperous stream into the opera. The simpler cultures have simpler and smaller problems to meet. Much of the eighteenth-century admiration of the romantic and unspoiled savage, and our own occasional hankerings after South Sea island idylls, stem from a vague sense of this fact. To be sure, it is well to remember that if the Ifugao and the Yurok and other nonliterate people did not evict, they did enforce debt slavery; and that others practiced war enslavement, human sacrifice, and cannibalism. Yet the total range of activities remained small enough so that even a slave might participate in more of the culture than a serf elsewhere, or than a free outcaste in India. Larger and richer cultures just do have bigger and harder social problems to solve.

125. CONTENT AND FORM; ETHOS AND EIDOS: VALUES

It is worth while to examine briefly certain overlapping distinctions among several aspects of culture. They are: content and form of culture; eidos and ethos; and material and nonmaterial culture.

The content of a culture is the sum of the items of which it is composed: things present in it—whether present or lacking in other cultures. For instance, kingship, hereditary titles of nobility, a state church, stringent libel and divorce laws, driving left on the road, spelling labor and honor with a *u,* are several big or little items contained in British civilization but not in its close American counterpart. However, British and American culture share as content steam engines and railways, alphabetic writing, representative parliamentary government, dairy foods, and many other items that until recently were wholly lacking in, say, China. It is content like these items which tends to increase and accumulate in the aggregate cultures of mankind, and to a certain extent even in one culture, and thus to give the impression of progress taking place (§ 127) though the process may actually be one largely of quantitative enlargement.

Cultural form is harder to describe or illustrate. We might approximate it by saying it is what is left over when we subtract cultural content from culture. What is this remnant? It may be a rearrangement, a transfer of an item or a group of items to other departments of the culture, to another of its jurisdictions. Thus education can be in clerical or in lay hands; schools may be parochial or public, as we say in America, parish or board in Britain. The education given may be very similar. In its elementary stages it is bound to be practically identical: *C a t* will spell *cat* and $3 \times 3 = 9$ whether the school and the teacher be democratic, religious, communist, or fascist. Yet we all know that the tenor or purport and the outcome of the schooling will be different—different enough to fight for, often. This is not wholly an affair of totalitarian propaganda aiming to thrive by liquidating everything else. Such extreme propaganda began to be developed chiefly some years after World War I. Yet even before then it obviously mattered who controlled the schools. Besides content, such as reading and arithmetic, education inevitably imparts an ideology, a *system* of beliefs and sentiments and values, which if accepted is all-important for its influence on conduct. An ideology or a system might also be called a pattern or configuration; that is, a way of arranging things.

Theoretically, one might conceive of two cultures whose itemized content was identical, and which yet differed in the form or arrangement or system or pattern of this content. Actually, form and content are far too interwoven for just such a situation to arise; but the hypothetical example will help point out what is meant by cultural form. A system or configuration is always, in its nature, more than the mere sum of its parts; there is also the relation of the parts, their total interconnections, which add up to something additionally significant. This is well recognized in "Gestalt" or configurational psychology. The "form" of culture may therefore be regarded as the pattern of interrelations of the contents that constitute it.

Somewhat related to the foregoing are a contrasting pair of aspects that have been called the *ethos* and the *eidos* of culture. Greek *eidos,* from which we have "idol" as a derivative, denotes form or appearance or likeness. The eidos of a culture would therefore be its appearance, its phenomena, all that about it which can be described explicitly. This would primarily coincide with cultural content as just discussed. The Greek word *ēthos,* from which we have "ethics," denotes first of all disposition. With reference to a people, it means their ways or customs, corresponding nearly to the Latin *mores.* Like that term, it carries an implication of what is sanctioned and expected. Hence the connotation of right or rightness, on which we have centered in our derivative Christian use of the words "ethical" and "moral" in their everyday sense. However, when we speak of the ethos of a culture, we revert at least part-way to the original Greek meaning, and refer not so much to the specific ethics or moral code of the culture as to its total quality, to what would constitute disposition or character in an individual; to the system of ideals and values that dominate the culture and so tend to control the type of behavior of its members.

Thus, we might say that the ethos of Italian Renaissance culture was sensuous and passionate, but that of the northern-European Reformation, puritan and ascetic. Hindu civilization is not only otherworldly but mystical, rationalizing, and extravagant in its ethos; Chinese, this-worldly, prosily moralistic, and matter-of-fact. The Japanese ethos differs from the Chinese in putting more emphasis on action, precision of form, and neatness.

It will be evident from these examples that ethos deals with qualities that pervade the whole culture—like a flavor—as contrasted with the aggregate of separable constituents that make up its formal appearance and are the eidos. The ethos includes the direction in which a culture is oriented, the things it aims at, prizes and endorses, and more or less achieves. We are here getting into metaphors that personify culture as if it had a will and a purpose of its own. That is a fault of the language of our day. Scientific thinking has penetrated so recently into these fields that it has failed as yet to work out its own more exact expressions. When we say that a culture aims at, prizes, and achieves certain ends, that is a shorthand way of saying that most of the members of a society, through having been molded by its culture, aim at, prize, and help achieve those ends. The ends or things referred to, the qualities that differentiate one culture from another, are undoubtedly distinctive, are genuine attributes of phenomena of history and nature. The difference between Western, Indian, and Far Eastern civilizations obviously consists of more than a diversity of content as exemplified by items of the order of eating with forks, fingers, and chopsticks respectively. Beyond these concrete facts, there is a pervading difference of character and outlook in the three cultures. That is what is meant by ethos.

It is evident that the ethos of a culture is pretty close to what a philosopher or a historian might call its system of values. This somewhat technical term denotes something that physical and biological scientists are agreed they cannot properly deal with by their methods, and therefore ought, as scientists, to leave alone—though most of them admit that there are such things as values, moral or otherwise, and personally try to live up to them. Whatever "values" are, it is clear that they have some relation to culture. Cultures differ in their values; each one shapes, or at least colors, its own. Values in this technical or philosophical sense might be informally defined as those things—cultural products, standards, or ideas—which men living in societies prize and hold as having a high importance, for them, for their group and descendants, and in themselves, over and beyond their practical utility. Christianity is one of the great values of our society and culture; so are the works of Shakespeare, and our democratic institutions and liberty—even the Liberty Bell, as a visible and tangible symbol. In China, Confucius would represent a similar value. No one would deny that these values influence human conduct and constitute real phenomena and effective forces in the world of history, and therefore of nature. This is true even though these same values have not been measured, and are regarded by the physicist and biologist as beyond the scope of their sciences. For the present, let us carry in mind that values exist and that they are tied up with culture. We shall be coming back to them again.

126. MATERIAL AND NONMATERIAL CULTURE

A distinction often made between material and nonmaterial culture is mentioned here only as probably having no first-rank significance. The literal difference is of course obvious: physical objects as against institutions and ideas.[6] But do they stand for something basically different? Do they function with significant difference in culture? The answer seems No. What counts is not the physical ax or coat or wheat but the idea of them, the knowledge how to produce and use them, their place in life. It is this knowledge, concept, and function that get themselves handed down through the generations, or diffused into other cultures, while the objects themselves are quickly worn out or consumed. It is the ax itself that is effective in chopping, the idea of the ax that is effective in getting axes made and available for use. In fact we can almost conceive of the ax as an institution, as we can certainly speak of lumbering and wearing clothes and grain farming in a sense entirely parallel to the institutions of marriage or churchgoing.

The attempt to segregate material from nonmaterial traits of culture perhaps derives from a white-collar distinction unfortunately long made in Germany between Naturwissenschaften and Geisteswissenschaften: sciences dealing with nature and sciences dealing with the human spirit. The latter corresponded to what we call the humanities and the social sciences. But there is nothing gained by implying that since humanistic and social studies have to do with the "spirit" or "mind," whereas natural science deals with tangible objects, the latter is therefore of a different and lower order. Such a point of view smacks of old-fashioned theology with its contrasting of body and soul. Genuine science is characterized first of all by its method, only secondarily by subject matter, except that this must be in nature and must consist of phenomena. My having learned how to write

[6] Material culture and content of culture partly overlap, but are conceptually different. Objects of material culture are part of culture content; but a lot of culture content is not material; monogamy, for instance, or mother-in-law avoidance, or belief in ghosts.

or being a Christian are phenomena; and equally so are the alphabet and Christianity and ax-using; and so are axes and clothes and chairs; and they are all parts of culture. Accordingly we may forget about this distinction between material and nonmaterial culture, except as a literal difference that it is sometimes of practical convenience to observe.

127. THE IDEA OF PROGRESS

One of the most widely held preconceptions is that culture is progressive. "The progress of civilization" is a familiar phrase—almost a trite one. Simple or primitive peoples are labeled "unprogressive." The implied picture is of a continuous moving forward and onward. Popularly, evolution is almost synonymous with progress; and progress means advance to something better.

Actually, the idea of progress is itself a culture phenomenon of some interest. Strange as it may seem to us, most of humanity during most of its history was not imbued at all with the idea. An essentially static world, a nearly static mankind, were most likely to be taken for granted. If there was any notion of alteration, a deterioration from the golden age of the beginnings was as frequently believed in as an advance. A definite system of belief in progress began to acquire strength only in eighteenth-century Europe. Reinforced by the French Revolution, it became a sort of article of liberal faith in the nineteenth century. It entered into the philosophy of Comte and Spencer. The latter saw evolution as a manifestation of progress. Darwin, who propounded a mechanism by which organic change might be explained—a mechanism about which the man in the street is mostly still a bit hazy—was popularly acclaimed as having "proved evolution"—that is, progress. The Unitarian profession of faith is interesting in this connection: "I believe in the Fatherhood of God, the brotherhood of Man, the leadership of Jesus, salvation by character, the progress of mankind, onward and upward forever." There is a certain nobility about this sentiment of liberalism; but it is as indubitably a sentiment and a dogma, and not a scientific conclusion, as are the Apostles' Creed and the Thirty-nine Articles. Progress has largely taken the place of Jesus in this most denatured branch of Christianity. But the concept of progress is far from being limited to that. If a poll were taken, devout Methodists and other Trinitarians would undoubtedly favor progress overwhelmingly and believe it to be enjoined by religion. So widespread is the modern attachment to the idea that even many strict fundamentalists would be shocked if told not to believe in "progress," in spite of some remaining inclination to balk at "evolution" as non-Biblical.

These instances are mentioned to show, first, that the concept of the progress of humanity is a special characteristic of contemporary Western civilization; next, that within this civilization it generally has the force of an a-priori assumption; and finally that, like most a priori's, it is adhered to with considerable fervor of emotion. All this does not disprove progress; but it does show that progress is something to be analyzed rather than taken for granted.

Now in a grand, over-all sort of way, there has undoubtedly been progress in human culture in the last quarter-million years. We are undeniably "higher" or "more advanced" culturally than the Acheulians, in much the same way that a mammal is higher than an Ordovician sponge or brachiopod. The real questions in this connection are: In what does progress consist? and, Is progress continuous and inevitable?

Let us consider these interrelated questions.

We have seen that, broadly speaking, the process of cultural development is an additive and therefore accumulative one, whereas the process of organic evolution is primarily a substitutive one. When men acquire flight, they add it to their former faculties; when birds acquired it, they converted a pair of legs into wings. One might thus fairly enough suspect that new culture tended to be incremental and not replacing; and that therefore the total stock of culture of any society, and of humanity as a whole, would show a normal inclination to grow. All in all, the verdict of history confirms such a judgment. There may have been occasional periods of stress for this or that society in which its total inventory of cultural items diminished. There is nothing to show that such hard times and shrinkages ever extended simultaneously to all the societies on earth. While one particular form of civilization is undergoing atrophy or decay, neighboring ones are usually coming into vigor. What Egyptian culture lost from 800 to 1 B.C.—if it did lose in total bulk—was more than made up for by the successive inventions and acquisitions of the contemporary Mesopotamian, Persian, Greek, and Roman cultures. The Dark Ages of western Europe, around A.D. 450 to 750, denote a period of breakup of an old pattern system before the patterns of a new system had been developed very far, with a resulting loss of political stability, intellectual and aesthetic achievements, urban refinement, and wealth; and in consequence very few superior men were able to realize themselves as "geniuses." But the historians most conversant with the era would probably find it difficult to say how much the total stock of western-European culture contracted during the Dark Ages, or to be wholly sure that it did contract seriously. Knowledge of Plato and Aristotle certainly was both less and rarer, and roads were not kept in as good repair; but useful and important new things like horseshoes and water mills (§ 183) became commoner. In any event, while Europe was perhaps receding, China was inventing printing and otherwise advancing.

Recessions in civilization, in short, either are local and likely to be compensated for elsewhere; or they primarily affect patterns or organization and the values of their products—cultural qualities.

And it does seem clear that in an over-all sort of way the sum total of culture of mankind has pretty continuously grown in bulk through history. As new artifacts and faculties are developed, the old ones tend to sink to a relatively more limited or humbler sphere, but rarely become entirely lost. Candles survive in the age of electricity, horses alongside motorcars, the bow beside firearms (§ 159); bronze has its special uses and virtues in the age of iron, and iron in that of steel. We use stone in more ways in modern civilization than Old Stone Age men did, although it was of primary significance to them but is only subsidiary to us.

Quantitatively, then, civilization advances because it tends in its nature to be accumulative; and to this extent the modern a priori of progress is justified. But will the admission of a mere swelling of bulk satisfy those who wish to believe in progress? Mostly, progress is taken to mean advance in higher qualities or toward more ideal values.

And there of course we get on subjective terrain. Is the philosophy of Plato or St. Thomas or Kant the highest and most valuable? Answers are obviously going to be colored by nationality and religion. A good Hindu might put all three of them lower than Sankara. Everyone will appreciate the values his own civilization has developed. Egocentricity in the form of ethnocentricity is inevitably injected into the problem, and makes the objective attack difficult. It is pleasant to believe in progress—which makes my times and my ways superior to all others—as it is pleasant to believe in the superiority of my nationality, my religion, my race, my language—my town or county even, my family, and myself.

Let us try, however, despite this emotional cloud, to discover something scientific or objective to justify a degree of acceptance of the progress idea. There are three approaches that seem to yield at least a partial standard of what constitutes "higher" or more advanced culture, apart from mere quantity of it.

The first is the criterion of magic and "superstition." In proportion as a culture disengages itself from reliance on these, it may be said to have registered an advance. In proportion as it admits magic in its operations, it remains primitive or retarded. This seemingly dogmatic judgment is based on the observation that beliefs in magic, such as are normal in backward societies, do recur in cultures that by profession have discarded magic, but chiefly among individuals whose social fortune is backward or who are psychotic, mentally deteriorated, or otherwise subnormal. When the sane and well in one culture believe what only the most ignorant, warped, and insane believe in another, there would seem to be some warrant for rating the first culture lower and the second higher. Or are our discards, insane, and hypersuggestibles perhaps right and the rest of us wrong?

For instance, a Lassik Indian woman in California lost and buried her baby. The next afternoon she heard a child crying overhead and fell over in a faint. She was revived, but she kept hearing the crying of the baby, and got progressively more ill. She engaged a shaman doctor to cure her, who finally said: "It is your own child's shadow (soul) coming back to urge you to accept him as a spirit helper aiding you to become a shaman yourself." This woman did not happen to want such supernatural power, and so she began to argue with her baby's shadow when its voice reappeared to urge her. She remained firm and told him to leave her alone, until finally he desisted, and she became well again.

To be a shaman is an honored and respected status among most of the Californian tribes, and many individuals accept such spirit offers. In this event they gradually learn to tolerate association with the spirit, therewith recover their own health, and then profess and try to cure other people with the assistance of their invisible helper. It is clear that in these societies there is complete social and cultural acceptance of spirits and their ability to talk and aid; acceptance also of the power of the shaman who is so aided, and of the place of the shaman in the community. But in our culture a person who falls sick, hears voices, communicates with shadows, and acquires special abilities from them is inevitably classed as deranged.

Thousands of similar cases might be cited. They provide a consistent criterion of distinction between primitive or folk cultures and advanced or high cultures, apart from the respective quantity of content. The backward cultures in their magic, shamanism, animistic ritual, recognize as objectively effective certain phenomena that the advanced cultures regard as objectively unreal and as subjectively psychotic or deranged. The limits of relation of personality and world are differently drawn in the two series of cultures. What higher cultures stigmatize as personal, nonreal and nonsocial, abnormal and pathological, lower cultures treat as objective, conducive to ability, and socially useful.

It will be seen that the difference is in terms of socialization as well as reality. Backward peoples assume as actual certain phenomena to which we grant only a mental or subjective existence that is not real in the sense in which tangible human bodies or animals or stones are real. Or perhaps it is more accurate to say that retarded peoples are also aware of a distinction but invert the emphasis. To them a child or a hawk or a stone seen or heard in a certain kind of dream or trance is much more important than a physical child or hawk or stone that one can touch and handle, because it is the possible source of much more power. Certain things we classify as unreal the primitive considers superreal—with the result that his world often seems "surrealistically" fantastic to us. From this follows the difference in socialization. To us a person who hears the dead speak, or who thinks that he can turn into a bear or a wolf, is socially subnormal, socially useless, and likely to be a burden and an upset to the community. But among primitives he is a personality of special, enhanced, and productive powers, which he may indeed abuse in witchcraft, but which ordinarily are believed to help the community to better health, surer food supply, victory over enemies, and similar benefits. So the primitive weighs and favors the magical where we reject and try to exclude it. Our values rather than our perceptions differ from his. He recognizes, standardizes, rewards certain psychotic or neurotic experiences—socially channels them—which we regard as well outside our socially approved channels.

It is important for a clear grasp of the foregoing view to realize that it has no reference to the supernatural as such. Belief in God is not a sign of backwardness. All that is contended is that the bestowal of social rewards for the inability to distinguish subjective experiences from objective phenomena, or for the deliberate inversion of the two, is a presumable mark of lack of progress.

In so far, then, as the mentally unwell in modern advanced cultures tend to correspond to the well and the influential in ancient and retarded cultures, at least in certain situations, we can accept objective progress as having taken place.

128. MORE ABOUT PROGRESS

There is a second group of traits that characterize backward as against advanced cultures. These have to do with the obtrusion of physiological or anatomical considerations into social situations, or with the related matter of the taking of human life. Some of these practices are: blood or animal sacrifice; segregation of women at parturition and menstruation as being contaminating to others; contamination by death or corpses, often with segregation of mourners until purified; puberty crisis rites, especially for girls at the onset of physiological puberty; preoccupation with the dead body, including mummification, skull preservation and skull cult, wearing of skull or jaw by widows, disinterment and reburial, eating of bits of the body or of cremation ashes; ritual prostitution and inversion; human sacrifice; retainer burial; head-hunting; cannibalism. These practices almost invariably contain an element of the magical or the supernatural, and so far as they do they are allied to the class of traits we have just reviewed as being apparently characteristic of cultural retardation. But they contain also a second element, toward which cultures that have once abandoned such practices react with aversion, disgust, revulsion, or the shame of bad taste. This other element has as its common denominator what strikes us as the gratuitous obtrusion into public recognition and the social order of physiological happenings, including blood and death and decay, which we tend to regard as matters best kept private and unemphasized, and their public obtrusion as unpleasant and useless. Deformation of the head by pressure, filing or knocking-out of the teeth, pattern scarifications, distention of lips and ear lobes and other anatomical mutilations, can perhaps be included here because they also have to do with the human body and tend to arouse shock or disgust in us; though mostly they affect anatomy rather than physiology and sometimes have little or no magical motivation. At any rate, they constitute a set of folkways allied to the class we are considering. It is true that our fashions have developed strange coiffures, cosmetics, corsets, and such, but they lack the element of permanent bodily defacement, of mutilation.[7]

All in all, retarded cultures seem infantile both in their unabashed preoccupation with bodily functions and in their disregard of other human lives as compared with the gratifications of the ego. In this sense, advanced cultures may be described as psychologically more adult. Hence their unwillingness to interest themselves in personal physiology, but their concern about humaneness. The latter is manifest also in trends like those of opposition to slavery, torture as a judicial procedure, beatings as legal punishment, execution with torture, slaughter of prisoners of war.

While, apart from deformatory practices, the primitive folkways enumerated almost always have ritual approval or supernaturalistic association, it is equally significant that the advanced "universal" or world religions, Buddhism and Mohammedanism as well as Christianity, have consistently and positively thrown their weight on the prohumane and anti-infantile side. In other words, what primitive religion approves or enjoins in this field, civilized religion forbids. This suggests that the role of religion is secondary in these matters: it tends to fortify such standards of decency, humanity, cleanliness, and propriety as each culture has attained or only partly attained. It sanctions the mores more than it causes them. The present class of criteria of progress, then, consisting of adult attitudes toward physiological function, in which the magical and supernatural elements appear to be only indirectly contributory, accordingly differs from the class discussed in the last section, in which the animistic and surrealistic element is basic and essential.

Of course, we are dealing here with exceedingly broad trends or drifts, which cannot be uniform in particulars. Retarded cultures form an enormous class, advanced ones another, and there is bound to be a deal of variation in each. For instance, the Eskimo, as nonliterate, nonmetallurgical hunters, are always reckoned as primitives. In fact it was long fashionable to begin the scale of civilization with Australians, Bushmen, Negritos, and Eskimo at the lower end. Yet the Eskimo do not possess in very emphatic form any custom of the class now being discussed, and lack some of them altogether. Judged by this criterion alone, Eskimo culture would have to be rated as more advanced than some high civilizations—possibly that of much of India. In short, what we are dealing with is not a handy yardstick, but a probability tendency that holds good on the whole or in the long run.

Among the North American Indians, the Western ones were particularly

---

[7] Chinese foot-binding seems to be the only case of serious mutilation practiced in a great recent civilization. Ear-piercing and circumcision are after all anatomically negligible. Foot-binding is rather a special phenomenon. It is consciously erotic with a tingeing of the perverse to the point of making overt discussion of its motivation taboo; and its disabling effect limited the practice to certain economic classes.

obsessed by notions of contamination through birth, menstruation, and death. The Eastern tribes took these fears more lightly, but, here and there at least, went in for retainer burial and human sacrifice, ossuaries and reburial, and scalping as perhaps a partial equivalent of head-hunting.

But the total trend of development in the area and the era of the great religions is unmistakable. The way in which the blood sacrifice of the ancient Mediterranean peoples, and of South and East Asiatic ones, is perpetuated among marginal primitives is discussed in § 165, 192, and 238. The hecatombs and libations and feasts of Achilles and Agamemnon survive as sacrifices and feasts of water buffalo, chickens, and palm wine among the pagan Igorot of the Philippines and in West African Dahomey. In China, ritual bloodshed and funerary deposit of valuables have long since been replaced by offerings of symbolic paper figures. In Japan, more distant from the advanced center, retainer burial went on until the early centuries of our era, when it was replaced, on avowed grounds of humanity, by pottery imitations of the living retainers. Leviticus, one of the later books of the Old Testament in date, is still full of blood sacrifice. "Whatsoever man of Israel that killeth an ox or lamb or goat . . . and bringeth it not unto the door of the tabernacle, to offer an offering unto the Lord . . . blood shall be imputed to that man . . . he shall be cut off from among his people. . . . And the priest shall sprinkle the blood upon the altar of the Lord . . . and burn the fat for a sweet savour unto the Lord." [8] These practices were still in full blast when Titus destroyed Jerusalem in A.D. 70. They did not differ, save in deity worshiped and place and detail of manner, from the sacrifices that Titus and his pagan Romans made. Graeco-Roman paganism died out; Judaism lived; but, after the obliteration of the Temple in Jerusalem, sacrifices quietly dropped off from Jewish cult: they were becoming contrary to the spirit and attitudes of the times. Since more than a thousand years ago the most orthodox Jews no more think of slaughtering animals on the altars of their synagogues than do Christians in their churches. A tacit dropping of this part of their law was no doubt a condition of their being able to survive at all within the pale of civilization.

The first great religion to break resolutely with all the ancient ritual obsession on physiology was Buddhism.[9] One of its cardinal injunctions is against the killing of animals, even for food. This was part of its fundamental revolt against its parent, Vedic Brahmanism, in which sacrifice and bodily purification were basic. Five hundred years later, Jesus seems never to have sacrificed on the altar nor to have mentioned such sacrifice; and therewith it was tacitly, but decisively,

---

[8] Leviticus 17: 3-6. For more on blood and burnt offerings, see Leviticus, Chaps. 1-9; for defilement and purification from childbirth see Chap. 12; menstruation, Chap. 15; death, Chap. 21.

[9] Jainism did so equally, is coeval, and still living; but it became an Indian sect instead of a world religion.

eliminated from Christianity.[10] Six centuries later still, Mohammedanism followed suit completely. Even the minor religions and hybrid sects of the period, such as Manichaeism, discarded the practice. The one exception was Mithraism, which stressed not only the sacrifice of a bull but baptism in its gushing blood. Mithraism, an offshoot of Persian Mazdaism, began earlier than Christianity, which is perhaps why it retained the blood feature. Up to the third century after Christ, it still competed with Christianity, but it weakened, lost out, was suppressed in the fourth century, and died without trace or survival: it was literally too raw for its times in the civilized parts of the world.

Illustrations could be multiplied, but these examples may suffice.

Finally, there is a third way in which the idea of progress in culture can be justified by objective evidence. This is in technology, mechanics, and science, whose accomplishments have definitely more cumulative quality than other civilizational activities. It is true that high scientific productivity appears to come in bursts or pulses as definitely as art (§ 136). But there is the difference that each art, or for that matter each philosophy or religion, very largely has to begin all over again, whereas each of the intermittent periods of discovery in science can begin, and generally does begin, just about where the last one left off. Science, and in the main technology, are evidently accumulative by nature, while philosophy, religion, art—and empire and nationalism too—tend strongly to be substitutive: a new product replaces an old one. Consequently, once technological or scientific achievements have been made, they are likely to be retained, even through long sterile intervals, until there is a new flashing-up of inventions. A pulley or a water wheel, geometry and the laws of the lever, do not usually get themselves wholly forgotten or abandoned, even in times of wrack and misery. There may be lost mechanical arts or lost branches of science; but they are certainly neither numerous nor important, as will appear in a following chapter (§ 156-160).

Here then is a third manner of progress of civilization. But with it we are back largely among aspects that are quantitative—like growth in population, growth in size of states and nations, growth sometimes in the number and complexity of their political subdivisions. Similar perhaps also is growth in stocks of wealth—more gold, diamonds, farmed acres, houses in the world: part at least of the old are physically preserved, and new ones added. But we have already seen that there is serious doubt whether magnification as such, mere quantitative swelling-up, can be legitimately construed as progress. Size is easy to boast about, but does it bring with it wiser living or greater happiness? Only so far as it does can quantitative increase of culture be considered as making for progress.

[10] The only mentions of sacrifice or offering in the New Testament, other than references to Jewish and pagan sacrifice, are symbolic: as when St. Paul says that Jesus "appeared to put away sin by the sacrifice of himself" (Hebrews 9: 26); or the "blood of the Lamb" in Revelation.

In summary, the quantitative expansion of the content of total human culture; the atrophy of magic based on psychopathology; the decline of infantile obsession with the outstanding physiological events of human life; and the persistent tendency of technology and science to grow accumulatively—these are the ways in which progress may legitimately be considered a property or an attribute of culture. They are the residuum supported by fact when the emotional and aprioristic idea of a continuous and inherent progress of civilization is subjected to analysis. More will be found on this in the discussion of cultural losses already cited. And of course the folk-sophisticate polarity considered in § 121 partly overlaps with the idea of progress.

129. FUNCTION

Function has been increasingly dealt with in cultural anthropology, as in other branches of study and science, in recent years. The basic meaning of "function" is activity or operation that is natural, proper, or characteristic, such as "secretion of bile and storage of sugar are functions of the liver." From this there is a shading into the popular meaning of purpose: such as the function of a broom is to sweep. Between is a whole series of vague and elusive meanings; consult any unabridged dictionary in confirmation. Through most of these meanings runs the idea of a relationship that is active but not causal.

Linton has tried to clarify these variable concepts by distinguishing form, meaning, use, and function in culture. The *form* of a culture trait or complex is what can be perceived by the senses and objectively described.[11] The *meaning* is its subjective associations in the culture, implicit and explicit. Its *use* is its relation to things outside the society and culture, as expressible in physical terms; its *function* is its relation within the society and culture. For instance, the form of an ax comprises the blade and the handle, the curve of the bit, the steel of which it is made. It is this sensory aspect of a trait or complex that obviously passes or diffuses most readily from one culture to another. The use of an ax, according to Linton, is to chop wood; its function, to keep members of the society warm by providing fuel, and to make carpentry possible by providing logs. It is evident that if consideration of purpose has not already crept into the statement of use and function here, it is not far distant. As to the meaning of an ax, while Linton does not expatiate on this, it is evident that this is variable, not only between different cultures, but according to context within one culture. An ax is not only a household and a vocational tool, but a weapon and the instrument

---

[11] Obviously, "form" as used here is that aspect of the *elements* of culture which has to do with their *sensory* appearance; whereas in § 125 "form" means the *organization* of the contents of a *whole* culture. A more discriminating terminology will presumably come into usage someday—perhaps "appearance" for Linton's "form," and "organization" for the form that is contrasted with content. At present, the context will usually leave no doubt as to which meaning is intended.

of the executioner. In the primitive parts of southeastern Asia and the East Indies, it has powerful meaning in connection with head-hunting. In ancient Rome, in Fascist Italy, in Republican France, the lictor's ax, in conjunction with the bundle of rods or fasces, is a well-known symbol of punishment, and therefore of governmental authority. In ancient Crete, the double-bitted ax or labrys was a sign of divinity and a cult object. Axes of bronze, jade, and polished stone have meant wealth or treasure to people emerging out of primitiveness, in ancient Greece and elsewhere.

The form of a ballot would comprise its material, size, shape, columns, arrangement of offices and candidates. Its meaning might be said to be popular freedom and sovereignty; its use, to elect officials; its functions, democratic and representative.

A song would have its form given by its melody and rhythm: it is a succession of particular notes. The meaning or association would be patriotic, sentimental, or religious according as the song was "The Star-spangled Banner," a blues, or a hymn. The use would similarly vary from opening a patriotic meeting, entertainment at a night club, or conduct of a church service. In fact, the national anthem has repeatedly been used to prevent incipient riots by compelling everyone to stand still at attention. The function of songs is, as usual, the vaguest aspect: to strengthen patriotism, make a drink more enjoyable, further piety.

The mother-in-law taboo of many nonliterate peoples is characterized as to its form—or its substance too, if one will—by silence, looking aside, moving away. Its obvious use is to prevent contact between in-laws of opposite sex and different generation. The meaning is, according to the usual testimony of those who practice the custom, an expression of respect, or conversely of shame if the respect were violated by familiarity. The function is usually believed to be avoidance or easement of social strain. However, it is well to observe that this functional relation is one-way: wherever the custom obtains, relief from strain is likely to be its function; but where it is not customary, its *practice* would immediately cause strain, of much the same kind and strength as would result from nonobservance of the custom where it is mandatory. Opposites can therefore fulfill the same function in different cultures, or in different situations. So can wholly diverse acts: making a gift, inviting to a meal, speaking politely or flatteringly, or tabooing one's mother-in-law, all can ease social strain.

A wreath may be defined as a ring of floral elements, either worn on the head or hung. We use bridal, funeral, and Christmas wreaths, whose connotations and meanings are certainly even more diverse than their materials or colors. Not so long ago, in Europe, the bridal wreath was definitely a prized symbol of virginity. The ancients wore chaplets or floral wreaths as a party dress, and hung them on sacrificial victims. They also gave laurel wreaths as honors, and called them crowns when they were imitated in gold. For wreaths, meaning and use are evidently pretty much coextensive. And the function of wreaths?

Can we say much more than that it is to express by a visible symbol an emotion of joy or sorrow appropriate to a given situation? But one might also wonder whether such a statement means anything more than that wreaths, like a hundred other kinds of things, serve as symbols of feelings.

It is evident from these examples that the function of a cultural act or trait differs from its form, use, and meaning in that these three all reside in the culture, but the function is something we read into the culture. The "meaning" of a trait may be literally "subjective," as that of a mourning wreath, or of "The Star-spangled Banner"; but everybody in the culture is agreed on it, so that the fact of the meaning can be ascertained objectively. Indeed many of us are none too sure of the whole tune or words of the American national anthem—that is, we often do not securely control its "form"—but no one doubts that its significance is patriotic. Similarly, we all know what a black or white wreath hung by the front door means, though many of us might be somewhat hazy as to the material it was made of, or wonder whether the "use" might be to express respect, to give warning that a corpse lay in the house, or to keep tradesmen and solicitors away. Still, everyone in the society is at least roughly informed as to such points. By contrast, function is something that the student or analyst of culture finds out about. Function is an interpretation, something in *his* mind, which he attributes to a culture; but the form, use, and meaning of artifacts and institutions are actually part of the culture.

This is not so different, in one way, from the role of physiology. A healthy body functions without awareness. True perception of physiologic function is the result of dissection, observation, test, experiment, and the laboratory. Even some highly civilized peoples have been quite random in distinguishing nerves and veins, let alone veins from arteries, and have variously associated emotions, feelings, and thought with the bowels, the liver, the heart, or the brain. The difference between physiological function and cultural function is that the physiologist has his laboratory and can experiment, and the student of culture has not this advantage. In many cases he can only guess as to function—as the Greek, mediaeval, and Chinese physicians largely used to guess as to physiological function.

Professedly functional studies of culture accordingly tend to contain a maximum of theory, interpretation, or opinion, often based on a relatively narrow selection of facts seen as significant. Their value as well as their weakness lies in this point.

130. PURPOSE AND NEED

At bottom, much of the preoccupation of anthropologists with cultural function seems to boil down to two things: concern with purpose, and concern with integration. Integration has already been considered (§ 122). It remains to consider purpose; or, as it is more fashionable to disguise it: need.

Preoccupation with purpose appears for one thing to be due to the fact that there are many cultural beliefs and institutions which serve no visible utility, or at least no utility that could not equally well be attained by other means, and which are adhered to merely because they are customary and "right," like the mother-in-law taboo just discussed; or which are destructive and unprofitable, like most war. Why are there exogamic groupings? Why are these often totemic? Why is eating their totem often forbidden to members of a group, but perhaps enjoined in special cases? Why are uncles called fathers by many peoples? Why are adolescents initiated into the sacred mysteries of adults, where they learn that apparent spirits or gods are only disguised fellow tribesmen? Why does a Yurok not eat in a canoe while it floats on the ocean? To all these questions there is no obvious answer of the sort of answer there is to why an arrow is feathered or what use a fish net has. Moreover, the practices cited are all limited to certain societies and do not occur in others, including our own. Accordingly, the practices cannot correspond to any universal need, bodily, emotional, or social; at any rate, not to any real or objective universal need. A native may think his baby will die if he does not observe the couvade taboo restrictions (§ 225). But since the babies of non-couvading peoples also live and these nations manage to multiply, the quite genuine problem remains for the reflective student: What actual need is fulfilled, what good or purpose subserved, by people's believing in the necessity of the couvade? Or for that matter, in the necessity of clans, totems, initiations, taboos, and all the rest.

The simplest and soundest answer is that the need, good, use, or purpose is often imaginary; that a lot of culture is irrational, and that collectively human minds are as full of aberrations as individual minds—or fuller. But most of these irrationalities are harmless, or at least not destructive. It may bore a man, or be inconvenient to him, to lie around the house inactive for days after his baby is born. But he has the compensating satisfaction of believing that he has strengthened the child's life; and there will normally be brothers or friends around to see that the needed household and living chores get done. What we call the more primitive cultures are full of such extravagances, of strange, unpredictable, exotic doings; variable, and suggestive of the habits of children, of neurotics, and even of psychopaths; sometimes highly charged with emotion, but quite unreasonable; often vehemently backed by the mores or ethical sentiments of society. Quite likely our civilization has its share of counterparts, which we cannot segregate off from the more practical remainder of the business of living because we are engulfed in this civilization of ours as we are in the air we breathe. Some centuries may be needed before the full recognition of our own nonrational couvades and totems and taboos becomes possible.

Obviously, it is going to/be very difficult to explain all these extravagances and absurdities on the basis of any coherent system of specific needs that they satisfy or purposes which they serve. The phenomena are too variable, the presumable motivations too diverse. Some nations follow the couvade, some do not;

some set up social groups to forbid intermarriage, some merely specify the forbidden kindred. Certain of the practices seem actuated by fear or lack of assurance, others by hope of a positive gain or reward; still others may spring from restlessness, from the pleasure and excitements of change (§ 166-167). Or they may have originated from one of these motivations in a particular, transient situation; but the situation having passed, the practice continues to be followed—without motivation, or with a new one. It is plain that any general explanation of phenomena as variable as these is bound to be thin, commonplace, and trite; it can be vivid and satisfying only as it is particular and special.

For instance, let us consider one of the most widespread of these "aberrations," the belief in and practice of magic. No culture has been free of it; in no two cultures has it been identical. An older view, that of Frazer, sees in magic an impersonal counterpart of religion, a sort of applied pseudo-science that deals with cause-and-effect relations; the supposed causal relations are untrue, but they contain a logic, in that, like the cause and effect of our science, they recognize and deal with similarities and with proximities or contacts. A later interpretation by Malinowski construes magic as a response to the human sense of helplessness in a world beyond control: we invent a control, however fictitious, to reassure ourselves and make living more endurable. Incidentally, the two interpretations are not contradictory; they differ in emphasis rather than in being exclusive. Malinowski goes on to assert that where people feel competent in a situation, they tend not to invoke magic. Pacific islanders fish inside the lagoon without bothering with spells, charms, and amulets; these are reserved for fishing beyond the reef, where boats can founder or be blown away, where sharks bite, and the surf pounds, where the prizes as well as the risks are greater.

This explanation may hold for some Pacific peoples but it is not a universally valid principle. In that event the Eskimo, who have to contend with far greater dangers from ice, currents, waves, drowning, freezing, and starving than the Melanesians, ought to make much more use of magic than the Melanesians; whereas, in point of fact, they use it less. They are far more practical, competent with tools, and self-reliant. They may make magic for a whale; they do so occasionally for seals if these leave them altogether in the lurch; perhaps never for fish. One might pick up the point of self-reliance and say that it is precisely there that the Eskimo broke loose from magic, relatively speaking: that their subsistence problems were so tough that no bolstering of their courage with magic would have sufficed for their survival. They had to find techniques that actually killed the seal and brought the hunter back alive, or perish; and with such techniques, they became self-reliant, and discarded much of their magic. But with this concession, the explanation by need is weakened. Magic is no longer a regular response to an automatic human need for assurance (§ 250). This need is itself a variable, dependent on degree of technological invention, and perhaps on other factors as well. Contact with a new people may result in the learning of new weapons, tools, or techniques, increased competence and self-assurance, and a falling-away of the cumber of magic. Contact with a new people is certainly among what we call the accidents of history; and if such accidents can influence the amount or kind of magic or animism practiced, it is plain that the explanation of magic as a function of a constant and imperative need, universally intrinsic to the human psyche, pretty much falls to pieces.

Of similar import is the fact that, in the same Pacific Ocean, Polynesians are on the whole less magic-ridden than Melanesians; and among Polynesians the Samoans are described as taking their animism with comparative lightness (§ 250), and the Hawaiians as having been bored with their religion to the point of wanting to discard it (§ 168). Here we are within the range of almost identical environments and therefore presumably very similar needs and problems.

Another irregularity is furnished by the Yurok and the Karok of native California. These tribes lived in a climate of no rigors, on a river that gave them abundance of salmon, in a land full of acorns that were their staple, and for centuries no foreign foes nor even pestilences invaded them. Their food supply was greater and their population denser than in most of California, yet they had hedged themselves in with a thousand do's and don't's of magic. You didn't drink river water because it might have been poisoned, nor drink in strange places; you didn't eat in a boat on the ocean, nor on the river-mouth spit, nor before going hunting or doing the day's heavy work. You did not eat deer and whale meat at the same time, nor bear meat and salmon. After eating venison, it was obligatory to wash your hands, but in a basket, not in a stream. You might sleep with your wife in the brush or in a camp, but not in your house, else your shell money took offense and left you. Your bow had to be made from that side of a yew tree which faced away from the river. And so on ad infinitum. Yet need cannot be invoked as cause, as we have already seen. The elaboration of all this magic and taboo system of the Yurok and the Karok is due to an orientation of the culture that has nothing to do with any necessities or actual problems. For some unknown reason the culture just had gone hypochondriac, and all members of the society, whatever their congenital individual dispositions, had fear and pessimism pounded into them from childhood on.[12] They were taught by all their elders that the world simply reeked with evils and dangers, against which one sought protection by an endless series of preventive taboos and magical practices. (See also § 253.)

We must conclude, accordingly, that there is no relation of simple function between specific organic needs rooted in the body and the mind or in the en-

---

[12] One might also try to explain such pervasive timidity by frequency of social fears or interpersonal strains. The Yurok had a good many person-to-person quarrels and enmities, but few class or communal clashes. It is difficult to say whether they experienced more social strain than tribes of courageous and optimistic outlook, such as the Dakota or the Mohave. Beyond this—is it a tense, hypochondriac disposition that leads to clashes with people, or is it actual enmities which make a people hypochondriac even toward nature? It would be hard to say. In most cases of this type, the causality tends to be circular: each effect tends to become a reinforcing cause.

vironment of man on the one hand, and his cultural activities, such as magic, on the other hand. Whether it be magic or art, mythology or elaboration of social structure, or what not, cultural activities differ so much, from people to people and from period to period, in their strength and in the forms assumed, that it is impossible to derive these activities from, or even to relate them rigorously to, any intrinsic organic necessities, which must in their nature be far more constant. Of course, organic factors are always present and operative. But as soon as we have culture at all, another set of factors also becomes operative: ideas, beliefs, and the practices and affects attached to them—cultural manifestations such as no subhuman animal shows. And these factors being highly variable, their expression in specific but unstable cultural traits and complexes must be variable and complex, with considerable play or give-and-take. The most immediate functional relations of cultural phenomena are to cultural variables and epiphenomena, not to organic constants such as physiological necessities or psychobiological imperatives.

CHAPTER EIGHT

Patterns

PATTERNS are those arrangements or systems of internal relationship which give to any culture its coherence or plan, and keep it from being a mere accumulation of random bits. They are therefore of primary importance. However, the concepts embraced under the term "pattern" are still a bit fluid; the ideas involved have not yet crystallized into sharp meanings. It will therefore be necessary to consider in order several kinds of patterns. We may call these provisionally the universal, the systemic, the societal or whole-culture, and the style type of patterns.

131. THE UNIVERSAL PATTERN

The *universal pattern* was proposed by Wissler, with the alternative designation of "the culture scheme." It is a general outline that will more or less fit all cultures. It is therefore fundamentally different from the other kinds of pattern, since these all apply either to particular cultures or only to parts of cultures. The universal pattern consists of a series of nine heads under which all the facts of any culture may be comprehended. The nine heads are: Speech, Material Traits, Art, Knowledge ("mythological" as well as "scientific"), Religion, Society, Property, Government, and War. These subdivide further, as desirable. Thus under Society, Wissler suggests marriage, kinship, inheritance, control, and games; under Material Traits, food, shelter, transport, dress, utensils, weapons, and industries; Government is divided into political forms and legal procedures.

It is apparent at once that this universal pattern with its heads and subheads is like a table of contents in a book. It guides us around within the volume rather than giving us the essence or quality of it. Except for minor variations, the universal pattern is in fact identical with the table of contents of most books descriptive of a culture, such as a standard ethnographic report on a tribe. The main heads are conventional captions for those classes of facts which common sense and common experience lead us to expect to be represented in every culture. We know of no people without speech, food habits, artifacts, property, religion, society, and so on. We can say therefore that these captions represent a sort of common denominators found in all cultures, and that the universal pattern consists merely of the series of these common denominators expectably represented in any culture—represented perhaps very variably but represented somehow.

It is evident that the greater the range of cultures considered, and the more diverse these are, the more will the universal elements or common denominators shrink or become vague. The proportion of universal or common traits in the total range becomes less and less as this total grows more diverse, while at the same time the concepts corresponding to the captions have to be increasingly stretched to accommodate the facts or traits. Thereby the most characteristic features of each culture get blurred out. The Yurok, and again the Ifugao, have a highly intricate legal system, but a minimum of political institutions— in fact it might be argued whether they properly have any. This is certainly an interesting situation in that it differs so radically from our own culture, where not only both law and government are highly developed but law is made to depend on government or to derive from it. This characterizing distinction, which is obviously significant for the understanding of Yurok or Ifugao culture, and almost certainly significant also for understanding our own culture better—this and similar distinctions are lost in the degree that one does one's describing in terms of the common denominators of the universal pattern.

This universal pattern thus boils down to a rough plan of convenience for a preliminary ordering of facts awaiting description or interpretation. No one seems to have developed the idea since it was set forth in 1923, or to have made serious use of it toward deeper understanding. We will therefore pass on to other kinds of patterns.

132. SYSTEMIC PATTERNS

A second kind of pattern consists of a system or complex of cultural material that has proved its utility as a system and therefore tends to cohere and persist as a unit; it is modifiable superficially, but modifiable only with difficulty as to its underlying plan. Any one such systemic pattern is limited primarily to one aspect of culture, such as subsistence, religion, or economics; but it is not limited areally, or to one particular culture; it can be diffused cross-culturally, from one people to another. Examples are plow agriculture, monotheism, the alphabet, and, on a smaller scale, the *kula* ring of economic exchange among the Massim Melanesians. What distinguishes these systemic patterns of culture—or well-patterned systems, as they might also be called—is a specific interrelation of their component parts, a nexus that holds them together strongly, and tends to preserve the basic plan. This is in distinction to the great "loose" mass of material in every culture that is not bound together by any strong tie but adheres and again dissociates relatively freely. As a result of the persistence of these systemic patterns, their significance becomes most evident on a historical view.

As we mentally roam over the world or down the centuries, what is impressive about these systemic patterns is the point-for-point correspondence of their parts, plus the fact that all variants of the pattern can be traced back to a single original form.

The alphabet is an example. Its history and variations are set forth in § 206-221. But we may anticipate here by pointing out that the alphabet was invented only once, by a Semitic people in southwestern Asia previous to 1000 B.C.; that it operates on the principle of a letter symbol for each minimal acoustic element of speech; that the letters for most sounds in any form of alphabet, no matter how specialized, always resemble the letters in some other alphabet, and through that, or still others, they resemble and are derived from the letters of the original alphabet; and that for the most part the order and often the names of the letters are the same, or where different, it is evident where and why they were altered. Thus Hebrew aleph, beth, gimel, daleth, correspond in sound, order, and name to Greek alpha, beta, gamma, delta, and to Roman and our A, B, C, D.

The pattern of plow agriculture comprises the plow itself; animals to draw it; domestication of these beasts; grains of the barley or wheat type sown by broadcast scattering, without attention to the individual seed, seedling, or plant; fields larger than gardens and of some length; and fertilization with dung, primarily from the draft animals. This system originated in the Neolithic period, probably in western Asia or near it, and by A.D. 1500 had spread from Morocco to North China—since then to the Americas and Australia as well. There are two other and parallel systems, both without plows originally: the rice and maize types of agriculture. The former involves small fields flooded by nature or irrigation, hand planting of seedlings and hand weeding; the associated animals, pigs and buffalo, were not formerly utilized in the rice-growing, though the buffalo is now put before the plow in some areas. This rice pattern began as a hoe-and-garden culture and still largely is such. Native American agriculture, centering around maize, also did not attempt to use the available domestic animals—llamas in the Andes—and therefore was also hoe farming, or even digging-stick farming. The planting was done in hillocks. Irrigation and fertilizing were practiced locally and seem to have been secondary additions. The plants grown in addition to maize were, with the exception of cotton, wholly unrepresented in the plow or rice patterns. The histories of the three systems have remained essentially as separate as their origins, except for some relatively recent transfers of draft animals and plows from the plow pattern into the two others where these began to be drawn into modern international, metropolitan civilization.

The exclusive-monotheistic pattern is Hebrew-Christian-Mohammedan. The three religions are outgrowths of one another and originated in a small area of southwestern Asia. The pattern comprises a single deity, of illimitable power, and exclusive of all others; so far as there are other spiritual beings, such as angels or saints, they are derivative from him; the deity is proclaimed by a particular human vessel inspired by the deity; and worship according to this revelation excludes and forbids any other worship. Cults and philosophies outside these three organized monotheisms have repeatedly attained to monotheism, or to a pantheism or a henotheism that would be hard to distinguish logically from monotheism. And many religions, even of backward peoples, recognize a supreme deity. But all these others regularly lack some of the features of the exclusive-monotheistic pattern, and their resemblances are thus only partial convergences of an analogical type. This merely analogical similarity of these "high-god" and miscellanously monotheistic religions goes hand in hand with their diversity of origin: they are not connected with the exclusive monotheisms, nor for the most part with one another. By contrast, the three exclusive monotheisms are homologous—structurally or part-for-part similar—and they are connected in origin: Jesus was a Jew, and Mohammed took his ideas from Jews and Christians.

The systemic type of pattern accordingly not only partakes of the quality of a system, but is a specific growth. It originates in one culture, is capable of spread and transplantation to others, and tends strongly to persist once it is established. It recalls the basic patterns of structure common to groups of related animals developed from a common origin, with the original pattern persisting through all superficial modifications as they occur under evolution. For instance, the basic vertebrate pattern includes a skull with lower jaw, vertebrate column, and, above the level of the fishes, two pairs of limbs each ending in five digits. Within the range of this pattern, there is endless variation. A snake has no legs, whales and some reptiles and amphibians possess only one pair. Birds have converted the front pair into wings; seals, into flippers; and moles, into "shovels." The digits carry claws in carnivores, hoofs in running mammals, nails in ourselves. They number five in man as in the salamander, never more than four in birds and in pigs, three in the emu, two in the ostrich and the cow, one only in the horse—not counting nonfunctioning vestiges. Not one of the thousand of species of amphibians, reptiles, birds, or mammals ever possesses more than two pairs of limbs or more than five digits; any six-fingered vertebrate is an individual malformation.

By contrast there are the arthropods, among whom the higher crustaceans have five pairs of legs (modifiable to claws or paddles), the spiders four, and the insects three pairs of legs and two pairs of wings; but none of the hundreds of thousands of species of arthropods ever show a five-digited limb. Such are the basic arthropod plans, which are endlessly modified according to order, family, and species. Thus many butterflies have only two pairs of legs; bees have two pairs of wings, but the related ants break theirs off after mating; flies have only one pair; beetles have two pairs but fly mainly with one, the other having become converted into a protective shell; worker ants, fleas, lice, and many others have long since become wingless. We might add that all arthropods have definitely segmented bodies, a skeleton on the outside, antennae, and pale bluish blood containing copper-protein haemocyanin, as compared with the nonsegmentation, inner skeleton, lack of antennae, and blood reddened by the iron-protein haemoglobin of all vertebrates.

It is true that these fundamental plans of structure of the subkingdoms of life such as the arthropods and the vertebrates, or of their classes like insects and mammals, constitute something very much bigger than the system patterns of culture. They are hundreds of millions of years old, expressed in thousands to hundreds of thousands of species and in trillions upon trillions of individuals. The culture patterns muster an age of only a few thousand years. Once established, the great biological patterns predetermine, as it were, the main frames within which evolution will operate. No arthropod can give rise to a vertebrate, or vice versa; their patterns are separated by profound, unbridgeable clefts. Evolutionary change takes place in the domains between these chasms—strictly speaking, between their subchasms. By contrast, cultural system patterns, such as exclusive monotheism, plow agriculture, the alphabet, pass from one race or society, from one major culture, to another, and rather freely. Each year men who otherwise remain in their ancestral culture are for the first time learning to plow, to read letters, to fixate on a single God. Such a transfer of pattern to new kinds of carriers is of course impossible in subhuman organisms, whose forms are dominated by irreversible heredity. But the transfer is characteristic of the very nature of culture, which is plastic, reversible, and capable of unlimited absorptions, anastomosings, and fusions. Hence the patterns within cultures impress us as shifting and often transient. They are so, in comparison with the grand patterns of organic life, just as everything cultural, being an epiphenomenon, something superadded to life, is relatively unstable, modifiable, and adaptable. What the present type of cultural pattern system shares with the fundamental organic patterns is that they both embody a definable system, in the repeated expressions of which, no matter how varied, there nevertheless is traceable a part-for-part correspondence, which allows each form or expression to be recognized as related to the others and derived from the plan as it originally took shape.

In fact, the peculiar interest of these systemic patterns is that, within the endless kaleidoscope of human culture, they allow us to recognize things that are actually related in origin as against things that appear similar but are not connected in origin. The patterns differentiate homologies from analogies, the biologist would say. Thus, the several examples of exclusive monotheism are both homologous and historically interconnected through derivation of one from the other. But the Chinese Heaven, the Indian Brahma, the Egyptian Aten, "god" in the abstract of the Greek philosophers, the supreme deities of many primitive religions, represent analogies or convergences. They are distinct, separate developments which led to results that seem similar. And so, Egyptian hieroglyphs, Mesopotamian cuneiform, Indus Valley, Mayan, and other ancient ideographic or mixed systems of writing, and the surviving Chinese system (§ 202-205) are like alphabets in that they function as more or less effective methods of visible-speech communication. But they are like them only in that functioning. All alphabets are genetically one—derived from a single source; the other methods of writing have separate sources, operate on different principles, are built on different plans. They resemble alphabets as a whale does a fish—both communicate or swim—but without genuine similarity of structure or meaningful relationship. But alphabet resembles alphabet as whale and porpoise and dolphin resemble one another.

It is in the working-out of these real relationships, structural and genetic relationships as against mere functional similarities, that the recognition of culture patterns of the systemic type finds one of its chief uses.

133. TOTAL-CULTURE PATTERNS

Next, there are patterns that relate to whole cultures. There is an Italian, a French, a British pattern or form of European civilization. There is an Iroquoian, Algonkin, and Siouan aspect or facies of North American Indian Woodland culture. This Woodland culture in turn has its own larger total pattern, which, together with the Southeastern, Southwestern, North Pacific Coast, Mexican, and other patterns make up the still larger native North American pattern (§ 326). It is evident that we are here dealing with culture wholes, not, as in the last section, with specific complexes or systems that form only part of any one culture but can be grafted onto others.

East is East and West is West, Kipling said in vivid allusiveness to the different physiognomies or qualities of Occidental and Asiatic civilizations. When he added that never the twain shall meet, he was technically overstating things, in that civilizations do borrow and learn from each other, do assimilate or "acculturate"—which fact he was perfectly aware of when he went on: "But there is neither East nor West, Border, nor Breed, nor Birth, when two strong men stand face to face." But the "never-meeting" is also a poetical way of saying that civilizations are vast things like great ocean currents flowing past each other, and perhaps of implying that the sets or trends of civilizations as wholes vary profoundly, quite apart from the sum total of the items which make up their content. Civilizations differ in "configuration," in modern scientific jargon; "spirit" would have been an earlier word, "genius" before that.

There is of course nothing new in the fact that civilizations are distinct. Innumerable items can always be cited, either of differential or of likeness. To engage a button, we cut a slit in the cloth; the Chinese sew on a loop; and so on. But what do a hundred or a thousand or ten thousand such items mean? What do they add up to that is of wider import or deeper significance? If the items just scatter with equal randomness in two or more cultures, their effect will be equivalent, in spite of the endless variation of detail. Obviously, the specific items must concentrate in some peculiar way in each civilization, must gather or weight themselves along certain lines, if they are to have a larger meaning. And therewith we have a pattern or configuration.

There remains a difficulty, however. Items like buttonholes are definite and are readily ascertained or established, but their significance is limited. The pattern or physiognomy or trend of a great civilization is certainly an important thing to know, but it is difficult to formulate accurately and reliably. Such a pattern has in it breadth and complexity, depth and subtlety, universal features but also uniqueness. In proportion as the expression of such a large pattern tends to the abstract, it becomes arid and lifeless; in proportion as it remains attached to concrete facts, it lacks generalization. Perhaps the most vivid and impressive characterizations have been made by frank intuition deployed on a rich body of knowledge and put into skillful words. Yet this does not constitute proof and is at best at the fringe of the approved methods of science and scholarship. These difficulties will explain why the formulation of whole-culture patterns has not progressed farther, though it is surely one of the most important problems that anthropology and related researches face.

A spirited depiction of the total pattern of any culture possesses much the same appeal and interest as a portrait by a good painter. Some cultures, like some faces, are more interesting than others, but all can be given an interest and meaning by the hand of the skilled master. This gift of "seizing" character, with its suffusion by insight, admittedly partakes as much of the faculties of the artist as of those of the scientist. Excellent delineations of culture patterns have in fact been presented by nonanthropologists, by historians and travelers. More than eighteen hundred years ago Tacitus gave to posterity one of the masterpieces of this genre in his analysis of German custom and character. So keen was his penetration that many qualities of his subjects are still recognizable in the Germans of today. Other notable examples are the mediaeval Persian Al-Biruni writing in Arabic on Indian civilization; and in the nineteenth century, Burckhardt's *Renaissance,* Doughty's *Arabia Deserta,* Codrington's *Melanesians.* The first was a historian, the second a crotchety Semitist, the third a missionary bishop. At the risk of making invidious distinctions, Malinowski, Benedict, Mead, Evans-Pritchard, might be cited among recent avowed anthropologists. Through the medium of fiction, Pierre Loti, Freuchen's *Eskimo,* Maran's *Batouala,* and Mofolo's *Chaka* have done something similar with exceeding vividness.

A requisite for the recognition of the whole-culture type of pattern, besides of course insight and articulateness, is willingness to see a culture in terms of itself, of its own structure, values, and style. There must be an interest in the culture for its own sake. Without this, the depiction tends to degenerate into a recital of oddments, or of those features in which the culture's standards differ from our own—to its own worsening, of course. The disengagement from the biases and values of the describer's own culture should be complete, at least for the time being. Such preconceptions should never block his sympathies for the culture he is describing, where its qualities call for sympathy. Of course the account must not be a laudation, but an appraisal of what the culture's own standards and valuations are, and how far they are adhered to.

This process is akin to recognition of style in art; to "appreciation" in the stricter sense of that word, before it acquired its popular meaning of mere liking. There too we do not judge Michelangelo by the standard of Rodin, or Mozart by that of Shostakovich; nor, for that matter, Shostakovich by the values of Mozart, though unconsciously that is what conservatives may tend to do. What is in question in such endeavors is the recognition of the art of a certain region and period as expressed by its best exponents, the evaluation of how far it achieved its aims, and the definition of what these aims and values were. Attempts to recognize and define whole-culture patterns are of the same kind, but are larger in that they try to grasp the totality of styles—the nexus of social, ethical, intellectual, and economic as well as aesthetic styles or manners which together constitute the master pattern of a culture.[1]

134. EXEMPLIFICATIONS IN LANGUAGE

As so often, language, which is one specialized part of culture, can be used advantageously here to illustrate the total cultural situation. An author's style—literally his "writing-rod" or pencil—refers to his consistent ways or habitual manners of expressing himself distinctively enough to be recognizable from others. We have also superindividual styles, such as that of Elizabethan and of eighteenth-century English as compared with that of contemporary English. Going still farther, we may say there is a Latin style, an Anglo-Saxon style, a Germanic style, in English; and beyond these, there are styles characteristic of the Latin, English, and German languages. These whole-language styles consist of more than degrees of elaborateness of sentence structure, or the posi-

[1] Kluckhohn proposes to distinguish patterns from configurations. Both refer to structural regularities of culture. But to him patterns are objective and explicit ("overt"), or readily brought into social consciousness, whereas configurations are implicit ("covert") sets or trends akin to attitudes or motivations, and have to be dissected out by analysts of the culture. In part, though only in part, Kluckhohn's "patterns" correspond to what are here called systemic patterns (§ 132), his "configurations" to total-culture and style patterns (§ 133, 137).

tion of the verb. By insensible degrees they involve the whole of what we ordinarily call the grammar of a language. Latin has six distinguishable cases, German four, and English two. Latin conjugates its verb by a long series of complex suffixes, whereas spoken English has only three living conjugating suffixes and performs its main business of conjugation by the equally effective mechanism of separate auxiliary words, as set forth in § 97, 109. What are such grammatical peculiarities but crystallized stylistic idiosyncrasies? The grammar of a language may be viewed as its total specific style compared with the styles of other languages, or as its total pattern of structure.

It is true that what we ordinarily call "style" in language is more limited, superficial, optional, and perhaps individual than what we ordinarily call "grammar," and for many purposes it is desirable to observe the distinction. But there is no absolute line between the two, and both are ways or manners or patterns of expression. Just as the grammar of a language is its total pattern of fixed forms, so we might conceivably refer to the total pattern of a culture as its cultural grammar. That is not usage; but the comparison may help clarify what we mean when we talk of total patterns. The trouble is that there is as yet no word in English, or in any other language, to express this concept except vague or metaphorical terms like "genius," "spirit," "style," "trend," "direction."

Comparison with language may also help clarify the difference between the systemic patterns (§ 132) and the total-culture patterns (§ 133). Much as grammar corresponds to total pattern, so lexical content corresponds in one way to system pattern and to miscellaneous unpatterned material. It is lexical contents, words, that are often borrowed by one language from another, as when English takes over *Gestalt* from German or *chic* from French, or thousands and thousands of earlier words from Latin or French or both—all without the form or grammar or pattern of English being appreciably changed. Similarly, innumerable items or traits of cultural substance, such as corn-planting or seasoning with curry or voting on Australian ballots, can be taken over into a culture without its basic pattern or "grammar" being affected in principle. Moreover, we have seen cases of a system pattern such as the alphabet passing over into culture after culture but its various forms there being recognizable as derived from one common source by their part-for-part correspondence. Well, just as in the alphabet aleph, beth, gimel, correspond to A, B, C, and help prove their joint derivation, so in the relationship of language. English *nose, tongue, two, three* correspond to Spanish *nariz, lengua, dos, tres,* and to German *nase, zunge, zwei, drei,* in sound as well as meaning; but none of them correspond to Japanese *hana, hita, futa-tsu, mi-tsu* in sound or form. Thereby these words help prove that English and Spanish and German speech have a common origin and relationship, which we call Indo-European, but that Japanese is outside the Indo-European origin and relationship. It is the parts or content of a system that can be used as evidence of this sort, and it is the parts or words or content of a language that can be used in the same way. Both kinds of content are receivable into larger entities—culture wholes or language wholes—without much affecting the forms or major patterns or styles or "grammars" of these.

On the contrary, resemblances in style pattern mean much less as regards connective relationship. The Japanese language compounds nouns, piles up and encapsulates subordinate clauses, and then finishes up its elaborate periodic sentence with a verb, in much the way German speech style does. English word separateness and English syntax or word arrangement in the sentence are much more like those of Chinese. It is evident from this example that these grammatical, stylistic, or pattern resemblances can grow up in languages quite independently of their historical connection. Of the four just mentioned, English and German are the only two related. In fact they are closely and recently related in origin; but both tie up in certain features of their style pattern with wholly unconnected languages at the far end of another continent.

As a cultural counterpart one might mention the sharing by early Romans and by Chinese of addiction to patriarchal authority in the gens or extended family, the strong economic functioning of this group, the use of gentile or family names, the cult of manes or ancestral spirits, the relative meagerness of other ritual and mythology, the high premium on sobriety, piety, self-control, and moderation. All these pattern resemblances of orientation or outlook or physiognomy are certainly not due to any specific or direct historical connection of Rome and China, which these two countries never had. The pattern resemblances are evidently convergent or parallelistic (§ 223). That is, the two patterns originated independently, and therefore their similarity is secondary, functional, and analogous only. For instance, early Roman culture put, and Chinese does not put, strong emphasis on bravery, on military training and success, and on a martial tribal god.

Again, the late Roman Empire, in its Byzantine phase long after the capital had been moved to Constantinople, shows interesting approximations to late Chinese civilization, say of the Ming and Manchu dynasties, roughly 1400 to 1900. In both instances there are present: a sense of old and thorough saturation in high civilization, leading to self-satisfaction and disdain of the achievements of other cultures; a competent and educated bureaucracy as the mainstay of the state and civilization; fatigue as regards war, coupled with tried defensive skill; a flagging of originality in the arts, science, and philosophy, side by side with real respect for learning and its quantitative reproduction in encyclopaedias, commentaries, and the like. Some of these shared trends may be the results of a sort of civilizational senility. At any rate, they could hardly occur except in cultures of some maturity. Nevertheless, whatever the causes at work, they do not include imitation influence of the one civilization on the other. And we have again a degree of physiognomic resemblance, of total-pattern similarity. And this is evidently analogous in kind to the patterning that makes the grammar of

English—and not of Latin, or Greek, be it noted—more like that of Chinese in its general character than is that of any other European language.

In summary, *systemic patterns* are blocks or pieces of culture or language sharing a content that is of common origin and is arranged in a common pattern persistent enough to be recognizable for a long time, even after direct historical record of the community of origin has been lost. (In the case of language, the block may be so large as to comprise the majority of the vocabulary.) *Total-culture patterns* are the over-all quality, set, cast, organization, or grammar of the whole of a culture or language—the direction in which it slopes, so to speak. The total patterns of separate cultures sometimes are perceptibly similar, even though differing considerably in their content; and they can become similar of themselves even though starting out independently and different. Or, conversely, they can begin by being alike and then diverge increasingly. Their value is thus low for tracing historical connections or proving relationships. Their significance lies in expressing the distinctive individuality and quality pervading a whole culture or language.

135. PSYCHOLOGICAL ASPECTS

It will be seen that the examples just cited of whole-culture patterns tend somewhat toward the psychological; they have psychological implications. This is inherent in physiognomic characterizations, whether these be of particular men, of racial types, of historical periods, or of cultures. A face may express sternness or majesty or raptness or serenity or benevolence or craftiness or intellectuality or sensuousness, or combinations of such qualities. In much the same way, in referring to a civilization or period or tribal culture or phase, we often use terms of psychological appraisal, such as fatigue, self-satisfaction, bravery, premium on sobriety, flagging of originality. Yet it is true that other characterizing concepts, such as family names, ancestor worship, bureaucracy, encyclopaedias, manual arts, obviously refer to specific institutions or concrete cultural phenomena. It would seem accordingly that formulations of the total pattern of cultures contain both strictly cultural and psychological characterizations. A formulation begins with the former, with institutions or folkways; and as these more and more weave themselves into a larger coherence, it gradually also becomes evident in what directions the culture is faced, what ends it looks toward, which qualities it is occupied with and prizes most. In short, its characteristic values and its characteristic attitudes or orientations become comprehensible. An attitude, or for that matter an orientation, necessarily implies psychology. Attitudes might be said to refer to the ways an organism sets or arranges or orients itself, adjusts inwardly and outwardly to its environment; anything in its merely internal physiological operations would hardly come under attitude and orientation. Where the boundary lies here between straight anthropology and straight psychosomatics has not yet been determined. We might venture that we are still within the jurisdiction or claims of anthropology if the environment—toward which human organisms react by an attitude or an orientation—is a cultural one, if it includes folkways or mores with societal pressure, or, in wholly untechnical language, institutions. If however the environment is unmitigatedly physical, like warm sunshine after exposure to cold, or the proximity of an angry bear when one is in the woods unarmed, the reaction toward the environment is primarily psychosomatic and outside the domain of anthropology.

In recent years attempts have been made to characterize cultures definitely in psychological terms. This does not mean that their cultural features were disregarded. On the contrary, their cultural traits were carefully studied for a selection and an enumeration of all those customs and institutions which would fit into a coherent pattern or plan expressible in psychological terms. In short, the procedure was to try to convert cultural phenomena into psychological formulations through the medium of total-pattern recognitions. This is of course the same procedure as we have been discussing, carried one step farther. Mead, Gorer, and Fortune have described cultures more or less along these lines, but the most comprehensive procedure has been that of Benedict. She began by contrasting two American Indian cultures, those of the Plains bison-hunters and those of the southwestern Zuni and other Pueblo farmers, as being respectively Dionysiac and Apollinian. The Dionysiac temperament—named after the god of wine—is outgoing, addicted to rushes of strong feeling and their expression in activity; the self is asserted. The Apollinian type of personality is calm, restrained, "classic"; it dislikes surges of emotion, vehement action, and insistence on the ego; this last should be muted in favor of group tranquillity. For example, among the Dakota each man was free to seek his own "vision" or inspiration from supernaturals, who instructed him in his personal ritual and made him a shaman. Among the Zuni, such personal experiences would be frowned upon, and personal rituals were socially taboo. Ritual was in the hands of priests holding established offices, transmitting traditional tribal lore and cults, and teaching younger priests to follow in their footsteps. The psychological formulation of Zuni culture as Apollinian is based on a large mass of cultural traits, such as these customs differentiating shamans from priests.

Later, Benedict went farther and passed verdicts on cultures outside her personal experiences: the Melanesians of Dobu Island, described by Fortune, and the Kwakiutl Indians of Vancouver Island, on whom elaborate reports by Boas were available. The Dobuan culture she found to be paranoid in its inclinations; the Kwakiutl, megalomanic. Individual temperaments tend to conform to the cultural set; they are molded by it. A Dobuan who may be suspicious and plotting by nature fits in with the trends of his society and becomes a successful member of it, a distinguished citizen. But one who has impulses to be confiding and amiable, and cannot overcome these impulses, will be taken advantage of by his tribesmen and be a social failure.

There is no doubt that these four cultures actually differ in the directions described, and that other cultures differ from one another in analogous ways. Also, the characterizations tend to be in more or less psychiatric terms, or at least clinical ones, partly because clinical psychology was the first recognized branch of psychology that attempted to deal with whole human beings, as distinct from their intelligence or learning ability or other parts or special aspects of the mind. Furthermore, terms like "paranoid" or "megalomanic" do not imply downright insanity in psychology, as they frequently do in laymen's speech. A man may have a definite megalomanic streak in him and yet be a "normal" and useful member of society. Most of us in fact can think of an acquaintance or two whom that cap just fits. Also, there are five or ten individuals with clinically recognizable paranoid or schizophrenic or manic-depressive tendencies for every one that actually breaks into such a psychosis. We speak of such persons, quite properly, descriptively and without stigma, as being for instance of manic-depressive temperament. Which is as much as to say that if they were to become insane, which they probably won't, their psychosis would take such and such a form; just as one man will show a phthisic constitutional type to a physician, and another an apoplectic one, and yet the betting is that both will ultimately die of some other disease, respectively, than tuberculosis and a stroke. So much then in validation of these translations of total-culture patterns into psychological "diagnoses."

However, there are limitations to this method. So far as it is valid, it ought to be applicable to any and all cultures beyond the four primitive ones cited. Benedict herself seems to think that only some cultures can be described in this way; the majority are not sufficiently "integrated" around a single psychological trend, not oriented exclusively in one direction. If that is true, then her Zuni, Dobu, Kwakiutl cultures are abnormal cases, and are of significance chiefly as showing to what degree of specialization culture orientations can be pushed. But it seems much more likely that every culture is psychologically characterizable; and that if only a few can be appropriately labeled, it is because our assortment of labels is inadequate, or our interest flags beyond the gaudy ones. Psychologists do not deny a personality to individuals who are complex, balanced, and well rounded, or allow it only to those who have warped themselves around a single impulse or idea. The same must hold for the personalities of cultures. Some will be more decisively one-sided than others. But all must have a psychological physiognomy of some kind corresponding to their cultural physiognomy.[2] This is because culture is itself the product of psychosomatic activity; because in turn it conditions and molds psychology, as we have seen (§ 123); and because its operation is necessarily accompanied by psychological functioning.

[2] Subsequent well-rounded characterizations of East Asiatic cultures made by Benedict during World War II (see § 245 for a Siamese example) avoid the single-label designation.

As a matter of fact all kinds of psychological emphases can be recognized in cultures, even though it is but a rare culture all of whose manifestations can be constellated around a single motif. For instance there are cultures, such as the Yoruba and the Dahomey in West Africa, that are marked by a passion for method and relational organization; others, such as the Nupe, also in West Africa, view the world matter-of-factly as consisting of an agglomeration of so and so many discrete events which they feel no impulse to order (§ 251). Acquisitiveness and retentiveness are certainly personality traits. Dobu culture is acquisitive and retentive as well as sensitive and paranoid; Ifugao, in the Philippines, is acquisitive but normally healthy in its outlook; Yurok, in native California, is highly retentive of property but neurotically timorous; the Polynesian and Australian cultures generally are not acquisitive, still less retentive, but geared to constant consumption. There is bound to be one pervasive psychology in a culture that puts a social premium on co-operativeness, but a quite different set of mental reactions when a culture really prizes and rewards ruggedly individual competitiveness. Still other colorings are reviewed in Chapter Fifteen, where this whole set of problems is examined more systematically.

There are thus all kinds of psychological concepts against which cultures can be graded, if not as yet by any system of measurements, at least by general consent. The recognition of some such psychic qualities flows almost inevitably out of recognition of total-culture patterns. Sound formulations are likely to involve various sets of concepts. Thus it might be maintained that there was a culture at one and the same time acquisitive, wasteful, competitive, intuitive, sanguine, and uninterested in relations and abstractions. Which one? Contemporary American civilization can be so appraised, perhaps without too much unfairness. At any rate it would be generally accepted that there are at least half a dozen distinct psychological strands involved in our national make-up. Such multiple-term characterizations as this, though less incisive, will in the long run be applicable to far more cultures, and are likely to be fuller and truer descriptions than the occasional instances in which a culture is so specialized that nearly everything in it can be disposed along one conceptual axis expressible in a single word.

There is a large field here waiting to be developed as more students of anthropology learn to make psychological characterizations, or more psychologists learn to deal with culture. In both sciences, the tools of method have been sharpened, for about the last two lifetimes, by pursuit of critical analysis. Apart from psychiatry as a branch of medicine, clinical or whole-personality psychology of more than mere introspective or guesswork caliber scarcely existed consciously, even in germ, before about 1920, and is still in its infancy; and the same is true of whole-culture or pattern anthropology. When both have grown farther, and interpenetrated each other more, the results are likely to be immensely interesting.

From what has been said about the conditioning or molding of men by their cultures, it is evident that to every total pattern or orientation of culture there must correspond a type of personality. In fact, strictly, all psychic action takes place not in the culture but in the people who participate in it, carry it, and are shaped by it. The culture, which from one angle is a sort of set of rules enabling a certain set of activities to go on, by its existence inevitably induces certain habits in the members of its society; and these habits aggregate, in any individual, into a particular kind of personality. This personality will tend to be more or less alike in all members of a society, though varied by their purely individual conditionings as well as by their individual heredities, which are never wholly the same. The average or type or mode of these personalities produced in a society by its culture is, strictly, what the cultural psychologist tries to recognize or describe; the culture that produces the personality type is, strictly, the anthropologist's first concern. A potlatch and a thousand-guest wedding are cultural facts; but if a culture favors and rewards them, certain psychological attitudes, such as those toward lavishness and personal ostentation, tend to be set up in most people living in that society under that culture. This idea, of a type of personality always having to correspond to a type of culture, at least on the average, is after all a quite simple one, as well as being seemingly unassailable. It is the basis of the relation of anthropology and psychology, and the reason why examination of whole-culture patterns or physiognomies inevitably suggests psychological implications.

This rather simple relation has sometimes been obscured by premature attempts to explain the full causality of cultures or persons—which no one is yet in position to do—and sometimes by technical jargon, such as "basic personality structure." This phrase seems to mean nothing more than the personality type corresponding to a particular culture—the kind of person normal or average to the culture, one might say. "Basic" is unfortunate, because to biologists "basic" means what is hereditary and congenital, whereas this kind of personality is induced by the culture, not primary. If "basic" refers merely to being typical or average, it would better be called that. "Structure" appears to be just a yielding to a word that has a perfectly good meaning but suddenly becomes fashionably attractive for a decade or so—like "streamlining"—and during its vogue tends to be applied indiscriminately because of the pleasurable connotations of its sound. Of course a typical personality can be viewed as having a structure. But so can a physiology, any organism, all societies and all cultures, crystals, machines—in fact everything that is not wholly amorphous has a structure. So what "structure" adds to the meaning of our phrase seems to be nothing, except to provoke a degree of pleasant puzzlement. Moreover, an impressive phrase like this one tends to provoke an illusion that somehow knowledge of life histories of typical personalities in a society will explain why the culture is as it is; whereas in the main it is the culture that has made these personalities what they are (§ 123). However, apart from such putting of the cart before the horse, and from the matter of technical verbiage, the idea of some certain kind of a person or type of mentality corresponding to each particular culture is both simple and important. It will be developed farther in Chapter Fifteen.

136. CLIMAXES OF WHOLE-CULTURE PATTERNS

If we consider how cultures grow, by reviewing the course of those civilizations we know best through their history or archaeology, we are soon struck by a familiar phenomenon. Successful growth, which in retrospect is judged to have been productive, tends to come intermittently, in pulses or irregular rhythms. The word "cycles" is sometimes used, but it denotes a repetitive return, and return is more than is really characteristic of the phenomena now in question, or at least more than is sure about them. The manifestations are more like unpredictable swells or waves than like any wheel-of-fortune action in which an idea of retribution is implicit, or of a fate that eventually levels all things out. The "rise and fall of nations" is the familiar phrase that refers to the phenomenon; but there is actually a good deal involved beyond the success or failure of national fortunes. There is included, it is true, politico-military achievement: that is, success of the society in outright competition with other societies. But, more or less associated, there are usually: a growth in population; an increase in wealth; technological advances; and bursts of productivity in the aesthetic and intellectual fields, all the way from sculpture to literature, from philosophy to science. The peaks in these several activities may come simultaneously, or overlapping, or in close succession. Sometimes the total rise is gradual, as was that of ancient Rome; sometimes it comes suddenly, or seems abrupt, perhaps because the initial stages have not got into the preserved record of history.

An almost supertypical example is provided by the ancient Greeks:

Military success: 500-250 B.C.
Politics: progressively democratic constitution building, 600-400
Population: increasing to probably 300, decrease by 200
Philosophy: 585-200; peak: Plato, Aristotle, 400-320
Science: 585-150; peak: Euclid, Archimedes, 320-220
Medicine: 500-100; peak: Hippocrates, 420
History: 500-200; peak: Thucydides, 420
Tragedy: 500-400; peak: Sophocles, 450
Comedy: 480-280; peak: Aristophanes, 420
Poetry: 650-200; peak: Pindar, 450
Oratory: 450-300; peak: Demosthenes, 340
Sculpture: 550-100; peak: Phidias, 450
Painting: 500-100; peak: Apelles, 330
Architecture: 600-100; peak: Parthenon, 450

It is evident that for a few centuries Greek cultural activities were much heightened in the quality of their values achieved: the near-concurrence of dates is striking.

The five centuries involved include everything the Greeks produced which the world since their time has thought important, with the following few exceptions: Around 850-800 B.C., well before the main growth, there were the Homeric epics. Under the Roman Empire, two or more centuries after the great growth, there occurred an aftermath of science, largely in the nature of codifications (Ptolemaic astronomy, Galenic medicine, A.D. 100-150); a philosophic revival (Neo-Platonism, A.D. 250); and a "silver-age" prose literature (Plutarch, A.D. 150). All the rest of the Greek contribution falls in the period 650-100 B.C.; much the most of it, in fact, is comprised in the three centuries 500-200, with practically all the peaks or climaxes between 450 and 300. And this happened in a quite small area, as well as in the quite brief time. To put it a little differently, there was an enormous concentration of culture energy and innovation, of production of high cultural values, and of flourishing of men of the first rank of genius, in a very limited space and period, in contrast with much less of the same that the Greeks did before or after or elsewhere.

Quite so intense a condensation was perhaps never again accomplished in history. But the number of less extreme examples is indefinitely large. In Rome, the "Augustan" age around the time of the birth of Christ corresponded to the Greek "Periclean" age. All the most notable Roman achievements cluster around this Augustan climax, within a century or two before and after it: Cicero, Caesar, Lucretius, Virgil, Horace, Ovid, Tacitus; the world's first truly realistic portrait sculpture fifty to a hundred years after Augustus; Trajan, the emperor who brought the Empire to its greatest extent; and the culmination of Roman architecture, road-building, engineering, and probably population and wealth, in the first two Christian centuries.

Sometimes such bursts come repetitively within one area and population, as in China of the Chou, Han, and T'ang dynasties;[3] or in Egypt of the Pyramid Age, the Middle Kingdom, and the New Empire, with an aftermath renascence.[4] Sometimes successful activities string along spottily and successively, or somehow fail to appear altogether. Thus England was musically productive until 1700, musically imitative or second-rate thereafter; but began painting successfully only after 1750; and never had a first-rank sculptor. Holland's great men all came in the 1600's: Spinoza in philosophy, Rembrandt in painting, Huygens in physics, Vondel in literature. This was also the century of successful Dutch aggression against Spaniards and Portuguese, of the founding of their colonial empire, and of an unusual accumulation of wealth. In a small country it seems to be easier for everything to pile up simultaneously. The much more numerous

---

[3] Most productive about 550-300 B.C., 200 B.C.-A.D. 200, A.D. 600-800.

[4] At peak around 2600, 1900, 1400, 600 B.C., respectively.

adjacent Germans toward 1800 had in Kant, Goethe, Beethoven, the greatest contemporary European philosopher, poet, and musician, respectively; but politically they were mediaeval and disunited, and militarily Napoleon buffeted them around. Their famous science was only just beginning to function successfully at the time. During the nineteenth century this science flourished, Germany became politically organized and strong in war, population and wealth increased faster than in most of Europe—but German philosophy, literature, and music were progressively on the downgrade. Nevertheless, on the larger view the significant thing is the close time association of these somewhat separate German culminations. Some merely happen to reach their peak a little before the others— some during 1750-1825 and some during 1825-1900.

It will be seen that there are two related aspects to the type of phenomena we are considering. One is the fact of the production of great men and great cultural achievements; the other is their normal concentration in time, space, and nationality.

It used to be customary to "explain" such happenings as these, especially literary ones, by referring them to the stimulating effect of great victories, or other national events. It was said, for instance, that Shakespeare was somehow helped to write great plays by the defeat of the Spanish Armada; Phidias, Sophocles, and the other Athenians similarly were pushed forward to higher achievement by Marathon and Salamis; Augustus at last ended civil war and brought peace. But in many cases closer examination of the facts shows that the literary or other burst had already begun before the political event. And even if the burst is wholly subsequent, it is hard to see why and how better painting, or a discovery like Harvey's of the circulation of the blood, should be "produced" by a victorious war. The present-day view is that this kind of working from specific cause to specific effect will mostly not hold water in these complex matters of civilization. Modern opinion sees correlations or functional interrelations between a group of historical phenomena, rather than saying that A "produces" B. The Armada, Shakespeare, the playwriters who preceded both, the poet Spenser, Harvey with his circulation of the blood, Napier and his invention of logarithms, the composers of madrigals, the freebooter Drake, Raleigh and his colonial expansion, are all interconnected in making the Britain of 1575-1615. Each of them represents or expresses part of a successful pattern; and the group of patterns together constitutes the national culture-whole pattern of England in its temporary "Elizabethan" phase.

These national spurts of success and concentrations of cultural productivity may accordingly be regarded as constituting a phenomenon that recurs through history—and presumably through prehistory—even though separate occurrences never manifest wholly identical forms. The bursts have considerable significance in illuminating the dynamics of style patterns, the nature of genius, and the causes of invention. Their bearing on these three matters will now be considered in turn.

137. STYLE PATTERNS [5]

The basic reason for the concentrations of productivity seems to be that for things to be done well they must be done definitely, and definite results can be achieved only through some specific method, technique, manner, or plan of operations. Such a particular method or manner is called a *style* in all the arts, as we have seen. And "style" is perhaps the best available word that will cover also the corresponding methods or plans in other activities. We can speak of styles of governing, of waging war, of prosecuting industry or commerce, of promoting science, even of speculative reasoning. For instance, all modern Occidental business is carried on in a style that includes banking and credit. But ancient and Byzantine and Islamic businessmen necessarily followed a quite different style or pattern because they did not seriously employ credit, and actual money had usually to be collected or moved for any and all transactions. A style, then, may be said to be a way of achieving definiteness and effectiveness in human relations by choosing or evolving one line of procedure out of several possibles ones, and sticking to it. That means, psychologically, that habits become channeled, facility and skill are acquired, and that this skill can then be extended to larger situations or to somewhat altered ones. This process may mount for a while, the original skill itself being developed farther or giving rise to subsidiary ones. Or it may mount through enlargement of the field to which it is being applied, and therewith the product achieved perhaps increases in quantity as well as improving in quality. But the process cannot go on mounting indefinitely, because it began with a limitation of choice, a selection among possibilities. Therefore every style is necessarily prelimited: it is an essential commitment to one manner, to the exclusion of others. Accordingly it cannot encompass everything. The range of its channeled skills will extend so far; beyond, they fail. Then we say that the style has exhausted itself, its characteristic pattern has broken down. Or the style may be able to maintain itself for a while, but without any longer increasing the range of its control or improving its achievements. When this termination has been reached, accordingly, there is either decline or a freezing. The style either loses its skill of touch and its products deteriorate; or it becomes frankly repetitive, which is usually equivalent to a slowed-up deterioration, interest and feeling having been lost when further change is eliminated. A pickup in quality will normally be possible only with a new start toward a new style. And the evolution of a new style is likely to be easier to outsiders or novices than to the group which has been reared in an old style. That is why nations replace one another in their achievements; or if one does repeat, it is usually after a considerable interval.

This course of development will be familiar to anyone who has ever followed through the history of any art style, whether in literature, sculpture, paint-

[5] This is the last of the four kinds of patterns listed in the introduction to this chapter

ing, architecture, or music. It is a commonplace that all aesthetic styles rise and fall and perish. All art has constantly to get itself reborn with a new set of impulses, and then run a new course. Why that is so is what has just been set forth. But, as has also been just said, the arts are by no means something wholly set apart from the rest of civilization. The same principles of style or method, and therefore of pulsation. tend to hold for most or all cultural activities except the basic day-by-day and year-by-year repetitive ones like plowing and reaping, making a living, cooking and eating, marrying and dying. And even in these day-by-day activities, style patterns do intrude: we certainly have changing styles of cookery—usually dignified as cuisines; of marrying—early or late, for love or convenience, and so on; of funerals and corpse disposals. However, let us consider a cultural activity that is obviously neither of the repetitive kind nor aesthetic, one that passes as cumulatively progressive: science.

We have seen that Greek science and mathematics came in a four-century spurt and then stood still. The Greeks never did achieve much in simple arithmetic, probably partly because their method of writing quantities—by letter symbols denoting certain specific numbers instead of by position numerals—made ordinary computations of any size difficult. Even less was accomplished by them in algebra, of which the imperfect rudiments began—or first appear to our view—some four hundred years after Greek general mathematical progress had stopped. The branch of mathematics the Greeks did wholly originate and develop was geometry—plane, solid, and spherical. Here they substantially "exhausted the pattern," fulfilled its possibilities, and left nothing for others to discover. Now geometry is a special way of doing mathematics—with a compass and rule and nothing more, the Greeks insisted. It visualizes properties and relations; it can be pictured, as algebra and arithmetic cannot be. Although already truly abstract, geometry easily retains the most concrete aspect of all branches of mathematics. This geometric approach was the Greek "style" in mathematics. One part of the style was the Greek emphasis on proportion, which can also be diagramed; and the Greek avoidance, where possible, of all but integral numbers, which can be handled like visible and tangible blocks; and the avoidance also of negative quantities and irrational fractions, which cannot be handled in this way. On the positive side again, the Greeks pushed on from their geometry into conic sections—dealing with plane cuts across cones, resulting in curves such as ellipses, parabolas, hyperbolas. This is a branch of mathematics which we still call by the original name of "conic sections," although we mostly express its concepts algebraically now. The further limitations of the mathematical style of the Greeks are shown by their failure to develop anything at all in the field of logarithms, analytical geometry, calculus, or the concept of function. What they could do with their geometrical and whole-number manner or style, they achieved. Other mathematical possibilities, like these mentioned, were simply left to be realized by other peoples and times—chiefly by western Europeans in the last three or four centuries.

A style of mathematics quite different from both the ancient Greek and the modern Occidental was briefly developed in China around 1300 but was soon dropped, then taken up in Japan around 1600, and carried farther there during the following two centuries. This was an algebraic approach, though quite different in detail from Western algebra and very likely unconnected with it. This method was used ingeniously enough; but as neither China nor Japan had ever discovered or learned geometry, their method or style of mathematics was subject to limitations as great as was the Greek method, though the limitations were in many ways almost opposite. For instance, the native Chinese-Japanese algebra handled negative quantities as freely as it handled positive ones, but it concerned itself very little with the properties of shapes, such as triangles, cylinders, or tetrahedrons.

In much the same way, the style of ancient Greek science as a whole and the style of European science are distinguishable. The Greeks observed, but without instruments and without standard measures; and they did not experiment. These aids to the prosecution of science were developed only after A.D. 1500, as part of the western-European method of science. Galileo's trials with bodies falling from the leaning towar of Pisa were made about 1590. The telescope, invented in Holland in 1608 (§ 140, 152), was used for astronomical discovery by Galileo within two or three years. The microscope was almost simultaneous. Since understanding of the subtler forms of energy and of the qualitative properties of matter seems to depend on systematic experimentation, the basic discoveries in electromagnetism and chemistry were made still later, about 1750 to 1800, after the modern European pattern or style of science was becoming mature.

We can assume, then, that the higher values of human civilization tend to be produced in bursts or spurts of growth. This is because their achievement is dependent on the development of specific methods or styles somewhat similar in kind to styles in art; and, like art styles, it is limited or exhaustible. Further progress, beyond the potentialities of a given style and pattern, normally requires a pause, followed by a fresh start with a new style or pattern—a new approach to the problem, we might say. This principle seems to apply almost equally to aesthetic activities, to intellectual ones, to politico-military or national fortunes, and even to major economic achievements. At any rate, such related items as machine versus manual manufacture, mass production, and credit suggest that industrial progress can also be due to the fact that a "style pattern" has been devised.

138. BASIC PATTERN AND STYLE VARIABILITY

Dress obviously is heavily involved in the matters under discussion. The first association of many women to "pattern" is likely to be the paper model from which dresses are cut and shaped. Vulgarly, the word "style" refers to dress first of all; and it is certainly plain that dress in general is heavily conditioned by style. But beyond all this, dress excellently exemplifies even basic pattern and its influence.

For instance, Occidental civilization, Ancient Mediterranean, and East Asiatic are each characterized by a distinctive, long-term basic pattern of clothing. In comparison with our fitted clothing, Greek and Roman clothing was draped on the body. While this statement is not wholly exact, it is true comparatively. Sleeves were little developed, trousers lacking, the waist of clothing was not fitted in to follow the body, the general effect accentuated the fall of drapery and the flowing line. The Roman toga was a wrap-around blanket. One did not slip into it like a coat, one adjusted it to hang in proper folds.

After prevailing for many centuries, this basic pattern of dress began to crumble and become transformed toward the end of the Roman Empire, when the old Hellenic-Latin religion had yielded to Christianity and the total Mediterranean civilization was disintegrating and at the point of gradually being replaced by the beginnings of our Occidental one. Trousers, in spite of protests and counterlegislation, were adopted from the barbarians. Sleeves came into general use. During the Dark Ages, the transition was gradually accomplished. The fitted clothes might be pretty well concealed under a long coat or cloak, as in the sixth-century mosaics of the Eastern Emperor Justinian and the Empress Theodora; but they were there. By the Middle Ages, they were in the open; and their pattern is still the fundamental pattern of our own clothing. The characteristic of this, in contrast with ancient clothing, is that it is cut and tailored, fitted to the figure. Our word "tailored" is from French *tailleur,* one who cuts, carves, or trims; and *taille* still denotes both the figure as a whole and the waist. The plan of Western clothing for men is that its parts follow the limbs as well as the figure. For women, on the contrary, the legs are withdrawn from sight in a skirt that during most centuries has been ample. From the hips up, however, the pattern of Western women's wear makes up for the loose skirt and has a bodice or an equivalent that follows waist, bosom, shoulders, and arms fairly closely.

How thoroughly this is our basic type of dress even today, underneath all local or national variations and fluctuations of period and fashion, is evident when we compare Western dress as a whole for the past thousand years with the East Asiatic in the same millennium. Chinese and Japanese dress is also cut and tailored, but it is not fitted. It is cut loose, with ample sleeves, or kimono style, to suggest a broad figure. Trousers are ample, so as to have almost a skirt effect. The use of clothing to model or suggest women's bust, waist, and hip contour is wholly outside the Far Eastern pattern. Witness the Japanese *obi* sash and bow intended to conceal these features, while European women for four centuries or more have worn corsets and girdles to accentuate them.

Of course dress is notoriously subject to fashion change. But it is remarkable how virtually all changes of fashion, alike in Classical, Western, and East

Asiatic costume, have consistently operated each within the basic dress pattern of its own civilization. Fashion creates a thousand bizarre forms and extravagances; but it never has produced, among Occidentals, a man's type of dress based on toga instead of trousers, nor a woman's with a Japanese silhouette. The matter of fashion changes, which represent a minor sort of restless and anonymous innovation or invention, is discussed elsewhere (§ 164), with emphasis on a concealed rhythm or regularity much greater than the participants in a fashion are ordinarily aware of. But there is another aspect of fashion change—what may be called the intensity of its alteration, its momentary degree of variability—that both defines the basic pattern and helps to explain variation from it. Variability is high when the fashion of one year differs considerably from that of the year before; it is still more so when a series of particular dresses, all of the same year, differ considerably from one another. Low variability of course is marked by small differences of this sort. Such variabilities are easily expressed statistically.[6]

The underlying fashion swings or trends change what might be called the total silhouette of dress rather than its details. These minor features may come and go quite rapidly, and are what give the impression nearly everyone has that dress fashions are highly unstable. On the contrary, the total silhouette shifts rather steadily for perhaps fifty years toward one extreme of proportion, such as a narrow skirt for women, and then for about fifty years toward the opposite, giving a wavelength of close to a century for the periodicity, which seems to be adhered to with fair consistency in case after case.

It might be thought that the basic pattern (for Occidental women's dress during the last hundred and fifty years) would lie somewhere between these proportion extremes. Occasionally it does. But mostly the basic pattern proves to coincide with one of the extremes. The other extreme then represents a sort of opposition or aberration from the pattern. One might describe these aberrant extremes as the proportions still just inside the pattern but as far away as possible from its center of gravity. Or one might say the aberrant extreme is antithetical—almost perversely antithetical—to the ideal or saturation point of the pattern, though still barely remaining within its range. Thus, as the permanent Western pattern aims at amplitude from the hips down but slenderness above, the silhouette-extremes conformable to the pattern would be: full or wide skirt, long or low skirt, narrow waist, and therefore waistline just at the waist proper. The antithetical extremes would be: narrow skirt, short skirt, wide or full waist, and waistline moved from the anatomically narrowest part up toward the broader breast or down toward the broader hips. In this last proportion—position of the waistline—pattern saturation evidently falls at the midpoint between extremes. In the three other proportions, pattern saturation coincides with one of the extremes.

[6] By the standard deviation or sigma, converted into a percentage of the mean as the coefficient of variability.

A glance at the silhouettes in the upper row of Figure 19, showing characteristic dress at twenty-year intervals during the latter and larger part of the nineteenth century, reveals what characterizes the pattern—its consant stable features underneath temporary fluctuations. The lower row gives two silhouettes from the period of the French Revolution and Napoleon, and two from the period of the World Wars—two eras of sociopolitical restlessness enclosing the relative calm of Victorian times. Here skirts are in evidence that are narrow or high or both, and waists that are thick or ultrahigh or ultralow— the aberrant extremes.

VARIABILITY IN EUROPEAN WOMEN'S DRESS SILHOUETTE DURING
FOUR YEARS OF PATTERN CONFORMITY AND STABILITY
COMPARED WITH
FOUR YEARS OF PATTERN STRAIN AND INSTABILITY

Stable Pattern Years: Low Variability *

	1839	1859	1879	1899	Mean of 4 years
Skirt length	27	0	55	0	21
Skirt width	61	22	73	61	54
Waist height	53	40	53	53	50
Waist width	170	107	43	138	115

Unstable Pattern Years: High Variability *

	1789	1813	1916	1935	Mean of 4 years
Skirt length	164	492	219	109	246
Skirt width	61	235	151	162	152
Waist height	93	253	106	186	160
Waist width	277	107	128	256	192

* Figures express 100(V for year)/(mean V for 150 years).—V = $100\sigma/M$

When we look at the statistical expression of fashion variability in the same selected eight years as given in corresponding position on the facing page, it is at once clear that the years and decades of pattern saturation or concordance are marked by definitely low variability, indicative of stability; and the years and eras of pattern antithesis or stretch are marked by a surprisingly great variability, indicative of instability. Stability and instability here refer to the dress style pattern and its behavior. Since the periods of dress-pattern instability were also periods of marked sociopolitical instability and churning, there is presumably a connection.

The connection or relation seems functional rather than causal. There is nothing to indicate that the mere presence of wars and revolutions will make designers deliberately plan consecutive dresses as different as is possible within

FIG. 19. BASIC STYLE PATTERN IN WOMEN'S CLOTHES

Transient fashions conforming to basic pattern in upper stagger contrast with intrinsic departures from pattern in the lower. Also, upper figures are accompanied by low variability of fashion, and date from the calm Victorian era; lower figures show high variability and date from Revolution, Napoleonic, and World War periods.

the mode, whereas in times of calm they design them as alike as they can make them and still keep them from being identical. What evidently happens is merely that in periods of general stress, when the foundations of society and civilization seem rocked, the pattern of dress is also infected and subject to strain. It expresses this strain by moving from stable saturation to aberration, antithesis, restlessness, and instability.[7]

This example may make more concrete the role of patterns—both style patterns and total-culture patterns—in cultural change and stability. Not that patterns are the beginning and end of everything about civilization. But practically everything in culture occurs as part of one or more patterns. Hence whatever happens in the way of accomplishment, alteration, succession, or persistence in any culture is likely to happen through the mechanism of patterns. We do not yet know too much about them, because awareness of patterns is relatively recent in anthropology. But it is already clear that understanding of culture as something more than an endless series of haphazard items is going to be achieved largely through recognition of patterns and our ability to analyze them.

139. THE CLUSTERING AND NATURE OF GENIUS

We have seen that the higher values of civilizations, their greater accomplishments, tend to be achieved spasmodically, in intermittent bursts. Also, these bursts can be associated with the growth and fulfillment of style-type patterns. Yet there is something else equally associated with the bursts of cultural productivity. This is frequency of genius, frequency of extraordinarily gifted individuals.

Personalities of the very highest ability—whether in ruling, thinking, imagining, innovating, warring, or religious influencing—have long been known to occur in concentrations of country and period. The list in § 136 is not only a tabulation of when drama, sculpture, war, philosophy, and other activities of culture flourished in ancient Greece; it is equally an enumeration of its great men, its outstanding geniuses. The philosophy, for instance, is *exemplified* by Plato and Aristotle, by their predecessors like Democritus and Socrates, by their successors like Epicurus and Zeno the Stoic. Or we can equally well say that it is these men who *produced* the philosophy. These are but two ways of describing the same phenomenon. Obviously, there is not going to be much important philosophy without able philosophers around, nor able philosophers without important philosophy to show for it.

[7] Literally, of course, it is the minds of designers of dresses that are affected and show strain in their creations. But since such individuals tend to be affected and to react more or less alike, it is their common behavior, and the common drift of their products, that are historically most significant. This significance in turn justifies the use of short-cut metaphors like "patterns being infected," "straining," "moving," "saturating," "freezing."

Of these two related aspects, the philosophy and the philosophers, the activity and product or the personalities, there is no doubt which is the easier to grasp: the concrete persons. All sorts of Athenian contemporaries saw, heard, and perhaps touched Socrates, and had quite definite reactions to him and judgments of his merits—Athenians who nevertheless knew little and understood less of his thoughts. Through the accounts of Plato and Xenophon, Socrates remains today a very living and real personality whom one can never quite forget even if one's interest in philosophy be zero or negative. Hence ordinarily we tend to think first of Socrates the man and secondarily of what new ideas he produced. To put it on a lower level, a child cannot comprehend a philosophy, but it can comprehend events like being married to Xantippe or drinking hemlock in prison. The first recognition of the two-faced type of phenomenon we are dealing with, accordingly, was in terms of great men and their near-simultaneity or clustering. This fact was already recognized by the later Greeks and the Romans. Velleius Paterculus, a historian contemporary with Augustus, has quite a little passage on it. No one since appears to have doubted it.

However, as long as the matter is viewed simply as one of persons, it remains rather meaningless—curious but inexplicable. It came to be accepted that there are golden ages thickly studded with great men achieving unforgettable products; silver ages with somewhat lesser men attaining smaller performance; and ordinary times when men of ability or talent are still available though the great lights of history just do not put in their appearance. But no reason was manifest, through many unstatistically minded centuries, for such fluctuations, which glaringly violate the principle of random distribution or accidental occurrence, and therefore suggest that there must be specific factors at work to produce the unevennesses.

Biologically we know that hereditary races are constant to the degree that if a thousand morons and one man of genius are born per million in this generation, the proportion is unlikely to be seriously different in the next generation or for a number of generations following. If Athens for a thousand years had no great men, began to have a few in the sixth century, produced an astonishing number of geniuses of absolutely first rank in the fifth and fourth centuries, tapered off in the third, then became sterile again and has remained so until now, there is no known mechanism of heredity which can explain this fluctuation of incidence of high ability; nor is it within the reasonable bounds of mere statistical possibility. Galton, who still argued for a change to inherent race superiority in the Athenians (§ 90), because little was known before his time about the heredity of intelligence and ability, already recognized that the brief upcurve could not be a statistical accident, but that it must indicate some factor at work. Nor is there any serious doubt now what that factor is, among the ancient Athenians and in similar cases. It is, in general, what is variously called the milieu, the social environment, the cultural context, the condition of civilization. More specifically, the involved factor may be supposed to be the nature and degree of development of the value or style patterns of the Greeks, and among them of the Athenians in particular, around 500 B.C. There was a style of tragedy, for instance, in the making then. Aeschylus developed this tragic style farther in the grand manner, Sophocles freed it from the last traces of archaism, Euripides introduced the final psychological finesses and tendernesses—and in this style of tragedy there was nothing essential or important left to be done. If there had been an unfinished remnant to be achieved, it is expectable that this remnant would have been contributed. With the exhaustion of the Greek tragic pattern, no very great Greek tragic poets could arise, it may fairly be argued. There was nothing left for them to do in the Athenian pattern. Nor could they, as children of their time and place, conceivably invent Elizabethan or Japanese tragedy, not even in Attic Greek language dress.

Now this explanation does not mean that the state of the dramatic pattern in Athens around 400 B.C. prevented the *birth* of men endowed by nature with high potential ability of expressing themselves in tragic poetry. Such a direct reaction of a momentary condition of culture on organic heredity would be an even more unreasonable belief than Galton's belief that the heredity turned itself on and off again within a dozen generations like a playful faucet. What the situation does warrant us in inferring is that when general cultural conditions and specific dramatic pattern conditions were at their optimum in Greece, there would be an average of one individual of the poetic potentiality and caliber of Sophocles or Euripides born among so and so many thousand or million Athenians; and also that these rare individuals would be able to realize or express their gift by writing tragedies. When the general and specific pattern conditions were not at optimum, there would continue to be just as many potential poetic geniuses born among the same number of Athenians, but they would not become tragedians, or if they stubbornly tried to, they would find that their say had already been said, and that instead of fame they were acquiring mainly a repute for being somewhat dull repeaters. Conceivably, if they had a somewhat different vein in them also, they might still become great comic poets, since Athenian comedy ran a somewhat later course than tragedy. Or if their gifts were not too narrowly specialized but were plastically adaptable, these potential geniuses might have become actualized geniuses in oratory or history-writing, or perhaps even in philosophy. Here we are at the border of certainty of opinion, because no one yet knows how far the high capacities that we call genius are congenitally specialized—say for poetry and not for prose—or on the contrary how far these capacities are general—like articulateness of expression, for instance, or originality of ideas—and it is a matter of conditioning after birth that determines whether the inherent genius is to become a writer of tragedy, comedy, lyrics, or prose.

In any event, within a very few hundred years there was no form of literature left active in Athens, and soon after that no form of cultural activity anywhere among Greeks, in which a congenital super-AAA genius could any longer hope to attain super-AAA rating. This was because the possibilities of Greek civilization were so used up, its pattern so exhausted, that no super-AAA achievement was any longer possible in that civilization. The same one-in-four-thousand or two-hundred-in-a-million births of top-flight ability presumably continued to take place in Greek society in subsequent times as before.[8] But these individuals simply no longer had any chance to become top-flighters. They very likely became the leaders of their day; but posterity would rate them only BBB instead of AAA, because what posterity can judge, or does judge, is accomplishment. What posterity cannot readily judge, of course, and ordinarily is too busy to try to, is how much of any accomplishment is due to innate or hereditary endowment and how much due to favorable cultural and environmental circumstance.

What we have in this whole matter, in summary, is first the fact that great men do constellate, or genius does cluster; and second, an explanation of that fact in terms of degree of development of patterns of the style type. A third consideration may be added; namely, the reflection that only a fraction of all the men congenitally equipped for genius ever actualize as such. Only a fraction are ever found out, or allowed the rank, by history. This fraction is the same as the proportion that the number of generations recognized as fruitful and genius-studded, in all lands, bears to the number of barren, geniusless generations. This proportion can hardly be reckoned as greater than one in four, and may be as little as one in ten, if we take into account all the regions and eras of the world in which it is customary not to recognize any geniuses as having occurred.

There is a point of impressive significance here. Human biological heredity runs good enough to produce, once in every so many hundred thousand or million births, an individual so highly gifted as to be capable of becoming one of the lights of our species, a benefactor or a creator whose work will live in history; and yet the nature of our culture manages to neutralize or frustrate from seventy-five to perhaps ninety out of every hundred such great geniuses, or to depress them into mere second-rank talents or transient leaders of soon-forgotten days. Ideally considered, this is a tremendous waste from the point of view of those concerned with human achievement. It certainly invites the consideration of eugenicists, to whom it offers the pessimistic prospect that even if they should succeed in improving the heredity of our species, three-fourths or more of the gain would be lost again by the shockingly wasteful way in which civilization to date has operated.[9]

[8] Galton computed 248 in a million, or 1 in 4032, as born in Attica 530-430 B.C.

[9] This over-all wastage of 75 per cent or more of the finest congenital talents born in the human species may seem to constitute a blasting indictment of human culture. But without culture, the waste would be a complete 100 per cent. Culture is admittedly still an imperfect instrument.

Logically, of course, what we have in this situation about genius is a distinction we have already considered in connection with race (§ 86, 90): that achievement and capacity for achievement are different things, and that they do not correlate in any outright one-to-one or other simple manner. We assume that achievement presupposes inherent capacity, though even here it is a problem to be investigated how close the correspondence comes to being a 100-percent one. We certainly cannot assume that capacity is always actualized in achievement.

One difference between the race problem and the genius problem is that differences in ability between races are still somewhat uncertain, and, being differences of averages, are likely to prove small; whereas individual differences within one race and culture are well substantiated as considerable by psychological and practical tests. Moreover, it is relatively easy to compare individuals of practically identical physique, culture, economic stratum, and social opportunities and yet find marked differences between them; whereas races are never the same in culture, social environment, and opportunities.

Recognition of the fact that potential capacity may not be inferred in regard to race outright from accepted achievement, especially not negatively, began to be well and widely established by 1900. But recognition of the parallel noncorrespondence as regards individual genius did not come until well along in the twentieth century. And the significance of the clustering of both genius and cultural florescence has at times even yet failed to penetrate where an unhistorical attitude of mind prevails.

One possible misconception will be guarded against by its mention. The naïve view of course is that great men do great things. The greater achievements of civilization are therefore "explained" by the great men's happening to come along. Why they come along when and where they do hardly seems to call for further explanation in a pre-culture-conscious period. But once we are aware of culture and begin to take note of its workings, the simultaneous clustering of genius and of style-pattern fulfillments is one of the outstanding manifestations of history, and seems to lead inevitably to the conclusion of the interrelation of genius and pattern. The admission of this interdependence may put some curb on our notion of genius. We can certainly no longer look upon genius as something wholly unaccountable, heaven-sent, exempt from the laws of nature, operative solely according to its own uncontrollable will. Genius is reduced to a phenomenon, and therewith relatable to other phenomena. But genius is thereby not abrogated or denied. The genius remains the superior man, even the supremely able one. But he is such at birth by the bounty of the variability of organic heredity; and he is such at death by the grace of the condition of his culture, which has allowed and helped him to realize his congenital potentialities. In short, understanding of how culture operates does not in the least "abolish" individual superiority. It merely helps to explain greatness while using it also to explain better the patterns of culture.

140. THE MEANING OF SIMULTANEOUS INVENTIONS

Allied both to pattern florescences and to genius clustering is the fact that many inventions have been made independently by two or more men, and often even simultaneously. If this happened just now and then, and were true of only a small minority of all inventions, it could be called coincidence and attributed to accident. But as soon as simultaneity and independence of origin characterize any considerable proportion of inventions or discoveries, it is evident on the basis of the law of averages that some specific factor must be operating in that direction. Now the number of cases is not small: Ogburn and Thomas as long ago as 1922 had listed 148 instances. It is therefore of interest to understand what is at the bottom of the phenomenon, and why it went unrecognized so long—until about the time of World War I.

The reason for the nonrecognition seems to have been the reluctance of our minds to see anything superpersonal in matters that involve persons. Acceptance of impersonal forces lying outside the individual, but driving him to this achievement or that failure, appears somehow to infringe on our personalities, to delimit our freedom. Particularly do we tend to resent such invasions when they concern great intellects.

After 1700, everybody who knew anything of the history of science was aware that Newton and Leibnitz had both devised the calculus, and each at first without knowing of the other's discovery. It was their respective followers and compatriots who fought over priority and insinuated bad faith.

In 1845, Adams and Leverrier separately predicted the discovery of the planet Neptune. Adams's computation was worked out a little the earlier, but Leverrier's was published first, and the planet was promptly seen where he had said it ought to be.

In 1858, Darwin and Wallace presented parallel papers at the same meeting of the Royal Society, setting forth the idea of natural selection as a factor accounting for the evolutionary formation and change of species. Darwin had had the germ of the idea twenty years before, but hesitated to commit himself publicly. When the same idea occurred to Wallace, who was exploring in the East Indies, he promptly wrote it out and sent it to London. This both forced Darwin's hand and strengthened his confidence, with the result of the companion papers as an immediate compromise fair to both men, and the publication of Darwin's *Origin of Species* the next year.

The year 1900 saw the discovery of the basic laws of heredity—it was really a rediscovery, but more of that later (§ 152)—by three several biologists: De Vries, Correns, and Tschermak.

These four instances, all of them relating to fundamental discoveries in science, will at least suffice to take the phenomenon of simultaneity out of the range of mere coincidence. The list on the next page, which could be increased indefinitely, will reinforce the principle. If practically all of the cases cited are from modern Occidental civilization, that is because invention records which are authentic, full, and exactly datable nearly all hail from that civilization. Also it will be seen from the list that technological invention, scientific discovery, and even geographical discovery all behave much alike in this matter of simultaneity—in line with their shading into one another otherwise, as set forth in § 145.

SOME SIMULTANEOUS DISCOVERIES AND INVENTIONS

Telescope: Jansen, Lippershey, Metius, 1608 (§ 137, 152)
Sunspots: Fabricius, Galileo, Harriott, Scheiner, 1611
Logarithms: Napier, 1614; Bürgi, 1620
Calculus: Newton, 1671, publ. 1687; Leibnitz, 1676, publ. 1684
Problem of three bodies: Clairaut, D'Alembert, Euler, 1747
Nitrogen: Rutherford, 1772; Scheele, 1773
Oxygen: Priestley, Scheele, 1774
Water is H_2O: Cavendish, Watt, 1781; Lavoisier, 1783
Steamboat: Jouffroy, 1783; Rumsey, 1787; Fitch, 1788; Symington, 1788 (§ 155, 186)
Theory of Planetary Disturbances: Lagrange, Laplace, 1808
Pepsin: Latour, Schwann, 1835
Telegraph: Henry, Morse, Steinheil, Wheatstone and Cooke, about 1837 (§ 187)
Star parallax first measured: Bessel, Henderson, Struve, 1838
Photography: Daguerre and Niepce, Talbot, 1839 (§ 187)
Planet Neptune: Adams, Leverrier, 1845
Surgical anaesthesia by ether: Long, 1842, results disregarded; Jackson, Liston, Morton, Robinson, 1846; N_2O, Wells, 1845
Sunspot variations correlated with disturbances on earth: Gauthier, Sabine, Wolfe, 1852
Natural selection: Darwin, Wallace, 1858
Periodic Law of Elements: Mendeleev, Meyer, 1869
Telephone: Bell, Gray, 1876 (§ 187)
Phonograph: Cros, Edison, 1877 (§ 187)
Liquefaction of oxygen: Cailletet, Pictet, 1877
Rediscovery of Mendel's Laws: De Vries, Correns, Tschermak, 1900 (respectively on March 14, April 24, June 2; see § 152)
North Pole: Cook,[10] Peary, 1909
South Pole: Amundsen, December, 1911; Scott, January, 1912
Flight orientation of bats due to hearing reflections of uttered sounds: Griffin and Galambos, U.S.A., 1941-42; Dijkgraat, Holland, 1943—during total severance of communications in war years

A list like this tends to instill a conviction that inventions may be inevitable, within certain limits; that given a certain constellation and development of a culture, certain inventions must be made. Such a conclusion involves

[10] That Cook's discovery was untrue varies the principle of simultaneity without invalidating it. Fifty years earlier it would probably not have occurred to anyone even to pretend the discovery; twenty, perhaps even ten, years earlier, the claim would have been received with such incredulity as to discourage a false claimant; 1909 was the psychological moment for a fake attempt—the whole world was agog for the discovery that Peary was actually consummating.

the recognition of superindividual forces—historical agencies or social currents transcending personalities. This is a matter which will be taken up again, and more fully, in connection with the nature of invention, in § 145-155, especially 152. Our more immediate concern here is with the clustering of able inventors around an important invention or series of related inventions, like the clustering of able or great men in a particular art or any phase of a nationally delimited culture growth. The two sets of clusterings are strikingly similar; and it is evident that they are both related to the development of culture patterns. The patterns must have a certain potentiality, and they must have reached a stage of "fruitfulness," before we can expect great men, great productions, or great inventions. But once geniuses, achievements, or inventions begin to arrive, they may be expected in bursts of concentration.

CHAPTER NINE

Culture Processes

141. CULTURE PROCESSES

BY PROCESSES of culture we mean those factors which operate either toward the stabilization and preservation of cultures and their parts, or toward growth and change. Changes, in turn, may consist either of increments, such as new developments, inventions, and learned traits acquired from outside; or of losses and displacements. Beyond these, there are minor alterations or fluctuations that are neither particularly additive nor deductive, as when the wheel base of automobiles is shortened, or the floor is lowered, or the engine is placed behind.

The main value of these formal distinctions of kinds of process is logical: they help us organize a large mass of facts into some sort of preliminary order. For that reason the topical sequence of consideration: persistence, invention, loss, in this chapter, and change in the next, will be followed here. But as cultures and their parts actually live, thrive, decay, and alter, and as they influence one another, these several processes, which in the abstract seem so neat and distinctive, are found to manifest themselves in association and interwoven. All of them are often at work at once, so that the same phenomenon may be seen as an example of two or three of them. This constant interrelation of processes is characteristic of culture. Their segregation has something artificial about it, and is justified chiefly by convenience.

For instance, one might expect innovations to cause displacements: for the steel knife to crowd out the stone knife. But the latter may survive in ritual; or the stone tool may have become associated with certain motor habits that it is awkward or unprofitable to change, as when the Yurok Indians eagerly took over our American knives for most purposes, but during a couple of generations retained their flint ones for dressing and splitting salmon. If there is such a retention alongside the addition, the culture of course now possesses two traits instead of one. Yet we may not assume that this always happens, else cultures would regularly grow additively or cumulatively. They do sometimes: our Western civilization undoubtedly has more content now than it had a thousand years ago. But it is probable that there are occasions when losses can and do exceed additions: for instance, in Italy during the first seven or eight centuries of the Christian era.

What happens in particular cultures may of course happen to their sum, to human culture in the aggregate. The total quantity of this probably does tend to increase, but certainly at uneven rates in different periods and areas, as already discussed in § 127. Variation and fluctuation of culture content are evidently more typical events than its steady increase. If any generic inherent force making for progressive cultural accumulation existed, it would be difficult to explain the fact that there still remain backward and lowly "primitive" cultures of meager content.

We may conclude that while innovations sometimes result in displacements, they sometimes do not; but that losses also can occur without gains. While there is a relation between the two currents, they are separate enough to justify their separate consideration.

Even changes and persistences blend into each other. The normal way in which culture continues is for one generation of a society to transmit its culture to the next generation, the process occurring in time, since societies and cultures are normally attached to an area. But when one culture transmits some of its content to another—when for instance porcelain or papermaking diffuses from China to Europe, or glass or surveying from Europe to China—the receiving culture has changed by acquiring something new, though the process of transmission is now through space instead of time. But from the angle of the total culture material in the world, there has been merely a continuance of a trait, accompanied by its geographical spread, conceivably without any change in the trait itself, or only minimal change. Ultimately a diffusing technique or institution or system may even die out or be displaced in its homeland, but survive where it was imported; as Christianity withered away in Palestine, and Buddhism in India, but they continue to flourish respectively in Europe and China. In Europe, however, Christianity crowded out all other organized religions; whereas in China, Taoism and Confucianism have maintained themselves alongside Buddhism.

These instances will indicate what is meant by the statement that conceptually distinct processes tend to come intertwined, and to interact, in the actual operations and history of culture.

142. PERSISTENCE

It has been asserted that the first problem of any culture is that of its survival or persistence, much as any society is always confronted by the problem of surviving. This allegation seems truer logically than important factually. If a culture perishes, there is an obvious end to its problems of adaptation and modification. But this does not by any means involve every culture's constant striving to avert disaster—least of all an awareness of being perpetually faced by a life-or-death problem. Nor are societies in chronically acute jeopardy. Their case is rather like that of individual organisms. These also have indispensable needs, but mainly they are organized to function as physiological successes, and on the whole they do so. The same with human societies and their cultures: normally they make a go of it, at least for a time. What is more, most peoples expect to make a go of it. They do not expect that they themselves and their institutions will have crashed to ruin by next year. Such overclouded, anxiety-ridden states of mind would have something of the abnormal about them. Perhaps the whole notion of their being usual is a reflection in the minds of some anthropologists of the uncertainties, strains, depressions, and threats of the period from World War I to World War II (cf. § 122).

What is true is that ordinarily societies cling with attachment to their cultures. Genuine revolutionaries are rare, the world over. They characterize particular periods and limited areas. Reformers are more numerous; but even these generally want particular improvements on top of a basic maintenance of the scheme of things. And a large part of mankind just is fundamentally conservative—which means that they like their culture and their personal stake in it. This personal stake and its rewards might well be bigger for the average man, and he is likely to be trying to make it a bit bigger; but mostly he does so without any notion of changing the rules, except perhaps at a spot or two. This is not a statement of what should be, but an attempt to summarize the attitude of most people, primitive, barbarous, and highly advanced, throughout history and all over the earth.

There are several reasons for this attachment of men to their cultures. One of course is habit adjustment. We have been molded by our culture until we fit it, more or less, have got used to functioning within its framework, and have channeled such functioning into habits. Then there is always education of the young, both spontaneous and deliberate. This inevitably exalts the ideals and values of the instructing generation. In most countries and times, these ideals of the elders are pretty generally accepted, without much criticism or serious revolt. The folkways tend to persist; the mores are held to firmly, with release of emotion if they are challenged. It must be remembered that the idea and ideal of progress, which we of modern Western civilization tend to accept as axiomatic

(§ 127), has not been in the least axiomatic to mankind at large. To most societies the notion has hardly occurred, at any rate not as a guiding principle. They rather take essential continuance for granted: the golden age is in the past, not ahead. There certainly is reassurance and comfort in the idea of continuance, unless one has been imbued with the contrary attitude that restless improvement is a desirable thing, or a sort of obligation.

The famous French sociologist Durkheim went so far as to maintain that what the "most primitive" people—meaning the Australians—really worship through their rites, sacrifices, and taboos is the bonds of their society and the institutions of their culture. The totems and the ancestors and their impersonations, the sacred spots and the hallowed paraphernalia of bull-roarers, the carefully screened mysteries—all these are not randomly worshiped ghosts, animals, rocks, and fetishes, but symbols of the total tribal society of the past, the present, and the future, and its successful adaptation in the universe through entering into mystic ritual relations with the universe. This interpretation perhaps fits the Australians more tellingly than it would fit most primitives and nonliterates, and is somewhat extreme even as regards them; but the view undoubtedly expresses considerable truth, and it would be more widely accepted today if Durkheim had not stretched it into a basic philosophy of all culture and society that savored almost as much of mysticism as did the beliefs of the savages. There is no doubt that most religious cults stress strongly the continuity with all the past, an accord or oneness of the individual or his group with the whole world, and the basic changelessness of these relations.

It is also necessary to remember how children—and adults—enter into assimilation and participation with their society and culture, as already touched on in § 123. One of two main mechanisms for this is voluntary adaptation—imitation, wanting to conform, learning from example. Some of this is conscious, or begins consciously; more of it is unconscious, or foreconscious. Perhaps it would be fair to say that normally there exists a strong emotional bent, which is latently conscious, toward participation, and therefore toward assimilation and learning, but that the actual imitating by the young is mostly done without much specific awareness.

The second mechanism making for participation of the young in their culture, and their fitting into society, is education, learning by being taught or trained. This is clearly in the main a conscious process, even though its implications may often be overlooked. In general, what elders teach the young is ways of becoming what they themselves are and have attained; or what they might have become and attained under the same cultural rules if their luck or their ability had been better. It is evident that both mechanisms are calculated to work toward perpetuation and persistence.

143. MOTOR HABITS

Among the factors that make for persistence of culture, in whatever form it happens to have anywhere, are motor habits. Such habits become established in all higher animals. Resting on congenital anatomical structure, they may be modified, and are channeled, in accord with the circumstances of environment. In the field of culture, motor habits become particularly conspicuous in the technologies and the arts. As long as these arts are studied chiefly through their products, such as museum specimens, the motor habits that went into the making of the objects do not obtrude. But if it is possible to give attention to production as well as to product, motor habits are quickly seen to be a definite factor. For instance, whittling, sawing, planing, and many other tool operations can be done either by pushing or by pulling. The Japanese carpenter pulls the plane toward himself, centripetally. The Western workman pushes it away from his body, centrifugally. Probably one method is as good as the other in most cases. But once a certain skill has become established in connection with pushing, it is impossible for a given individual to be equally skillful when he substitutes the pulling motion. He may attain such skill by deliberately trying to learn a new habit, but meanwhile his work is that of a novice. As there is usually no reward for a change, and likely to be an obvious penalty, because of temporarily decreased quality of performance, the change is not made, and the individual remains a lifelong addict to the particular set of habits that first became established in him. Just as he acquired these habits from older workmen, he is likely to transmit them to his apprentices or pupils. Thus not only does one habit prevail among a certain population, and the contrary or a different one among another population, but such habits may persist for hundreds or thousands of years. These habits are definite parts of cultures. The difference between pushing and pulling a plane is as much a culture phenomenon as the difference between smoothing with a piece of sandstone and with a carpenter's plane.

There are a great many situations in which one way of performing an operation is about as good intrinsically as the other; but it is frequently more efficient, or at least timesaving and effort-saving, to decide on one method and stick to it. Driving on the right or the left side of the road is a case in point. Where traffic is negligible or slow, it is quite possible to get on without any motor habit or rule. In proportion as traffic is heavy and swift, it becomes indispensable to make a decision once for all and then to establish the chosen habit as an individual automatic reaction, as well as a law of the society. It is notorious that since the nations of the world have felt it necessary each to enforce a choice in the matter, they have divided, some in favor of right-hand and some of left-hand driving. Any reasons for one being intrinsically preferable to the other are mainly rationalizations. What actually seems to have happened is that loose tendencies toward passing oncoming vehicles on one side or the other became crystallized as wagon traffic became heavier with the growth of population and the improvement of roads, and were then transferred to the automobile when the matter of uniformity of reaction had become imperative.

It is interesting that once such a rule becomes set among a population it may be easier to alter manufactured objects than to change the rule. The English began with the horse-driver sitting on the right side of the seat and turning to the left on meeting another vehicle. He could thus see whether the wheels of the two vehicles were clear. When horses and wagons and roads were introduced in British Colonial America, the driver presumably continued to sit on the right of the seat: he had an established motor habit on this point. Traffic, however, was at first so sparse that apparently any rules of passing fell into disuse; and when finally, with the increase of horse-drawn vehicles, a rule or custom became desirable, the right-hand pass of oncoming vehicles was somehow chosen. This put the driver away from his clearing wheel; but apparently this was felt only as a minor objection. Only after the automobile with its much greater speed came on the scene, was there seen to be an element of serious danger. Then the conflict was solved by altering the pattern of car construction so that the driver was now put on the left side of his seat. The rule of swerving to the right, in which instantaneous response to a motor habit is frequently vital, remained unaltered.

Even animals get their motor habits conditioned by human culture. In our civilization one mounts to the saddle by the left stirrup. Many horses become disturbed or alarmed by an attempt to mount them from the right. An animal taught to obey the jerk line in multiple-team plowing will not know how to respond to the rein, and vice versa.

Differences in motor habits are not necessarily between whole cultures or societies. They may exist between groups within the same society, or between the sexes. Among ourselves a man's coat or vest buttons from the left over the right. The buttons are on the right edge. The side that carries the buttonholes laps over this from the left. The rule in women's garments is the opposite. The left side carries the buttons and the right is laid over and outside it. The result is that men execute most of the business of buttoning with their left hand, women with the right. Habits get established, and transfer to the other hand would bring awkwardness and irritation.

In weaving cloth on a vertical loom it is possible to begin inserting the weft either at the top or at the bottom. In a basket the direction of progress of weave can be clockwise or counterclockwise. Here it is possible to set up explanations to the effect that most people are right-handed, and that it is natural to keep the defter fingers free for the insertion and pulling of the weft while the left hand holds or spreads the warps. A basket can however be woven at the near edge, with the worker facing its outside; or it can be woven across its hollow, facing the inside, in which case the progress of the same weft between the weaver's hands would be opposite. Ordinarily perhaps a basket is manufactured resting on what will be its bottom; but some tribes hang the foundation of the basket up on a cord and work downward toward what will be the rim. In the contrasting cases the same finger manipulations will yield progress in the opposite direction. These several variations in technical manipulation actually occur as standard among certain populations. They plainly are cultural differences, although they all preserve the normal supremacy of the right hand. In such instances, factors of organic equipment, such as normal right-handedness, must be recognized if the total situation is to be understood. Yet the direction of progress depends not on this alone, but specifically on how the basket is held. A particular congenital motor habit rarely suffices to explain the whole method of operation: this always remains partly or mostly cultural in origin. Motor habits have the limits of their range set by the human organic equipment, but their specific determination is overwhelmingly by culture.

144. OTHER HABIT CHANNELINGS

There are some persistences in culture that recall habit formations in individuals and into which the factor of habit channeling undoubtedly has entered through the constant overlapping of generations in every society. For instance, in ancient Peru the southern coastal districts early got into the habit of making their pottery vessels with round bottoms, whereas the northern areas favored flat bottoms. This difference was consistently maintained as long as native pottery continued to be made. Both Peruvian areas, as far back as we have archaeological record of them, developed tubular spouts: single, double, or united like a stirrup-shaped handle. This is a trait which persisted throughout the ceramic history of Peru.

On the contrary, in ancient southern Mexico and Central America, habit ran in the direction of providing bowls, pots, and even jars with three legs. This tripod arrangement has certain practical advantages when cooking vessels are to be set over the fire; but among the Mexicans it became a stylistic manner or trend, because the supports were put on vessels whose shapes or ornamentation shows that they were never set on the fire; and in some cases the legs have degenerated into functionless lugs or ornamental devices. Moreover, in this same Mexican region the idea of tripod support was extended to objects of totally different uses, such as the metate for grinding corn, and the stool or seat. The tripod habit was already established two thousand or more years ago in the earliest wares yet discovered, and it maintains itself today in the household inventory of Indians and peons.

Farther north, in the United States Southwest, whose archaeological history can also be carried back something like two thousand years, both spouts and tripods are characteristically absent. They do occur occasionally, as spouts occur sporadically in Mexico, and tripods in Peru; and these exceptions are significant because they prove that the ideas of spouts or tripods were not beyond the capacity or range of any of these pottery-making peoples. They were in fact tried, but did not take except each in the area where it became typical. In short, though traits like tripods and spouts are relatively unimportant, they can nevertheless be extremely persistent and characteristic. From the angle of the successful functioning of the native cultures of the three American areas, it was of course immaterial whether they went in for spouts or legs or neither. Yet, having made one stylistic choice or the other, they adhered to it over long periods during which more important features of government, technology, or subsistence were altered fairly drastically.

Such cultural happenings are comparable to the ordinary habits of a person— his nonessential mannerisms. An individual early in his life acquires a particular shrug or gesture, a posture or way of seating himself, a manner of articulation, of forming or spacing his letters in handwriting. He goes through periods of good luck and bad luck, his fortunes fall or rise; but the mannerisms persist. This is not to say that habits in persons and cultures consist entirely of insignificant idiosyncrasies. As a matter of fact, habit formation enters just as much into the bigger and more important features of human life and culture. But in such cases we think of habit as character or attitude system; and these, being large and complex things, not only are bound to be partially modified with the wear and tear of time, but their persistent core is less easily extricated and defined. The smaller habits, those of the type of mannerisms, are more easily traced just because they are discrete, and because, being of indifferent importance, their very neutrality sometimes enables them to go on practically unaltered for surprisingly long periods.

Further examples on the cultural level are teapot-shaped vessels, with a double-curved spout and a handle, which in Japan have an archaeological history stretching back of the introduction of tea into the early Iron Age and even the Stone Age; and pile houses in the regions around the Alps, as illustrated by the Stone Age lake dwellings of Switzerland, the Bronze Age terramare of Lombardy, and by modern Venice. The North American side of the Atlantic was a clam-eating coast in prehistoric Indian times, as attested by shell mounds, and is so today. By comparison the mussel was neglected as food, and still is, except for a partial change in tastes recently introduced by French and Italian immigrants. On the European side of the same ocean, on the contrary, the clam is little esteemed and the mussel is eagerly eaten; and this was true in the Stone Age as it is today. This difference may be due in part to the quality of the species available, or to environmental factors; but it cannot be wholly accounted for on such grounds because the same species of mussel, *Mytilus edulis,* occurs on both sides of the Atlantic—in fact has a nearly world-wide distribution. Hence it would seem that the factor of long-term taste habits has contributed to the picture.

145. INVENTION

The most incisive form of cultural addition is invention, the finding things out, or, etymologically, "coming into" something new.

In studies of culture the word "invention" is used with a somewhat wider meaning than its current popular sense. To the man on the street "invention" denotes a new machine or technological process. In anthropology and culture history it includes this and more. We can for instance speak of institutional inventions, such as the matrilineate, kingship, moiety organization, representative government, or written constitutions. If it seems that this is stretching meanings unduly, because institutions are social growths, usually accepted gradually, so are machines social growths, having antecedents and being accepted gradually, as we shall see. Then there is intellectual invention: a scientific discovery, a new philosophical idea. We can just as properly speak of the Copernican invention as the Copernican discovery; perhaps more properly, because if the theory should ever be found incorrect, it would remain an invention although disproved as a discovery of the truth. From here it is only a step to the discovery of a new planet, and from that to the discovery of the South Pole. The point is not that all these inventions are exactly identical in character, but that they grade into each other. Above all, that they behave much alike, as regards their causes, manner, and effects. It is thus wiser to direct attention to the common features of the behavior of societies when they do something new, rather than to spend much attention on distinctions that are mainly logical.

There is one idea it is necessary to be rid of in order to understand the process of invention in general. This is the assumption that our contemporary Western habit of seeking or planning inventions is at all normal. Deliberately planned or sought invention, in fact, is nearly lacking in most of the history of civilization. It began timidly to come up in Europe around 1300 or 1400, increased in the 1600's, but did not become systematic and important until the nineteenth century. It is therefore an exceptional feature of our own civilization. In fact it would have been extremely difficult to plan much invention until both theoretical science and practical technology reached a development, about the seventeenth century, such as had never before been attained.

146. NECESSITY

The old byword of necessity being the mother of invention must be heavily discounted. It is true only in so far as ordinarily there must be a need, or at least a use, for a new thing before it will be devised, and especially before it will be accepted by a society. Necessity may therefore be a spur; it is never a sufficient cause by itself. Above all, need is a relative and subjective factor. Your need may not be mine. We feel that we need three meals a day. Many ancients ate and primitives eat only two and are content. Some obtain food so irregularly that they may not average much more than one meal a day; when they get enough, it is eaten up. These same people will cheerfully eat three times if they are fed; but they hardly feel that they must or ought to have meals so often. Their circumstances and habits are different, hence their orientations and expectations also differ from ours.

A Negrito wants a little sloping roof over his head; it does not occur to him that he wants a house with walls. If a river is to be crossed and recrossed, he may build a suspension bridge that shows him possessed of mechanical ingenuity. But a house instead of a leanto windbreak would be extra work and would give him nothing that he really wants. His family is small, his possessions few, and in several days or weeks he expects to move elsewhere because food will be exhausted where he is now. So he does not sense a need that we might regard as imperative.

On the contrary, most primitives obviously desire certain things on which we are much less intent. They strongly want close and constant association with their kin. The floating laborer of our society who leaves his home folks, drifts about without ever seeing them again or without rearing a family of his own, is as good as unheard-of among them. If a savage leaves his home, it is to settle down and marry among another group.

Similarly with religion, which all primitive peoples evidently feel a need of, since they all possess one, and the overwhelming majority of individuals seem genuinely to believe in—not to mention the much greater number of men in societies that are beyond the primitive. Yet many Russians of today, and a fair number of people among ourselves, get along comfortably without religion. One might contend that the Soviet social program constitutes the prevalent Russian religion. But though a program that leaves no room for God or the soul, which does not recognize anything supernatural, may function emotionally as the equivalent of a religion, though it may surround itself with satisfying social rituals and with sanctions, it obviously does not quite constitute a religion.

In short, necessity is so largely a function of orientation, of goals already established by the extant culture, that it is too variable a factor to be invoked very often to explain invention. It is wants that determine what people do, and wants are states of mind, largely determined in their turn by already existing culture.

147. ACCIDENT

On the other hand, accident is unquestionably one factor in invention and discovery. There are a number of cases in the history of medicine. Sulfanilamid was first made as far back as 1908 as part of a dye fixative. In 1935, the dye was found to be powerful against streptococcus infections; research then isolated sulfanilamid as the active agent. Penicillin was "invented" as a result of Fleming's working with staphylococcus cultures and noting that where these became infected with mold the adjacent colonies of bacteria were dissolved away. The shock cure for dementia praecox was discovered through a schizophrenic's being given, by a nurse's error, an overdosed insulin injection for the diabetes that he also had. He almost died, but recovered improved, and the way was pointed. Pasteur was led to the theory and the method of immunization by happening to inject an overlooked and stale bacterial culture of chicken cholera and finding that it failed to kill. It then occurred to him that an attenuated culture might immunize. By contrast, it may be pointed out that for several generations medicine has felt the urgent need for a nonoperative, non-radioactive treatment of cancer, and has brought all the planned resources of several laboratory sciences to bear on the problem, without being able to find a solution.

Daguerre solved a crucial problem in the invention of photography through forgetting that he had an open vessel of mercury standing in a cupboard. Into this cupboard, because it was dark, he put away overnight an exposed bromide-coated silver plate. In the morning, the latent image had begun to develop. Daguerre, in a flash, suspected fumes from the mercury, and trial confirmed his suspicion. Other chemicals in time came to replace mercury vapor, but the essential and hitherto undiscovered factor of "developing" invisible images had been found (§ 187). Yet to see the situation in its entirety, it must be remembered that Daguerre was a conscious inventor, long seeking a way to a specific goal. That is why he was able to profit at once by his fortunate accident: he was alerted to take advantage of it.

Malus's discovery of the polarization of light came from his happening to be looking at a crystal as he turned it idly in his fingers against a reflection of the rays of the setting sun in facing windows; he noted that the refraction altered perceptibly with the turning. If he had held the crystal against un-reflected light—or even with reflection if the rays had not been coming in nearly horizontally—there would have been no alteration. Malus had his head full of refraction phenomena at the time, so he promptly verified his chance observation, and determined its meaning by experiments. Another physicist, preoccupied with different problems, might have filed the observation and only followed it up years later, or forgotten it. The average layman would probably have thought the phenomenon odd and have done nothing about it. It is evident that the degree of experience and the direction of interest of the person to whom the accident happens is at least as important as the accident itself.

Thus, one F. P. Smith was testing ship's screws. An unduly long one hit a snag, broke off, and the boat went faster. This accident might not have been profited by at all except for happening in the course of trials deliberately aimed at invention.

Similar was Goodyear's accidental discovery of hard or vulcanized rubber by heating with sulphur, a process he invented in 1839 and patented in 1844. Yet the "accident" only happened after Goodyear had been in the rubber-goods business and had failed because of the deterioration which articles of rubber underwent. He had in fact previously experimented to prevent this deterioration.

Farther back in the history of culture there are a number of instances on which direct evidence is lacking but which suggest the factor of invention by accident, or as a by-product of some other effort. Rye, for instance, is believed first to have been a weed in wheat or barley fields of western Asia. As the cultivation of wheat was carried farther north, or to higher altitudes, the hardier rye throve at the expense of the wheat. There are regions where the two are put in together: if the wheat fails in a bad year, there is at least a partial rye crop to fall back on. In still colder climates, rye, on account of its dependability, came to be sown pure as a crop in its own right. In the same way, oats seem to have begun as a weed in fields of emmer wheat.

So with the fire drill. It is an uncertain enough implement; in most primitive communities only the more adept individuals attempt to use it. It requires wood that is neither too hard nor too soft and is both seasoned and kept dry, and especially a rather delicate balance of manipulative strength and skill. This makes it unlikely that anyone who noted that friction produces heat, and who deliberately attempted to apply the principle in the fire drill, would have succeeded. Without previous experience or teaching, it would be perhaps a thousand chances to one that the trial would fail and that our putative inventor would discard his invention. It seems much more probable that in the boring of a hole not only would warmth be felt, but sooner or later the ground-out wood dust would collect in a little heap and send up a wisp of smoke and show a glowing spark; whereupon it would only be necessary to repeat the operation with a new purpose. Much the same holds for the other friction devices, fire plow, fire saw, and fire cord. While there is no proof that these inventions were actually made as unintended by-products, it is mechanically plausible that they were. In any event, it is inescapable that the "invention" had antecedents.

The occasional part that accident plays among apes in the solution of problems that are akin to simple inventions has been discussed in § 28.

That accident has an occasional hand in invention is certain, but its importance must not be overestimated. Without awareness of want or problem, favorable luck will be wasted. It is again true that states of mind determine inventions, in individuals and in societies. Only as against this background does accident become significant.

148. INVENTION AND PLAY

Inventions motivated by play impulses are fairly common. The old "high" bicycle, with a very large wheel, was purely an instrument of sport. When about 1890 the modern type, with two equal and smaller wheels, then called safety bicycle, began to appear, it was hailed with acclaim. Bicycle parades were held, bicycle racing became an intercollegiate sport, century runs were scheduled every Sunday, hundreds of clubs were organized, then federated into a great League of American Wheelmen. It was only later that the bicycle began seriously to be used as a means of getting around on business. From this position, in America, it was again partly displaced by the abundance and cheapness of automobiles; but in Europe, where relatively few people have been able to afford motorcars of their own, the bicycle has remained standard as a middle-class means of local transportation. In 1944, when the American forces re-entered a western Europe denuded of railroads and gasoline, it was about the only civilian means of locomotion.

The history of the automobile is parallel. It too began essentially as a vehicle of sport, luxury, and recreation.

Ballooning, the first form of aviation, commenced partly as a scientific demonstration and partly as an adventure. The practical and economic utilization of all aircraft came much later.

The first invention of the bow and arrow may fall into the same class. A bow must have passed beyond a certain threshold of effectiveness before it can have any utility as a weapon. It seems dubious whether any primitive, starting from nothing and thinking up a bow and arrow by insight, could give it the several points of efficiency needed for killing even a small animal. Besides, certain manipulative skills are required in addition to aim, such as an arrow grip and a string release. Our hypothetical inventor out of the blue would therefore quite likely have given up his idea as unworkable on first actually trying it out. On the other hand, a string on a bent stick is under tension and will twang. Just such a "musical bow" is used by many primitive peoples as a sort of "Jews'-harp" or jaws'-harp, set against the teeth. The same strung stick could also be bounced in a game, or have sticks bounced off its string. From that it would be a short step to sliding or shooting light sticks at a near-by mark. Now, with something to build on, both in the way of a working instrument and manipulative skill, a little more strengthening or improvement of both bow and arrow would much more easily result in a workable weapon. This reconstruction is wholly speculative, and no assurance can be put on any step in the process outlined. The suggestion is merely that something of the sort is likely to have been the development, because the invention in toto, at one stroke, seems over-difficult mechanically; and the play factor, perhaps aided by accident, seems the most likely to have entered into the transitional stages. The influence of pattern, of existing similar forms, must also be reckoned with, as antecedents: not only a musical or game bow, but the spring trap or noose holding down a bent-over sapling. In both cases taut cords and the elasticity of wood are utilized. Unfortunately, we have no more actual knowledge of the origin of the sapling snare than of the bow. We do know that the bow as a weapon is not really early in prehistory. Its first record is late Palaeolithic or Mesolithic (§ 274-276), and it was preceded in Europe by a well-developed spear-thrower in the Magdalenian (§ 269).

A second prehistoric instance is American. It has long been known that even the most advanced native cultures of the New World—Aztec, Maya, Inca—totally lacked several basic technological devices that had long been important in the Eastern Hemisphere. These included ironworking, stringed musical instruments, plows, and wheels.[1] In 1944 wheeled toys of pottery were reported from excavations in the Panuco River region in Mexico, near Tampico. They consisted of effigies of dogs with the paired legs perforated, presumably for insertion of a slender rod or reed, on the ends of each of which pierced pottery disks were jammed. The axles have decayed, but the baked clay figures and sets of disks remain. These are indubitable little four-wheel wagons in principle, though applied to toys (or possibly cult objects) on the order of the stuffed lambs or wooden horsies that our children drag around. Subsequently it was noted that similar pieces had previously been discovered scatteringly all the way from Michoacán to Panamá.

As compared with all the other instances here discussed, this case is incomplete. The principle of the device was achieved in play, but it failed to be applied for utility. Actually this nonuse of the wheel after its discovery makes native America stand out in sharper contrast with the Old World. Literally and mechanically, the ancient Mexicans made the invention; socially speaking, they refused it—threw it away.

Generically, all the discoveries and innovations of pure science and fine art—those intellectual and aesthetic pursuits which are carried on without reference to technology or utility—may be credited to functioning of the human play impulses. They are adult sublimations, onto a largely supermuscular level, of the sensorily exploratory and kinaesthetic activities that constitute play in children and mammals. They rest on the play impulse, which is connected with growth but is dissociated from preservation, comfort, or utility, and which in science and art is translated into the realm of imagination, abstraction, relations, and sensuous form.

149. ANTECEDENTS

The bow is of interest, not only because of its presumptive relation to play before utility, but also because it illustrates the necessity of antecedents to almost any invention. These antecedents, prerequisites, or conditions must be present—both before an individual can make a workable invention, and before a culture can accept it. These antecedents are of the utmost importance to recognize, because we men are by nature romantic and unhistorical-minded, and, except under intellectual discipline, we prefer and shape for ourselves emotion-

---

[1] There were indigenous spindle whorls, but these were only disk buttons or weights on a rod twirled free by hand. They might at best be called near-wheels. The axle did not spin in a bearing, and the wheel edge engaged nothing.

ally appealing stories of how inventions are brought about by sheer resolve, superhuman insight, dire necessity, or mere blind luck. On analysis every invention on which we have information proves to depend on antecedents, as regards both individual creation and social acceptance.

The essential feature of the modern automobile is the propulsion of a wheeled vehicle by an explosion engine. Wheels were known for thousands of years, the explosion engine for decades, before the combination was made. It is completely certain that the idea of combining a vehicle and an explosion engine occurred to hundreds of men long before any automobile ever ran. The problem was not to put one and one together, but to make them fit workably. This involved all sorts of complications, which had to be mastered gradually. We need not go into the mechanical complexities of transmission and gearshift; simpler features will illustrate the point. To be effective, the gas explosion must occur in an enclosed chamber or cylinder against a piston whose plunge outward moves the machinery. How introduce an intermittent flame rapidly into this tight cylinder? The most feasible answer is an electric spark, and this is what has chiefly been used in gasoline motorcars. It could be used when automobiles came along, because by then first static electricity, next current, and then electromagnetism had been discovered. Until these prior discoveries had been made, the *principle* or abstract idea of an automobile could have been invented, but hardly a car that ran.[2] The difference is like that between Leonardo da Vinci's dreams of flying machines and the Wright brothers' realization at Kittyhawk. Leonardo merits high credit for his imagination; but he was four centuries too early. His time could not have produced a machine that would fly. It possessed too few scientific and technical antecedents.

Patents, by the way, are not issued for an idea, but for a specific device, process, or machine that is presumably workable, and which is concrete enough so that it can be drafted or a model can be supplied. If the Patent Office believes a proposed device to be unworkable, it refuses the patent. It is true that if a device includes a new idea, this idea also becomes protected by its patenting; but only secondarily, by inclusion. It is easy to see why the law takes this stand. Without it, there would be a scramble to pre-empt all possible new ideas, largely by people incompetent to translate them into effective execution. Patents would be held by those working out combinations of words instead of working out parts of machines. The point is significant for the understanding of culture history.

Sometimes the prerequisite antecedents are indirect and unexpectedly remote. The really first automobiles did not have gas engines, but were steam-driven. This was as early as 1770 in France, soon after 1800 in England, long before the gas engine was invented. Some of these early road machines have been preserved and may be seen in the United States National Museum Annex. They

---

[2] Some progressive dates are: workable gas engine, Otto, 1877; Selden basic patent, 1879; practical automobile, Serpollet in France, 1889; first gasoline motor of present motor-car type, Daimler, 1892.

look something like monstrous steam rollers. Trevithick's car of 1803 ran on the streets of London with 10-foot drive wheels. By 1823 tubular boilers had been introduced. These road cars were not a practical success, and for several reasons; but one of the reasons was that roads were bad. Locomotives, which is what these contraptions really amounted to, were accordingly put on rails, where they no longer shook to pieces, could go much faster, and could better haul cars. Thus the steam railway was born about 1829; is really was a transfer from the idea of the free-ranging automobile, which was then dropped for nearly a century. The idea of rails was much older than that of self-moving engines. Wooden rails for hand-pushed cars are said to have been used in small-scale mining operations in Germany as early as 1546, and certainly were used before 1700 at Newcastle; iron-shod ones in 1716, and cast-iron ones in 1767, all these last in England. Passengers were hauled in horse-drawn cars on rails near London in 1801—the same year that Trevithick carried them in a steam-driven locomotive—a full twenty-eight years before Stephenson's steam locomotive proved practicable on the Liverpool-Manchester rail line.

It should be added that several factors were involved in the nonsuccess of the early road locomotives. In England, where industry had become heavier and more mobile than in France, and roads were far better than in America, the directors and promoters of steam railways exerted competitive pressure as soon as the railways had proved successful and were promising to make money. Beginning as early as 1832, they induced turnpike trustees to exact prohibitive tolls from road machines. When this was not sufficient, they got legislation passed which put a 4-mph ceiling on any road engine-vehicle—a rule that was not relaxed in England until 1896, when the gas-engine automobile was already successfully racing across France. Such blocking of the development of inventions by use of influence is not mere wickedness. The railroads did represent a growing investment, much larger than any for road machines; and money is like life in seeking self-protection. Indeed, the early railway-builders were genuinely farsighted in their fears, as the later automotive competition beginning in the decade 1920-30 was to show.

A weakness of railways is that they involve heavy capital for right of way, roadbed, track, and maintenance, and that they reach only a limited number of points. Recognition of the desirability of a mechanical vehicle that could range freely on all roads was therefore bound to recur. Shortly before 1900, the immediate ancestors of our modern automobile began to appear, in three forms. One used the newer explosion engine already discussed; another, the old steam engine, though in a shape extremely light for the power produced, with 1000-pound-pressure flash boilers; the third, a storage-battery electric motor. For years the three forms competed, until the gas engine won out through greater adaptability to most demands. One thing, however, helped the modern automobile, even in its infancy, as against its precursor of a century before: the solid rubber tire, which eased some of the jolts as speed increased. This tire had come in toward the end of the horse-and-buggy days for pleasure vehicles: "Bring out your rubber-tired hacks." Soon the hollow, inflated rubber tire took its place; this had developed with the low or safety bicycle a decade or so before, and had there proved its advantage and feasibility. Without rubber and pneumatic tires, the automobile would have had to take a racking pounding at speeds of more than six or eight miles an hour on most roads of that time; but now the automobile's tires were awaiting it. Undoubtedly if tires had not been ready, they would soon have been developed; but the progress of the automobile would in that case probably have been delayed some years.

A simple case of antecedents, though an ancient one, is the calendar, which could not have been devised without recorded observations and counts. Reference is to a genuine calendar that recognizes a specified number of days and of moon appearances within the year, and attempts to reconcile the three factors—days, moons, year—which are not related in integral numbers. Even if such a calendar is only approximately true, it must be preceded by observations whose cumulative count is carried on for many years, probably for several lifetimes. This in turn involves some system of notation or record. Hence any complex calendar can hardly be expected to have preceded writing by very long.

Greek astronomy underwent a splendid development for some centuries, then slowed and ceased progress. The Greeks had no real clocks with gears, pendulum, or escapement. They had only water clocks depending on drip, and sundials. They knew optics and the lens in principle rather than in practice, because they do not seem to have ground glass. Hence they had no telescopes. Their other observational instruments were of the simplest. Looking back now, it is evident that Greek intellect and imagination had developed astronomy about as far as they were able to until clocks and telescopes were available—and, let us add, until a mathematics with a computationally efficient number-symbol system like our positional "Arabic" numerals was also available. It was by lack of these antecedents that the further progress of Greek astronomy was necessarily checked. As a matter of fact, when basic progress in astronomy began to be made again, it was by Copernicus and his successors some centuries after clocks (§ 184) and position numerals (§ 189) and algebra were in use. Within another century the telescope was invented (§ 152) and was immediately utilized by Galileo and others. Similarly, contemporary astronomy builds largely on the photography and the spectroscope that the nineteenth century devised.

150. CUMULATIVE AND COMPLEX INVENTIONS

So important is this matter of antecedents that it is often difficult to determine reliably just what constitutes an invention or when it took place. The more the situation is analyzed, the larger do the antecedents loom, and by comparison the less outstanding does the new step or increment appear. This is contrary to the popular view, which condenses a complex and gradual process into a single dramatic act by one individual, with whom we can identify ourselves emotionally. Hence the anecdotes about Newton and the apple, or Watt and his mother's teakettle, which we are taught as children. We profess not to believe these stories seriously, but they nevertheless tend to influence our thinking.

It is true that there is always insight at work when something new is devised or understood. It is no doubt also true that usually it is great men, genuinely superior individuals, who have these insights. But there is also a long chain of antecedents involved, in every case of which we have knowledge, without which the insight and genius could have done nothing in the given situation. This intricate and largely impersonal build-up is precisely the anthropologist's or the historian's business to elucidate for true understanding of what happened; but it is horribly unromantic, and the lay mind shrinks from it, just as a child could not grasp it. The popular mind loves being off duty as regards criticism and skepticism, and has invested the whole matter of invention with an atmosphere of fascinating mystery. It imagines a great intellect rushing along out of nothing like a new comet out of space, and making a complete invention at one stroke. The more inexplicable this is, the more satisfying it is as a day-dream story. In reality, however, we may say that most so-called inventions are not a single act but a cumulative series of transmitted increments plus a series of new elements when these become possible in the culture in which they appear.

Kuznets neatly demonstrated this rule in a type study of the plow sulky. This is a plow with wheels. The addition of the wheels undoubtedly made it a new kind of plow, which we can define, and distinguish from other plows. Kuznets went over data extracted from United States patent records on the number of patents issued each year that had to do with plow sulkies—new parts, improvements, refinements. Each year after the initiating invention in 1865 the number of new patents grew more rapidly, then began to level off, reached a peak around 1882, then diminished, declined rapidly, and dwindled away by 1923. There was little more to perfect on the plow sulky, and inventiveness turned to replacing it by new types of plows. The year-by-year curve of additions to and improvements of the plow sulky suggests a somewhat skew "normal" frequency distribution.

Now it cannot be maintained that all inventions develop as regularly as this. A physical or an economic catastrophe may come along and chop off the curve; or a new and subversive invention may displace a still growing one. The line of development would also look different if one chose a wider category, say plows in general. In that case the line would be a composite of the curves for inventions of handled plow, share plow, plow sulky, disk plow, and so on; and it would presumably run more nearly level but with many minor fluctuations. Also, in the absence of Patent Office records, we cannot be sure of the precise growth of many inventions. Yet what analysis of the plow-sulky history does show is that many inventions are not single acts of mind, but cumulative results. They are social events, and therefore they usually are gradual events.

In the last analysis, the fundamental invention in the plow sulky was the combination of two antecedents, the plow and the wheel, and two very old antecedents at that. The rest of the history of the invention consists of improvements and modifications; in other words, developments or consequences of the original combination. A great deal of invention seems to boil down to just that.

The more analytically facts are gone into, the more difficult is it to isolate many really basic inventions. More and more do they resolve into combinations of old elements, or into modifications that are reapplications of other old elements. What is new is often a new function, which is culturally significant because it is socially accepted, and which we can name. Such are the plow sulky and the automobile, the bow and arrow, and the fire drill. Mechanically, it is often hard to delimit an invention. The mechanical principle or structure of the shooting bow is the same as that of the drill bow, the game bow, the mouth-harp bow. The bow becomes a bow when it is shot as a weapon. It is its use, its human function, that makes it a weapon, its name, "bow and arrow," that gives it entity. For most of us, other than engineers and inventors, the cultural history of the bow is more significant than its mechanical history. Similarly with the automobile. Mechanically, the early nineteenth-century steam road-locomotives were motorcars or automobiles, as much so as a White Steamer of 1908 or a Chevrolet of 1948. But they failed to be successful, they went out, and culturally the history of what we call the automobile begins in the decade before 1900 when flash-boiler steam models and gas-engine makes began to be produced.

151. SOCIAL ACCEPTANCE

This brings us to the matter of social acceptance of inventions. We may lay it down as a definition that, anthropologically, sociologically, and historically, an invention is not an invention until it is accepted in a culture. Until then it exists merely individually or mechanically; it actualizes historically only with its social acceptance.

It is notorious that a great many successful inventions have been claimed by and for different nations. Which is the right one is often difficult to decide. Where nationalism enters into the problem, it becomes still more difficult. Asked who the inventor of the steamship was, the average American will answer Fulton; the Britisher, Symington; the Frenchman, Jouffroy. A Spaniard may even propose Blasco de Garay, who is wholly mythical as regards the steamboat. Each is reacting to what he has been taught. But Fulton had well-known predecessors, both American and European. The story is set forth in fuller detail in § 185-186, but it might be said here that what Fulton really did was to build a steamboat which convinced people that it was or could be made economically successful. Historically, the definition of the inventor as the man who makes a utilitarian invention pay, or succeeds in persuading others that it will pay, has a great deal to be said for it, especially in our contemporary civilization with its heavy economic and technological slant. For all times and places the definition is a bit narrow, since some successful innovations do not yield a money profit, and some cultures have neither money nor profit. Broadened accordingly, the definition reads that an invention is only potential while its idea remains in the head of an individual, but that it becomes actualized when it begins to be socially accepted into a culture.

The bars to adoption are of several kinds. First there is the direct economic preventive. We know how to extract gold from the ocean, or power from the tides, but it costs more, in money, to extract them than the gold and the power are worth. Then there is the already discussed matter of antecedents, as with Leonardo's ideas of flying machines. In 1500 Europe was technologically not far enough along to execute his ideas. Next is the factor of resistance. A new religion usually encounters an established one. An attempt to induce Americans to eat taro meal for breakfast failed because they already had fixed eating habits and a sufficiency and variety of foods, so an unexciting novelty made no appeal. An efficient private express system may block institution of a public parcel post, or vice versa. The two are competitive in serving nearly the same ends, and economic, political, or monopolistic pressure will be directed against the newcomer. Finally, there are innovations that may seem intrinsically desirable to nearly everyone, but which are bound to exact a heavy toll of temporary confusion and disorganization: a radical reform of the calendar or the alphabet, for instance, as discussed in § 170 and 212.

Converse conditions of course further the adoption of changes. An established religion that has lost its hold, chronic food shortages, times of distress when reorganization is in majority demand—all invite reforms that normally include innovations and long-delayed inventions.

A cultural novelty always encounters existing cultural conditions, and it is these which determine whether, when, how, and in what form it gets adopted. These preconditions of course are so variable from instance to instance that it is difficult to attribute the acceptance of particular inventions to their intrinsic merit. In the realm of machines there certainly is something pretty close to intrinsic or absolute merit, in the degree of physical fitness, efficiency, and economy. But even as between machines, their acceptance is always in part conditioned by their relation to the local culture in which they are invented or into which they are introduced. Witness the story of the steamboat in § 185. In nonmechanical matters, innovations are of course even more influenced by the culture they are trying to enter.

In this matter of their fate, or at any rate their date, being determined by the cultural soil on which they fall, inventions from inside a society and diffusions from outside it (§ 171) are much alike.

152. SIMULTANEOUS INVENTIONS AGAIN

The frequent simultaneity of inventions has been discussed in § 140 as a manifestation of pattern growth, but it is obviously also a matter of antecedents. If the prerequisites for an invention are lacking, it cannot be realized, even if the idea should crop up. On the contrary, once the prerequisites have been supplied, if desirability of a contrivance continues to be felt, a whole series of individuals are likely to work on the problem, so that the prospects are considerable that two or more of them will find a feasible solution. In familiar metaphor, we say that the discovery is now in the air, or that the time is ripe for it. More precisely, inventions are culturally determined. Such a statement must not be given a mystical connotation. It does not mean, for instance, that it was predetermined from the beginning of time that type printing would be discovered in Germany about 1450, or the telephone in the United States in 1876. Determinism in this connection means only that there is a definable relation between a specific condition of a given culture and the making of a particular invention.

The history of science is full of instances. Sunspots were first discovered in 1611, independently and in different countries, by Galileo, Harriott, Scheiner, and Fabricius. The specific antecedent is highly definite: the telescope was devised in 1608. The telescope, in turn, has three claimants to its invention. All three were Dutch, probably because the manufacture of lenses was developed farthest in Holland at the time. Only a little later, Spinoza, now remembered as one of the great philosophers, was earning his daily bread as a lens-grinder. The compound microscope also originated in Holland; and the discoveries through it of animalculae, egg development, blood circulation, insect anatomy, and the like were made later in the 1600's by two other Dutchmen, Leeuwenhoek and Swammerdam. All this means that the culture of seventeenth-century Holland included a pattern in which lenses figured with more weight than elsewhere. In short, the Dutch were lens-minded and lens-making, which was the antecedent that led to the telescope, and this in turn was the antecedent to the discovery of sunspots.

To a certain extent we may even speak legitimately of the inevitability of inventions—provided we mean by this nothing more than that, given an existing sense of the desirability of a conceivable device, and the presence of the needed antecedents, the device will necessarily be invented soon. Given enough knowledge of optics, technological skill in making lenses, and astronomical curiosity, sunspots and the moons of Jupiter will be discovered promptly—if not by Galileo, then by someone else. Given knowledge of electric current and electromagnetic induction and of sound vibration—especially with telegraphs in successful operation for thirty years—and the idea of the telephone is bound to occur to a number of technicians. It is only a question of who will first work the idea out feasibly. Will it be Bell or Gray in 1876, or someone else in 1877 or 1878 or perhaps as early as 1875? To the individual inventor the "Who?" is all-important, because it means who is to get the prize. To his society, and to the world at large, the "Who?" is really a matter of indifference—except for sentimental partisanship—because the invention was going to be made anyway about when and where it was made. We cannot always see this fact at the moment, and still less can we judge in advance whether all the necessary antecedents have been gone through with and the economic requirements satisfied. But after the event, especially at some little perspective from it—provided it is not so long ago that the record has again begun to get dim or lost—we can recognize the piling-up of the antecedents until the invention or the innovation follows as their consequence. See for instance the histories of mills, of the steamship, of the telegraph and telephone, in another chapter (§ 183-187).

This view of the inevitability of inventions is now pretty generally accepted. That it is not yet common popular knowledge is due to the persistence of what may be called the "great-man theory" or fallacy. No one denies that there are great men and that they do great things. The fallacy is to infer from this that everything important in history must have had a great man as its specific cause. From the fact that the telegraph and the telephone are extremely important in the mechanics of modern living, it does not follow that Morse and Bell were outstandingly great men; though obviously they were more than mediocrities.[3] It is the personalizing, anthropomorphizing habits of nonscientific thinking that lead us loosely to assume not only that such men were supremely great, but that they were so much greater than all their contemporaries that we might still be doing without the benefits of their inventions if they had not been considerate enough to make them. This is patently absurd, since they had rivals treading on their heels, and in fact sometimes stepping out ahead. Let us examine another instance or two, where the circumstances are unusually clear.

We have seen (§ 140) that Alfred Russell Wallace was the independent co-discoverer in 1858 of the "Darwinian" concept or hypothesis of natural selection as a mechanism explaining the change and origin of species and therewith of continuous evolution. At that time Darwin had had the idea for twenty years, and had discussed it with a few of his friends; but, not sufficiently winning their approval, he hesitated to publish until his hand was forced by Wallace. Suppose that Darwin had died during his two decades of indecision. Wallace's would almost certainly be the name now on our tongues. Suppose he too had died, say in 1857. Does it seem more likely that in that event biologists would have gone on indefinitely believing in special creation for each species? Or that within a few years some third man would have had the concept of natural selection occur to him and have announced it? The idea of evolution was "in the air"—as a matter of fact it was more than that, Herbert Spencer having developed it before Wallace and Darwin. Their explanation after all is only that

[3] Morse was also an able portrait-painter.

of a specific mechanism by which the general process of organic evolution is supposed to have worked. Darwin's grandfather Erasmus, and Lamarck, had already had the idea of developmental transformation. It is evident that natural selection was really a link in a chain, one idea among several whose union made a broad system of evolutionistic thought possible. All of which together would seem to build up to this: that science and philosophy having got where they were in western Europe around 1858, it was inevitable that the notion of natural selection should be thought up by someone within a very few years of 1860 at the latest.

By contrast we have Aristotle actually imagining and mentioning the idea of natural selection as something logically thinkable, but immediately dismissing it as something not worth testing against evidence. The Greek way of thinking favored the finite and the definite; its world view was not evolutionistic. The set of the culture pattern—the "spirit" of the Greek times—was against anything like natural selection, and so it was rejected, and remained out for two thousand years. Incidentally, thinking of the idea when he did can be credited to Aristotle as a mark of his individual genius. But his rejection of it is not to his personal discredit, because that was the result of his Greek environment and social heritage.

The case of Mendel, founder of the science of genetics, is extraordinary because his genius almost did never get recognized. In 1866 Mendel published in the proceedings of a learned society at Brno an account of his experimental breeding of peas. In this he announced the basic quantitative laws of heredity, and correctly: they have been much elaborated since but still stand. Except for the Swiss botanist Nägeli, who went unheeded, no one took any notice. Darwin, Galton, and hundreds of other biologists were studying heredity, but they either missed seeing Mendel's paper or failed to realize its significance. Surely this is a case of the time being not yet ripe: Mendel was ahead of it. He died in 1884 as an abbot, but scientifically an obscure person. In fact, he was so discouraged by his failure to impress anyone with his discovery that he is said to have abandoned belief in it himself. Then, a generation later, in 1900, within three months three biologists, the Dutchman De Vries, the German Correns, the Austrian Tschermak, who were studying heredity, and evidently were now severally approaching the point of view that Mendel had reached in the sixties, made his discovery over again (§ 140), and clicked to its importance. Correns also rediscovered Mendel's forgotten publication, and announced it. Literally and personally, the Mendelian laws thus date from 1866; culturally and socially, from 1900. From the angle of understanding human history and the workings of civilization, which is the effective date?

This array of evidence may seem to depreciate the great man, to make him merely a function of his culture. This is both so and not so. As compared with popular thinking, it is largely true, because popular thinking wants to dramatize and build plots around conquering heroes. But recognition of cultural forces or drifts is obviously quite compatible with recognition of genius or individual superiority. They can and do coexist. We can be sure that no important invention is ever made by a dub. If he made one by accident, he would not know it; but some more intelligent person might see the significance and communicate it, thereby becoming the real discoverer. We can be just as sure that there are superior individuals, whom we call highly talented and geniuses, as that there are inferior ones who are incompetent and unintelligent. It is the talented and the geniuses who make inventions. But they make them only when and if their cultures permit; and they make only the specific inventions that their cultures allow, within a narrow range. Other inventions have already been made, and still others are as yet impossible, given the culture as it is. Biography is a recognized literary genre, which has usually been assumed to have a laudatory purpose, and of late has tended frankly to assume semifictional dress. Biographers thus are free to cut out any cultural analyses that would make the human interest of the plot drag, or again to admit bits of culture as picturesque background. If however our purpose is to understand the history of human civilization, the cultural factors loom as decisive, just because they are the larger determinants. They determine what, where, and largely when and how. The individual determines the precise date, the particular manner or coloring of the event, and the mnemonic label of his personality and name.

153. INVENTION OF INSTITUTIONS

At the bottom of every invention there is an idea or a principle, whether formulated or not. Fundamentally, therefore, invention is one in kind, whether it relates to implements and machines or to institutions and beliefs. When a concept like that of divine kingship first appears in human history, it is, in our sense of a new idea, an invention, though an anonymous one. We know nothing of the inventor or the circumstances that led him to originate the idea, but it exercised a profound influence on millions of men from ancient Egypt to modern Japan. Against this, its persistence into recent centuries in Europe is but a fragmentary survival. This king-godship became one of the bases of an extensive politico-economic-religious system or major type of culture in protohistoric times (§ 286). The first sure record of the invention's being accepted is in Egypt. It must have been a startlingly original invention—first to conceive that a human being was a god and then to persuade people to believe it.

Among modern institutional inventions may be mentioned the form of ballot that is officially prepared, marked in privacy, but deposited under control: a system devised to minimize intimidation and fraud. It originated in Australia, whence its name after its spread to the United States.

There are also the initiative and the referendum, which come from Switzerland. Their roots are mediaeval, in the small cantons where every citizen could personally participate in government, much as in a Greek democratic city-state or a New England town meeting. In modern form, the referendum was first worked out by the minute, rural, and conservative canton of Schwyz in 1848. The idea received impetus when larger, liberal, and urban Zürich accepted it in 1869. Five years later it was written into the Swiss federal constitution; and in 1891 the initiative followed. South Dakota in 1898 was the first American state to adopt both institutions.

An American contribution is the written constitution. There were Magna Cartas and the like before, but they were essentially confirmations of concession or privilege. The American constitution was an attempt not to modify or retain, but to create a new political order, and in unambiguous terms free from the interpretations of usage or custom. It took over from existing English practice certain features, such as the bicameral legislature. But it developed as a new feature the differentiation of representation in the two Houses of Congress—by political units and by population size. Also new was the explicit co-ordination of the executive, legislative, and judicial branches of government. But perhaps the most radical innovation of the American constitution was its outrightly creating the basic foundation of a political structure. By contrast, the English constitution is a cumulative growth. As such, therefore, it is unwritten: it is a sort of direction followed through centuries of development. The American constitution, on the contrary, being made up at one stroke, had to be explicit and written out. The parallel shows that conscious, abrupt efforts toward production of new culture form and content may have functions and results closely similar to semiconscious, gradual efforts, and that as processes the two may intergrade.

Analogous to these political inventions are socioeconomic ones such as banks, credit, double-entry bookkeeping, social security and old-age pensions, installment mortgages. There is no difference in principle.

All these institutional inventions cited spread widely. In fact it is their spread beyond the point of origin that has made them historically important. In thus showing invention and diffusion as closely associated, the cases are typical. Just as an invention becomes culturally significant only upon its social acceptance, so an innovation by one population obviously becomes significant in world civilization in proportion as it is accepted by other populations.

154. INVENTION BY STIMULUS DIFFUSION

There is one type of situation in culture history that is interesting because diffusion and invention enter into it equally. It can be called either stimulus invention or idea diffusion. In ordinary diffusion, as of the just-mentioned Australian ballot or the automobile, both the principle and its mechanism are taken over by a receiving culture from the inventing one. Occasionally, however, there are difficulties about acceptance of the mechanism, or the mechanism has not been fully learned. The idea or principle may then also fail to be accepted. But again, the idea may exercise an appeal that causes it to penetrate. An effort may then be made in the receiving culture to devise another mechanism that will produce the desired result. Thus an invention, or reinvention, is stimulated by contact transmission or diffusion.

It is in the nature of such events that they tend to leave little historical trace of the processes at work. But there is documented evidence of several cases, and there are a number of probable ones.

Porcelain is a pottery containing a feldspar clay, kaolin, which on high firing vitrifies all through the ware, instead of only on the surface like a glaze, and hence is brilliant, hard, and waterproof. The Chinese gradually evolved porcelain around 1100 after a long series of groping experiments. In these step-by-step inventions accident may well have played a part, as well as blind trials. By the time Europeans came into direct sea contact with China soon after 1500, the porcelain art was highly developed there. Its products were brought to Europe and admired; but they were costly. Attempts to imitate porcelain were made, but with only partial success. This was because European ceramics were still only in the stage of development of Chinese ceramics some centuries before: they operated with surface glazes. The seventeenth-century delftware, and similar developments, represent this incomplete European imitation. Finally deposits of the necessary ingredient kaolin were found in Europe, the techniques were mastered, and in 1708-09 true porcelain was reinvented by Böttger and Tschirnhaus in Dresden. That is why we eat off "china" plates today. But without a mark having been set by the previous Chinese invention, Europeans would have had nothing to shoot at, and conceivably they might not have devised porcelain until much later.

In the early nineteenth century a half-breed Indian called Sequoya in his native Cherokee, and John Guest by white people, realized the value of writing. He was illiterate. Perhaps this is what made it seem desirable to him that his people should possess an instrument comparable to that of the white man. Had he been sent to an American school he would probably have been content to write English as a substitute. He wrestled with the problem for years. Finally, about 1821, he evolved a Cherokee writing of which his fellow tribesmen were at first incredulous, but which proved to be entirely adequate and simple to learn, and which they adopted and used. The characters are derived from English: in fact Sequoya had in his house a spelling primer, which he could not read, but many of whose letters he used for his own purpose with entirely different values. Eighteen of the Cherokee characters are straight English capitals; some are modified or extended or inverted capitals; a few are lower-case letters or numerals; about a third or a quarter of the total of 86 are freely invented. That Sequoya's feat was however a genuine and singlehanded invention is shown by two facts. Not one of the characters has the same value as in English; and all the characters denote syllables, not letter sounds. Thus A is read as "go" in Cherokee, B as "ya," C as "tli," D as "a." We have thus a true and real invention, with a high degree of originality; and yet we also have the assurance that but for the influence and example of the alien culture, the invention would never have been made. It is another instance of "antecedents," though unusual ones.

An entirely parallel invention of writing was made by a West-coast African, shortly before 1849, for his native Vai language. He had had a bit of missionary schooling in his youth; but he made the invention in a dream, in middle life. It is also a syllabary, as against the alphabetic system of English that had stimulated him. But the number of characters is over 200, and they bear no resemblance to English, nor of course to Cherokee. The names of primitive inventors are rarely known, so this one is cited: Doalu Bukere.

Stimulus diffusion accordingly is also stimulus invention. Therein lies its interest.

This is perhaps not one of the most frequent processes in culture. However, its nature is such that its results look wholly novel and original even when they are not; and the factors involved tend not to get into the historical record and often become quickly forgotten. The number of occurrences of the process may thus be considerably larger than appears. Several instances can be cited in which derivation by diffusion has actually been suggested by one and another culture historian without their being able to find direct evidence of the derivation. Yet the resemblances and the space-time tie-up are such that the operative mechanism may quite possibly have been reinvention stimulated by previous foreign existence of the trait. Such possible examples are:

The seemingly independent invention of pottery by the early Basket Maker-Pueblo (Anasazi) in northern Arizona-New Mexico at a time when pottery surely was already being made in central Mexico (Archaic) and perhaps in southern Arizona (Hohokam; see § 323)

Monks in Christianity, some centuries later than Buddhist monasticism, with convents, celibacy, begging, and tonsure

Development of Greek grammar some centuries after Sanskrit grammar, and of Japanese two centuries after Latin and Dutch contacts

In converse direction, Sanskrit drama following the Greek

Quantitative meter appearing in Arabic poetry, and then by known transfer in Persian and Turkish, after it had long been established in Greek and Latin

None of these can at present be either proved or disproved as examples of stimulus diffusion, but there seems an inherent probability that some of them may turn out demonstrably to be such.

155. INVENTION BY REDUCTION-SEGREGATION

In general, more invention means more machines and more institutions—more physical and social apparatus to be handled. This somewhat dismaying prospect is partly relieved by a type of invention that works through simplification or reduction. Perhaps "extraction" or "segregation" more nearly describes the process. Metaphorically it would be a sort of curdling or clotting-out.

The most striking case is the alphabet (§ 206 and 207). Previous systems of writings consisted of idea signs, word signs, syllable signs, and, in the case of Egyptian, of sound signs also (§202-205). Moreover, a word might be spelled but according to its sound and then an ideogram for it be added, as if to make sure that one representation would be read if the other were missed—see the example in Figure 20. Not only was the writing of particular words cumbersome, but each method of writing required several hundred symbols. Thus Egyptian hieroglyphic comprised 460 characters, cuneiform Babylonian around 600, Indus Valley writing nearly 400. As against this, the true alphabet rests upon the realization that if pure minimum-sound symbols—true letters—are con-

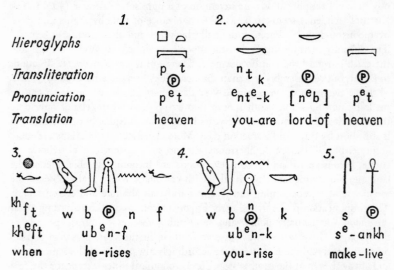

FIG. 20. MIXED PICTOGRAPHIC AND PHONETIC ELEMENTS IN
EGYPTIAN HIEROGLYPHS

Phrases from a page of Egyptian hieroglyph papyrus. The circled **P** denotes a pictograph or ideograph; the rest of the writing is by pictorial *consonantal letters*. In 1, heaven is written alphabetically and confirmed by a conventionalized pictographic "determinative" (the vault of heaven); in 2, by pictograph alone. The first words of 2 and 3 are wholly phonetic: pictographs for the ideas of "when" and "you are" would be hard to devise. The grammatical suffixes -*f* and -*k* added to *uben*, "rise," in 3 and 4 illustrate another reason for the development of consonant letters. In the first of these, the confirming pictograph (sun with rays) is put in the middle of the stem *uben*; in the second, between it and the suffix. In the first words of 2 and 3, the letters in the word read downward; elsewhere, mostly horizontally. The true alphabet was devised by a process of *segregative reduction* out of mixed-method writing such as this.

sistently used, all the characters for syllables, words, objects, ideas, and "determinatives" or classifiers can be discarded; and anything that can be spoken can also be written, and with complete intelligibility, by means of from two to three dozen simple signs. It took two thousand years for this realization to be achieved. In one sense the cardinal quality required by the inventors of the alphabet was resolution, the courage to break with the multiple reinsurance of ways of denoting meaning that was characteristic of the older mixed pictographic-ideographic-phonetic systems. In a rough sort of sense, the invention was like a cripple's finding he could walk free when he threw his crutches away.

If the Egyptians missed a bet by failing to discard all their writing symbols except their 24 true letter-signs scattered among the rest, they did achieve another mental simplification: the invention of a pure solar calendar (§ 291). The "natural" tendency seems to be to take cognizance of time by nights and days, by moons and their phases, and finally by years and their recurrent seasons. The difficulty bred by this is that the moon's revolutions around the earth and the earth's around the sun do not gear. There are more than twelve lunations in a year, but considerably less than thirteen. They average a bit over 29½ days, so that a twelve-moon year is nearly 11 days short. A rough correction can be made by putting a thirteenth month into every third year. Yet not only does this have the inconvenience of the years being quite unequal, but the correction is still short by three and a fraction days. More elaborate intercalations are more accurate, but also more cumbersome. But no such system can be wholly accurate, because earth and moon revolutions are incommensurable. Hence the Chinese, Mohammedan, and ritual Jewish calendars, which really observe the moon, are always beginning the year at a different absolute and seasonal date. The simplification made by the early Egyptians consisted in disregarding what the moon was actually doing, and substituting months—arbitrary periods of thirty days. There were always twelve of these in the year, plus five supplementary days; and the Egyptian year accordingly always was of the same length and always began at the same seasonal or astronomical time—except for the few hours' gain that we correct by a leap day. We still follow the Egyptian plan of months' being independent of the physical moon and its phases, though we do not use the supplemental days, and we have our months of unequal length— "Thirty days hath September," and so on. The cardinal act in the devising of the Egyptian calendar, and a feature that we retain, was the *discarding* of the moon's revolution from any relation to the earth's revolution or year.

Another example of the process is the way in which astronomy and astrology were originally associated in one system in Mesopotamia, as discussed below in connection with the origin of the week (§ 196-197). It used to be thought that the segregation was effected wholly by the Greeks, who discarded the omens and portents and developed the pure science. It is now known that in late Mesopotamian days, after the fall of Assyria and especially after that of Persia, there was a school of genuine or pure astronomy in Babylonia on which the Greeks were more dependent—both for observation and for interpretation—than their self-centeredness had led us to believe. But however the credit may fall between the two nationalities, they did manage to curdle a purely naturalistic science out from a previous amorphous, naturalistic-supernaturalistic mass of knowledge and beliefs regarding the heavenly bodies. This astronomy maintained itself for a number of centuries; but about the time it stopped progressing, by Roman Imperial times, it was reinvaded by a new wave of magic. This was astrology, of the type still followed by a remnant of the mystically inclined and the credulous among ourselves. The earlier Mesopotamians had been concerned mostly with eclipses as portents. The later astrology crystallized chiefly at Alexandria and dealt with the continuous fortunes of men as determined by the positional relations of the planets, or rather of the seven moving heavenly bodies visible to the human eye. From then on until about 1600 astronomy was astrology-ridden, among ancients, Arabs, and Europeans. Occasional astronomers disavowed the astrological component, more accepted it, some were ardent over it. It was close to 1700 before scientists were once more unanimous in repudiating astrology as wholly nonscientific.

The relations of alchemy and chemistry were similar except that here there was no ancient attempt at autonomy of a self-sufficient science. The result was that a wholly naturalistic chemistry never emerged as a productive and systematic activity anywhere until in the most recent centuries of European civilization. The magico-mystic ingredients in alchemy were the elixir of life, the philosopher's stone, and the transmutation of metals into gold. The search for these transcendentals was not calculated to encourage preoccupation with ordinary "base" substances and their humble quantitative properties. In the West, alchemy first appeared in the turgid atmosphere of Imperial Roman Alexandria about contemporaneously with planetary astrology.[4] In the East, substantially identical beliefs were rampant in China apparently a little earlier, during the first half of the Han period of 206 B.C.-A.D. 220. Alchemy still had some repute in Europe as late as the sixteenth century.

The type of inventive change by reduction or extraction has been called "etherealization" by Toynbee. The connotations of that word seem inappropriate, and perhaps unfortunate. But it is evident that the process deserves a name. It is not a process of outright specialization, though it somewhat resembles differentiation by specialization. For instance, medicine begins with general practice, from which after a time eye-ear-nose-throat treatments separate off. With added knowledge, instruments, and skills, certain doctors begin to limit themselves to the eye and are called oculists. The remainder for a while go on as a unit, but in time the aurists perhaps again split off as specialists. In

---

[4] This is the usual version. Another interpretation makes the Alexandrians crude chemists concerned with producing deceptive imitations of gold. Both accounts may be true.

this medical specialization there is no discarding or repudiation of one element or ingredient; they are all developed further, and therewith it became advantageous and desirable for individuals to choose among the subspecialties. In the process here discussed, however, the essential step is that an encumbering ingredient, which is either unnecessary or false, is got rid of. There is accordingly a *reduction* of total compass of a system or activity through a segregation of its more valuable or efficient elements from its inferior or impeding ones.

Apparently, a process somewhat reminiscent of this reduction-segregation is observable in technology. In the main this technological happening is obscured by the fact that many machines grow more complex as they develop, because their functions and powers increase. But as each kind of machine approaches the limits of its inherent possibilities as a type, it tends to revert to simplicity, to emphasize economy of means, and to achieve what engineer and artist would agree in calling beauty of design and function. An example in point is the clipper ship coming to its peak in the very days when steam was beginning to supersede sails. The superb swords of Japan in an era of cannon are another instance. We have here a field of social process that has been inadequately explored, but in which interesting possibilities can be glimpsed.

156. CULTURAL LOSS

Popular romance maintains a half-belief in supposed lost arts of the ancients, such as hardening of copper to equal steel, miraculously lifelike embalming of mummies, and the like. Actually, it is likely that no art of serious consequence has been lost from total human civilization. Copper can be hardened by alloys most of which the ancients did not possess; it can be somewhat hardened by hammering, a quality which we know as well as they did but do not utilize precisely because we have very much harder steel. Lenin's body in Moscow is probably preserved much better than any Egyptian master embalmer would have known how to preserve it. And so on.

There is considerable cultural "loss" that is actual, but it relates to particular cultures rather than to human culture as a whole. Most of it, as will be seen presently, is displacement, properly speaking: a new custom, art, worship, or belief crowds out an old one. Utilitarian arts, such as hardening copper, dyeing with cochineal or with Tyrian shellfish, retire to a humble spot in the technological background as metallurgy improves steelmaking and chemistry devises anilines. Most of what we shall have to consider as cultural "losses" possess this character of replacement or displacement. In addition, particular societies do at times undergo genuine or downright losses of specific items of their culture, owing to environment, loss of materials or skills, shrinkage of population, impoverishment, and other or unknown causes. Some instances of both kinds will be briefly analyzed.

157. DISAPPEARANCE OF USEFUL ARTS

In 1912 Rivers demonstrated a series of convincing examples of the disappearance of useful arts in Oceania. The things given up were of unquestionable utility: canoes, pots, bows. The canoe went out of use in Torres Island in Melanesia, was replaced by·sailing rafts in Mangareva. In a series of Melanesian islands—Malikolo, Pentecost, Lepers, Ambrym—potsherds are found in the ground, but pottery has not been made in the historical period. In several areas the bow was still known recently, but it was used only as a toy, in sport, or in small-game hunting of rats, birds, or fish—not in war. These areas of fighting without bow and arrow covered nearly all Polynesia except Tonga and Samoa; in Melanesia, most of New Britain, New Ireland, and the Admiralties; and some of the coast of New Guinea. The causes of the several disappearances were various. Lack of material was the least common cause. It would be applicable chiefly to canoes, but was not the reason for abandonment in either Torres or Mangareva. Sometimes the guilds or families of tohunga or craftsmen who had been taught magic as well as manual skills by their elders died out. This happened to the canoemakers in the Torres Islands, and to the stone-adz producers in Woodlark. Sometimes in Oceania a single community specializes in manufacturing one article, such as pots, and supplying it by trade to a large area. A catastrophe overwhelming such a village might result in the whole area's coming to use wooden vessels instead of pottery. As to the bow, there was generally no large game in the Oceanic islands to sustain one customary economic utility of the weapon. Of warfare there generally was enough, but it was sometimes ceremonial rather than waged for practical advantage. And in Polynesia war tended to be dominated by standards of bravery, chivalry, or manners of fighting: fashion exalted the hand-to-hand club.

All in all, the array of cases is significant in showing that the actual historical behavior of cultures cannot be predicted from an a-priori notion that practical utility—economic motivation—is invariably determinative.[5]

There also are conditions of natural environment under which particular utilitarian activities can wither away fast. In 1818 the explorer Ross discovered some two hundred Eskimo along the east shore of Smith Sound in northern Greenland—later also named Peary's Eskimo, or Eta or Polar Eskimo, because they live farthest north of any permanent human community, at Igita beyond latitude 78°. Ice and cliffs had long cut them off so effectually that they no

[5] One consideration that Rivers did not stress is that the Oceanian continent of native Australia also lacked canoes, pottery, and bows, and almost universally so. Australia seems to be a case not of having possessed and lost, but of never having had the inventions—in the main perhaps of not wanting them (see § 253, 310). Nevertheless, the proximity of Australia to New Guinea, Melanesia, and Polynesia makes it seem that the two negative distributions may be connected, according to the principles of distributional evidence set forth in § 223-224.

longer had clear knowledge of any other people. They possessed no kayaks—the decked-over boats of skins stretched on a light wooden frame which were so widely prevalent among the Eskimo that it is assumed that all once had them. This group lacked them because driftwood does not carry into Smith Sound. From 1818 on, they got wood from Ross, and from subsequent explorers and whalers; but still they made no kayaks: they no longer knew how. About 1868 a vigorous, restless Baffinland Eskimo took his family, pushed north with sledges, crossed Smith Sound on the winter ice, and found a new home among the Polar Eskimo. Then the kayak reappeared among them: this newcomer from a region of driftwood and knowledge of the kayak taught them how to make it. During the fifty years preceding this Baffinlander's coming the Polar Eskimo had again got the necessary material through the whites. But this had not helped them, because the design and art of joining a seaworthy frame had been forgotten in the preceding centuries of their isolation.

Technological skills can generally be taught only imperfectly by words. There must be visible example and, above all, manual practice. That is one reason why the teaching of chemistry and other science insists on laboratory periods. Useful technologies do not tend intrinsically to disappear faster than other parts of culture; the weak link in the matter of transmission of technologies lies in the acquirement of manipulative practice, the formation of motor habits. Interfere with these and the continuity of the art is broken and may be lost.

It was a deficiency of environment that was at the bottom of the Polar Eskimo's losing their boatbuilding ability. But having once lost the skill, the fresh accession of the needed wood did not suffice to cause them to reinvent the art. And meanwhile their lack of boats helped to pen them in their habitat.

However, nature gave the Polar Eskimo something else. Three large meteorites, now carried to New York City, had fallen in their habitat. From these they managed to whack off slivers of nickel-iron with stones; these they beat to an edge and set end to end in a groove in a bone handle and thus made themselves iron knives—something that no other Eskimo group had, except for rare pieces of drift or trade iron coming from Asia into Alaska. Here then we have both an invention and a loss connected with the same environment—an apt illustration of how complexly culture operates.

158. EFFECTS OF ISOLATION: SOUTHAMPTON AND EASTER ISLANDS

Small, isolated peoples are especially interesting because of the unexpected things that happen to them. While contacts remain open, complete losses are less likely to occur. Wholly localized increments, and fixations at an ancient level, are also less expectable under open contacts. because knowledge and customs have a chance to spread both in and out.

On Southampton Island, at the entrance to Hudson Bay, lived a second Eskimo group who had lost boats from their culture. They were therefore cut off from intercourse with the world unless other Eskimo, or subsequently whalers, ventured to them. They did have a makeshift substitute for alongshore hunting: inflated sealskins that they paddled, riding them like hobbyhorses. But with only these they could probably secure nothing more than occasional small seals. Their main dependence accordingly was on a large herd of wild reindeer that roamed the two-hundred-mile-wide island. With this herd once eaten up, reduced by disease, or impossible to get at, the Southampton Eskimo were doomed. In fact, this fate overtook them in 1902, when they starved to death. All in all, their tools were not those of the other eastern Eskimo, but represented a somewhat deteriorated form of what is called the Thule phase of Eskimo culture. This phase is estimated to have flourished quite widely in the American Arctic around A.D. 1000-1300, after which it became superseded elsewhere by the more modern or historical Eskimo culture. It looks therefore as if the Southamptoners, once they had settled down with their simplified and boatless version of the Thule culture, managed to get along and survived for centuries before disaster caught up with them.

The Polynesians of Easter Island, though they must originally have come in canoes, were also nearly boatless when discovered, because of lack of logs or planking. They had a very few small canoes, carrying from two to four persons, ingeniously sewed together of many patches and splinters of wood. The island is only ten by thirteen miles in size, is grassy and windswept, and very isolated. It lies sixteen hundred miles from Polynesian Mangareva, twenty-two hundred from South America. Tapa-bark cloth was nearly as scarce as canoes, because the paper mulberry withstands the cool winds of Easter Island only with considerable coddling. Breadfruit and coconuts are wholly prohibited by the climate; but bananas, sweet potatoes, taro, and yams were grown. All in all, the Easter Islanders had a purely Polynesian culture—as their speech was a pure Polynesian dialect—with its richness considerably thinned down by their small numbers and by environmental lacks and limitations. But the culture was thinned down more or less all over, without notable total losses at any one point. There were the usual Polynesian gods, chants, myths, kings or chiefs, wars, human sacrifice and cannibalism, houses, stone platforms, dress, foods, and the rest, in a somewhat meager provincial form.

What is really remarkable about this isolated culture is not so much what it had lost as certain unique positive increments that must have been local developments. Three of these stand out. The first was a peculiar bird cult culminating in a ceremonial race that was the great event of the year. The second feature was wooden tablets incised with lines of figures that look remarkably like a script and appear to have had some connection with prayers or chants, but which could not be read, and probably were not true writing but decorative symbols similar to large petroglyphs painted in connection with the bird cult

The third specialty consisted of gigantic rude statues of tuff rock weighing from four or five to twenty or thirty tons. These statues have partial parallels elsewhere in Polynesia in small stone carvings or fair-sized wooden ones. Consequently they represent a heightening of degree—the largest statues occurring on one of the smallest islands—rather than a radically new idea. But the bird cult and the tablets are without real parallels elsewhere in the Pacific and are accordingly indicated as having been devised in the isolation of Easter Island. In this case, therefore, loneliness had several unique and conspicuous results, though they are probably balanced by many minor losses or impoverishments.

The period during which Easter Island was occupied is not known, but is estimated to have been less than a thousand years rather than more. Assuming an average population of 3000, for which there is warrant in the reports of early white voyagers, we must credit this small number of islanders with considerable originality in having evolved their specializations in perhaps from five to eight centuries. Withal, the originality puts no strain on credibility, as do some of the fantastic theories which blow up the Easter Island situation into extreme improbabilities—sunken land bridges, vanished prior races, or "writing" mysteriously preserved from the Indus Valley script of five thousand years earlier.

159. DISPLACEMENTS

On the whole, "loss" appears often to consist of a displacement by something new, rather than being an outright disappearance or a mere melting-away. And the displacement is often only partial. Thus we still have candles and oil lamps though gas came in a century ago and electricity in turn has been generally substituted for gas. The older elements survive, though with diminished or specialized scope. The total culture is thereby so much richer than before. Much of the enormous variety of our technology is due to this preservation of the old alongside the development of the new. The established culture trait loses most of its functions but retains part, or even acquires new ones. It is a use that is lost rather than the trait or item itself. There is, especially in contemporary civilization, a constant tendency for utilitarian devices that are dispossessed by new inventions to persist in art, sport, luxury, religion, or symbolism.

Thus, in North America the automobile has virtually displaced the horse for transportation of both passengers and goods. Yet the horse is still used considerably in certain situations, such as for small-farm plowing. It holds its own without diminution in racing, horse shows, rodeos, circuses, polo, and as a form of pleasurable exercise. All these serve the ends of sport or play.

Similarly the bow still exists in our culture, but archery has become purely a sport.

Woodcuts used to be the ordinary method of illustrating books; only expensive works had steel engravings. Photographic reproduction has entirely displaced the woodcut for practical purposes. Even apart from screen plates that render light-and-shade values with transitions, the ordinary pen-and-ink drawing, which can be done by the artist in a fifth of the time required for cutting a block, gives the same effect, and if necessary a much finer one. Has the woodcut therefore disappeared? As a practical means of actually illustrating in print, yes. But it survives, in fact is having a bit of a cult, as an art form, as an aesthetic expression, as a conscious revival of what is antiquated and simple and comfortable and rude, something like eighteenth-century furniture or imitations of primitive utensils. We do not live by utility alone.

The horn lantern was used when people were poor and glass was expensive as well as brittle. There was always a cow's horn available, and in winter there were evenings in which the farmer could steam and pare and trim it. Glass being much clearer, as soon as its price came down through industrial improvements and mass production, it drove horn out; except that occasionally we still buy sheets of horn for our electric bulbs to shine through with a "natural" mellow amber glow while we talk in the living-room. The glass that was once available only for the wealthy has now become universal; horn, once the poor man's refuge, has become an article of luxury. Many of the losses of civilization, especially in our own of the past century or two, are really displacements, or even inversions of function, like this.

A curious analogy is found in the history of the dog, the almost universal domestic animal. Except where he is of specific value for transport, hunting, herding, or watching, most cultures other than our own may be said to tolerate rather than to protect him; he fends for himself and becomes a scavenger. There are a few groups of primitive tribes that are exceptional in being dogless. There was at least one of these groups in South America and another in native northern California. In this latter area the dog was by no means unknown, but one might have to travel through several Indian villages to encounter one or two. These had been bought or traded from outside, and they were pampered, fed, allowed in the house at night, named, and given formal burial when they died. They were too soft and valuable to be used for hunting. They seem to have been so scarce as to have had no chance, ordinarily, to breed; so the supply had to be kept up by import from outside. This primitive luxury manifestation strangely parallels contemporary New York, where tens of thousands of childless couples keep a dog in their apartment, and at night have the maid or a husband lead him about a bit to foul the public street. It is the attitude of overcherishing a pet that is common to the two cases. How did these California Indians come to have their attitude? Evidently it was because they were essentially dogless and knew no practical use for dogs when they did get them. They may have been this way for one of two reasons. Either they had never in their past history acquired a full-scale dog-keeping habit, or they once followed it and it went into disuse—a case of loss, or more exactly of near-loss displacement into a luxury. The latter seems more likely in view of the near-universality of the dog among American Indians, and the fact that the few non-dog-raising tribes in California must for thousands of years have been in some contact and communication with the much more numerous dog-keeping tribes (§ 165).

Displacements involving both loss and innovation occur also in situations other than those of attitude or function. With cosmetics there may be substitutions of bodily topography. Many primitives paint the body as well as the face. The ancient Egyptians concentrated on the eyelids, the nineteenth century on the cheeks. Lipstick was unknown. After this had come in, interest shifted to the lips, at first timidly; but after a time the cheeks were toned or browned in order to exaggerate by contrast the vivid redness of the lips. Painting of the nails also developed—a new area that primitives seem to have overlooked; but at least it is a reversion to cosmetics elsewhere than on the face. We tend to think first, in all such cases, of the new or intruding item; it is what attracts interest; but of course every innovation ordinarily involves a loss too. The whole cosmetic custom went out once in our culture, with Puritanism. It might go out again, though perhaps next time possibly as a change of taste rather than from moral scruple.

160. KINDS OF LOSS

There remains the more general, seemingly philosophical problem of how large a factor cultural loss is or can be. For instance, can the loss be entire for one feature? Beyond that, could losses be universal, so as to lead to cultural death? Actually, the questions are ambiguous.

First of all, entire loss of features from what? From the particular culture of a particular people? In that case, the answer definitely is Yes. For instance, "we" have lost slavery in the past century. That holds for the United States. But does it hold for the totality of human culture, past and present, everywhere? Such a loss will obviously come more slowly: witness Ethiopia, which is still de-facto slaveholding. And in many cases, even if universal loss had occurred, it might be hard to establish. Things have a way of hanging on long in the remote places; or they persist undercover, in the subcultures of unsophisticated social strata at home: as astrology, crystal-gazing, voodoo, and magic do among ourselves. Then, as we have just seen, an item of culture may be displaced by a novelty from most of its uses, even from its primary use, but persist in one of its uses, or even acquire a new luxury or play use.

Second, it is necessary to narrow the question by defining what it is that is being lost. Is it culture content or culture form? A specific element, a system, a pattern, or an attitude? Or indeed do we mean that a whole culture may disappear? In the sections on progress (§ 127-128), we have seen that among those civilizations which by common consent are reckoned as higher there has been an indubitable drift to discountenance behavior motivated by magic and animism, as well as that which is psychically infantile and unsocialized in its inhumanity and its crude emphasis on the physiological. We may expect, and most of us will certainly hope, that this drift toward the gain of reason, taste, and humanity at the expense of practices based on more infantile motivations will continue. But we certainly cannot prove that it will continue indefinitely, nor can we assert that there might not be conditions which would reverse the trend and cause increase of what is now diminishing.

On the basis of a breakdown into more precisely defined questions, some generalizations can be made as to loss.

Specific items, such as painting the eyelids, or hammer-hardening copper, are more likely to be lost, by outright giving up or by displacement, in any one culture or in all human culture, and to be lost more rapidly, than broad, varied activities such as fishing or animal husbandry, or than large systems such as a religion or a method of writing. The counterpart is that the small trait generally also gets accepted more readily than a big complex. This is logically obvious; and the chief significance of the point perhaps is to help us guard against dealing alike with noncomparables—little things and big, isolated bits and ramified networks.

Replacements, modifications, and substitutions are, broadly speaking, more characteristic of the changes of organic evolution; additive increments are more typical of the changes of human culture (§ 5, 127). But this difference is probably most accentuated in artifacts, tools, and technologies, where a whole array of devices serving similar but not quite identical purposes can easily exist side by side with advantage and without conflict—say tenons, pegs, nails, screws, rivets, lashings, which all hold parts together. Religions, writings, or social systems may also coexist—witness the three "religions" of China and the two writings of Korea (§ 221); but between such there is likely to be strain or conflict, and time is required for an adjustment, if one is worked out at all. And particular items are likely to be rejected or forced out where they are in conflict with a dominant socioreligious system: blood sacrifice in Christianity or Mohammedanism, for instance, or cross-cousin marriage in our Western society. But it is hard to imagine any socioreligious system so averse in principle to crank handles or screws as to force their abandonment from its culture.

The contrast of the organic process as substitutive, of the cultural as additive, is broadly true, but it must not be forced so far as to mean that organic novelties occur *only* as substitutions—that is, as accompaniment of losses—while cultural novelties are regularly incremental. It is true that when birds evolved out of reptiles they gave up a pair of running limbs to acquire a pair of wings, whereas when men learned to fly in airplanes it was not by sacrificing arms—nor even wagons, railroads, and motorcars. From the point of view of the history of birds themselves it is true enough that they acquired flight by a transformative substitution. But from the angle of the evolution of life as a grand total there was also an increment: running reptiles and flying birds where there had been only running reptiles before. And much the same had happened millions of years before when some branch of the ancestral anthropods, having developed air-breathing and come out of the water, somehow got two pairs of wings and soared away as insects. The natural tendency in dealing with animals is to consider what happens to a particular line of descent in its evolution, but in dealing with man to view a cultural change as if it affected the totality of human culture. And not without reason, since an innovation may and sometimes actually does spread to all cultures, whereas the wings developed by birds remain confined to descendants of birds: they cannot possibly spread to non-descendants. In short, the contrast of basic process of organic evolution and cultural evolution is valid and fundamental; only it must not be pushed to exaggeration by comparison of a single line of organic development with the whole breadth of cultural development. Culture also has its substitutions, and therewith its losses—especially the single or particular culture as viewed separately.

161. PROBLEM OF THE DEATH OF CULTURES

When we come finally to the question of cultural death, it is particularly important to define the problem so as not to get enmeshed in what is really a metaphor. There is presumably no possibility of all human culture "dying"; that is, disappearing from internal causes. Of course, the cooling of the sun, the loss of our atmosphere, a collision of the earth or its atomic explosion—any such event that extinguished the human race—would automatically extinguish all culture with it. But that would not be an inherent or a spontaneous death. It may be assumed that culture has sufficient survival value for our naked, unarmed species so that if any branches of man, for whatever reason, got into the way of somehow consecutively diminishing or destroying their own stock of culture, they would inevitably be eliminated in competition with those branches which advanced or even only maintained theirs.

At the opposite end of the scale, as concerns culture traits or items—customs, techniques, beliefs—it is obvious that these get changed, replaced, and lost, but that there is no need of applying to these matter-of-fact happenings any term so metaphorical, so charged with emotional connotations, as "death."

The situation in connection with which the phrase probably arose and has a possible meaning is the passing away of particular national cultures. If there really is a "decline and fall" of civilizations or peoples, there might well also be a "death." What seems to be actually involved in such cases is the dissolution of a particular assemblage of cultural content, configurated in a more or less unique set of patterns belonging to a nation or a group of nations. Such particular assemblages and constellations do unquestionably "die out"; that is, they dissolve away, disappear, and are replaced by new ones. The elements of the content of such cultures may have previously spread to other cultures and survive there. Or their place may be taken at home by elements introduced from abroad. Or they may survive, with or without modification, at home, in the different configuration that gradually takes the place of the old one as a successor culture. All that goes out of existence or "dies" in such cases is a particular, characterized, over-all configuration or pattern grouping.

Thus there can be no question that the culture of ancient Egypt is "dead"— though a more precise formulation would be that its specific pattern assemblage has long since ceased to function or exist anywhere. We even know a good deal of the circumstances of the dissolution. Toward 1400 B.C. there was a last great flourishing of the Egyptian patterns. True, there had been a premonitory symptom a few centuries before in the irruption of the Hyksos, the first conquerors of Egypt, even though transient ones. But there had been recovery from this, and on the rebound the greatest military might, expansion, wealth, excellence of art, and development of thought were attained by the Egyptians. The inherent patterns of their culture may be said to have been fully realized or to have been saturated then. After that, with pattern potentialities exhausted, there could be only diminished or devitalized repetition; unless the patterns can be reformulated in the direction of a new set of values—which would be equivalent to recasting the civilization into a new one or into a thoroughly new phase of one. This latter did not happen in Egypt; so more and more sluggish, mechanical repetition within the realized but fully exhausted patterns became the universal vogue. After about 1200 B.C., general decline is evident. There were civil wars and rival dynasties, failure of art, and evidently of wealth, with only temporary checks. The last line of fairly successful rulers maintained themselves through Greek and other foreign mercenaries, while foreign ideas seeped in. From 700 B.C. on, Assyrian, Persian, Macedonian, and Roman conquests succeeded one another, with the upper classes increasingly Hellenized, and finally all classes Christianized. By A.D. 600 the old civilization had disappeared substantially as completely as now. No one worshiped Osiris or the hawk-headed Horus, no one could read hieroglyphs, no one mummified his dead, no one was Pharaoh. The Arab conquest and Islamization beginning a few decades later merely superimposed one more stratum on the cultural layers under which the old native civilization was already buried forever. The moment of "death" may be impossible to specify, just because the process of "dying" went on so long and is so continuously evident.

Egyptian culture as a unique nexus and entity thus went out of existence. But the society to which it had been attached went on. The Hellenized Egyptians of Cleopatra's time, the Hellenized Christian Egyptians of A.D. 500, the Mohammedan Egyptians of A.D. 1000, and those of today are no doubt mainly the bodily descendants of those Egyptians who first shaped their distinctive civilization around 3500-3000 B.C. Especially is this true as regards the mass of the population, the rural fellahin. The stream of biological heredity rolled on through the millennia with only minor alterations; above it, civilizations grew, dissolved, entered, and replaced one another.

The components of the old Egyptian civilization did not perish equally. Here and there bits of it persist into the thoroughly different culture aggregate of present-day Egyptian culture: perhaps a water-bucket sweep, an ass under his load. Other elements, like the hieroglyphs and burial pyramids, have long since been abandoned everywhere in the world. Other content traits still exist in one or another of the contemporary living cultures, including our own. If it is difficult to name such, that is only because the expansive phase of Egyptian culture productivity took place so long ago—it ended more than a thousand years before Western civilization began to germinate—that transmitted elements have reached us indirectly, at second and third hand, in much altered dress. Original Egyptian traits perhaps first became Asiatic, then Minoan, Greek, finally Roman, before they filtered into incipient Occidental culture, with reselection and remodeling all along the slow, devious route. But elements, ideas, or stimuli of probable Egyptian origin are recognizable in our own calendar, writing, religion (influences contributory to the concepts of monotheism, dying god, afterlife, Madonna with child), architecture, plant and animal husbandry; and others reappear in modern native African cultures (§ 311).

This picture seems typical of what ultimately happens to cultures. Their content is partly superseded and replaced; partly it diffuses through space and time, in ever new settings and with endless remodelings, selections, and recombinations. The ethnically or nationally individuated pattern aggregates of culture material—what we ordinarily call civilizations or culture wholes—also change, though slowly. But beyond a certain point it is no longer a matter of wear and tear with them, of better or worse fortunes, but of either gradual dissolution or gradual ossification of the nexuses which have held them into an active integrated whole. Even before they have become mainly loose pieces or skeleton, another and younger civilization is usually ready to step into their place; or, if there is none such in the vicinity, a new civilization may slowly integrate out of the debris of its indigenous predecessor.

At any rate, such is, in outline, what history tells us of the aging and death of past cultures. The corresponding societies, the culture-carrying groups, have a way of going on; much of the cultural content continues to exist and function somewhere, and may amplify; it is the particular set of patterned interweavings of content characterizing a civilization that breaks down.

The question that inevitably comes to our minds is whether such an end is necessary, or whether our own civilization may perhaps escape it. An honest answer seems to be that available precedent is pretty solidly one-way, but that history is never a sure basis for prophecy, since conditions can never be exactly repeated and precedents are therefore always only partial. For instance, there might be a new influence of culture-planning. Of this we have so far had only rudiments as by-products of contemporary social planning; for most social planning to date aims essentially to freeze most of the existing cultural values while trying to distribute their benefits more satisfactorily among the members of the society—or among all societies.

What is of interest in this connection is the contemporary trend of other cultures to assimilate themselves to Occidental civilization, of Turks, Arabs, Indians, Chinese, and Japanese to "Westernize" in their ways of life and standards. Mankind has never before been essentially unitary in culture. It is not yet unitary; but at the moment it is traveling fast that way. A good many persons, as diverse as ardent Christian missionaries, Communists, generalized idealists, until 1945 even Fascists and Nazis, look forward to the universality of civilization—implicitly their kind of civilization—as a goal and a boon. But there is this consideration: Suppose we attain a single, essentially uniform, world-wide civilization that has supplanted the many diverse ones of the past. And suppose that in attaining this one civilization we achieve its aims, realize the values potential in its patterns. What then when the exhausted, repetitive stage is reached, and there is no new rival culture to take over responsibility and opportunity and start fresh with new values in a different set of patterns—what then?

There is no precedent, and no answer, optimistic or pessimistic, can be proved for this future contingency. But the question is worth thinking about.

CHAPTER TEN

Culture Change

162. TYPES OF CULTURE CHANGE

SO FAR we have considered culture as if it constituted a kind of world of Brahma, Vishnu, and Siva representing creation, preservation, and destruction: that being, in a sort of way, what invention, persistence, and loss might be called. But in the actual physical world, as compared to a logical one, there is a lot of change that ultimately is neither creation nor destruction, but just change. In fact change is more frequent and more certain in the natural world than either creation or destruction. Most physicists would deny both creation and destruction for energy as well as matter; but they would say that what physics is concerned with is changes and redistributions of energy and matter. So in culture too there are a great many happenings, such as the growth of swing music, of informal manners and casual greeting, of sitting with legs crossed, which are undoubted changes of recent decades and yet would be hard to fit with sense into any rigid scheme of invention-persistence-loss. Nor are such changes all trifling: drifts toward or away from totalitarianism or democracy, or fundamentalism or liberalism, or industrialism or laissez faire, are of the same order as these examples, in that they are gradual and growthlike instead of happening in jumps or steps.

We have accordingly to consider also cultural changes of the kind comparable to growths. For convenience of approach, we can separate off, among such changes, those which are due mostly to internal factors and thus seem "spontaneous" in a culture, and those due chiefly to factors external to a culture and therefore induced in it.

Among changes from inside we have, first of all, alterations on the subsistence-economic-technological level such as the Neolithic Revolution (§ 262), the Industrial Revolution of recent centuries, the increasing urbanization of contemporary times, and many smaller shifts. These seem to be distinguished by what may be called a distinctive circular causality, about which more in a moment. Another large group of changes can be attributed to the biological play impulse in its cultural expression. These include fashion fluctuations, but also many that are not ordinarily classed under fashion. Affective factors—restlessness, strivings, boredom, repugnances, fatigue—are often involved in this group of phenomena. In fact, the emotional associations are sometimes quite disproportionate to the seriousness of the actual change, so that we are here skirting the field of social psychology. Finally, we have growth changes, leading gradually to new religions, different idea systems, social reconstructions, basically altered culture patterns. Revolutions, whether affecting one institution or a whole culture, form an extreme and special form of changes of this last class.

Changes from the outside relate either to culture elements or traits, the spread and introduction of which is usually called diffusion; or to the spread of larger pattern systems or complexes, such as the alphabet or Islam; or to the increasing contact of culture wholes, with attrition, penetration, and adjustments of these. This last type of externally caused culture change can be subsumed as *acculturation,* that word being construed as having outgrown its originally narrower meaning of assimilation—as will appear in the final sections of this chapter.

In the technical literature of anthropology certain similar features occurring in cultures of different periods, or of widely separated areas, are attributed to processes called independent parallel development and convergence; but other similarities are attributed to contact, dissemination, diffusion, or dispersal (§ 108, 109, 223). Parallels and convergences are due to internal or "spontaneous" growth factors; diffusions, as just stated, represent influences on a given culture from others outside it.

163. SUBSISTENCE AND POPULATION CHANGES

There is a group of basic factors that can have deep influence on the fortunes of societies and may affect the whole of their cultures. These factors include serious alterations in the environment, sufficiently heavy growth of population within a given territory, and fundamental changes in subsistence technique. It is evident that these factors are, strictly, subcultural, except for subsistence; and this, of course, not only is basal in culture, but in the case of farming and stockraising the subsistence provision amounts to the creation of an artificial or man controlled floral and faunal environment.

An environment may alter with climate; or a people may abandon an old habitat, or be driven from it. If their new home is environmentally different enough to enforce a change in methods of subsistence, the rest of their old culture may alter profoundly. It does not follow that the new situation is inferior; it may be better or worse.

Changes in culture due to natural changes in environment undoubtedly occur. But this explanation for cultural change has probably been propounded ten times for every actual case of such change, especially in the long subarid belt from North China to southern and western Africa. Here there has been a mania or a fashion to posit pluvial periods followed by dry ones, with change from fertile lands to steppe and from steppe to desert, and with populations swarming out in consequence, or shrinking and impoverishing. If we go back far enough, there is no doubt that such climatic alterations have occurred. Yet it should always be recollected that ten thousand years is only a minimal unit in geology but an enormously long time in human history. Consequently, the two kinds of evidence barely meet; and it is where the evidential contact is poorest that the sparks of imaginative theory fly thickest. The explanation has certainly been worked hard, all the way from the Old Stone Age in Kenya to Jenghis Khan coming out of Mongolia, and there are very few scholars who really have enough control of all the data to separate the valid from the invalid guesses. There does seem to be general agreement that North Africa was moister about ten thousand years ago than it is now. But it is difficult to be sure of the extent of this change, or its precise effects on culture, which is infinitely more plastic and capable of rapid change than slow-moving climate is.

The transition from Palaeolithic to Mesolithic culture in northern Europe is now generally associated with the climatic change at the end of the last glacial period, which allowed forests to grow where there had been tundra, steppe, or grassland before (§ 276). The change in vegetation and fauna at the time seems well attested. That it was also the cause of the cultural change is plausible, but, in the nature of things, less certain: history is full of new culture phases without environment being involved.

More localized changes are sometimes well established. About 1425 the herring suddenly shifted their run and began to do their main spawning in the North Sea instead of the Baltic. The Holland fishermen profited economically, the Hanseatic Germans were the losers; and after about 1500, the Dutch, who till then had always trailed the Belgians in the Low Countries in prosperity and therewith in cultural productivity, began to draw abreast of them, and finally to forge ahead.

The general effect of increased population on culture has already been discussed in § 118 and 121. This is an expectable influence, a sort of reasonable a priori. It is validated at least partially by the fact that we find no very rich or advanced cultures among small populations.

That man-made new environment, the utilitarian domestication of animals and plants, which in prehistory is sometimes called the Neolithic Revolution (§ 281, 282), certainly provided a subsistence that for the long pull was more dependable than gathering and hunting had been, and it seems to have been followed by an increase of population. This new turn of culture became noticeable first in the Near East, the general region of southwestern Asia, and was followed there within a millennium or two by town life, building in brick, permanent structures for worship, metallurgy; and, in another millennium, by cities, rulers, states, writing, and records (§ 286). We are now, around 3000 B.C., at the beginning of history, in the narrowest sense of that word, as well as of higher civilization, in the Near East; but Europe of the time was only beginning to enter upon its first acquaintance with farming and the Neolithic. The regional difference is almost certainly due to the fact that ancestral grains and animals native to western Asia were first domesticated there. Here, accordingly, it was that the population gradually grew denser and that an advanced and partly urbanized type of civilization developed, while the diffusion of farming outward from this center was only commencing.

It is characteristic of this kind of culture change which advantageously affects subsistence that its causality tends to be circular,[1] or self-reinforcing, at least for a time. More and surer subsistence leads both to population increase and to specialization of skills and occupation. The specialization again makes for more stock of wealth, more varied and larger consumer demands, more concentrated productivity, and the chance for further population growth (see § 118).

Circular causalities similar to that of the ancient Near East seem to have been set going also in India and China and, more slowly, in Europe. Fairly soon after agriculture reached these areas, it was followed by metallurgical and other crafts, towns and states, and a population increase. In native America, again, massed populations, cities, conquest empires, and metallurgy characterize the areas between Mexico and Peru where farming was probably oldest and certainly most intensive. All these cases also are findings based on archaeological evidence.

However, these growth developments—except the American one—were all interconnected in some measure, as the identity of some domesticated plants and animals shows. They must therefore be construed as at least partly derived one from another. Consequently they cannot in fairness be counted as independent instances each reconfirming a law or generalization.

In fact, it appears to be the surety of ample food supply that is the primary factor in these circular situations, rather than farming as such. This is shown by the population of indigenous northern America, for which fairly specific estimates are available. These are easily highest for ancient nuclear Mexico with its intensive tillage: 7 to 8 people per square mile, or over 700 per unit of a hun-

---

[1] It might well be called spiral in many cases, but the technical term is "circular."

dred square miles. North of the Mexican high-density center, the figures drop to 26 souls per hundred square miles in the farming areas, and still further to only about 10 in the nonfarming areas as a total. So far we have corroboration. But from the nonfarming tracts there can be segregated out a narrow strip along the Pacific coast from Alaska to California, where the density was 65 per hundred square miles, as against less than 6 in the rest of the hunting-gathering areas. In this Pacific-coast strip the dependence was on sea and river fishing in the north, on gathering of acorns and seeds in the south. Neither procedure is likely to cut seriously into reproductive supply, whereas steady hunting on land does quickly exhaust game, as soon as the number of hunters becomes considerable. So population density was able to mount among the fortunate fishing and gathering tribes along the Pacific coast until it was two and a half times greater than the over-all among the farming tribes north of the Rio Grande. To be sure, most of the eastern groups were not too assiduous in their farming, leaving it mainly to their women, while the men hunted or warred. Also, farming had come to them out of the tropics probably not very many centuries before, and it was still unaccompanied by the cities, states, metallurgy, and calendars which had developed in Mexico along with, or soon after, agriculture. The relation of the farming Indians of the eastern United States of A.D. 1492 to those of Mexico was evidently quite like that of the Neolithic people of Europe around 2500 B.C.—when population was certainly not yet dense there—in comparison to the populous and literate kingdoms of contemporary Egypt and Mesopotamia. Left undisturbed for another thousand or two thousand years, these eastern and central United States farming Indians might have caught up; but when discovery overtook them, they were clearly less populous than the Pacific-coast fishermen. and probably not quite as far along toward a rich and diversified culture.

There is no doubt that, given time enough, and on the average, farming will lead to very much heavier concentrations of population than are possible under gathering, fishing, or hunting. Compare, again on the basis of 100-square-mile units: native Australia, gathering, 5 inhabitants; but Italy 39,000, Japan 50,000, Belgium 75,000 Kiangsi province 87,000, Java 90,000. In all of history there has never been a genuine city in a nonfarming culture. All that the foregoing citation on the northern Pacific-coast Indians proves is that the relation is not wholly automatic in favor of food-producers as against food-gatherers. Nonfarming at its optimum may be accompanied by heavier population than farming that is newly learned, indifferent, or inefficient.

164. FASHION CHANGE

A series of cultural activities seems ultimately rooted in the organic play impulses, which are most developed in the young of mammals—especially among the carnivores and the primates (§ 15). These cultural activities include, first of all of course, organized games and sports of all kinds; in addition, such

expressions of play and relaxation and humor as may be more loosely standardized in the folkways. Definitely to be included, as nourished at least partly from
the same organic root, are science and the arts and fashion—the sciences and arts
perhaps more so in proportion as they are less colored by utilitarian purposes.
Obviously, this is not saying that the fine arts and pure science are just play: they
are serious endeavors and mostly hard work. Yet in their primary nature they
are neither individually nor socially utilitarian, but are ends in themselves, and
in a way pleasures in themselves, and in this respect they resemble play; just as
the impulses toward, say, curiosity, or rhythm, which go into science or music,
are also found in play. Science and art may be conceived as cultural sublimations, on the adult level, of hereditary physiological impulses whose manifestations in childhood we unhesitatingly class as play.[2]

Even more directly than science and art does the realm of fashion, with its
constant seeking for something new, exemplify cultural play activity. While
fashion change may be sought with considerable eagerness, it is generally regarded with a certain lightness—we might literally say with a playful attitude.
Also like play, fashion is followed most actively when there is a surplus of food,
energy, and leisure—wealth, in cultural terms. In connection with fashion we
think first of variability in dress styles (§ 138); but it is evident that there are
changing fashions in houses, furnishings, gardens, and automobiles. In fact, it is
not difficult to recognize some degree of changeable fashions in political and
religious beliefs and in institutions. The sciences, especially the newer ones, are
subject to waves of fashion. The layman, standing respectfully outside, is likely
to be unaware of this: the latest "edict" of science is to him the latest truth. Run-
of-the-mill scientists may share this opinion: they are like the dressmaker who
believes that this year's mode is at last the complete combination of beauty, comfort, and serviceability—forgetting that if it were, next year's fashion would have
nothing left but to undo the ideal. The scholar with perspective of his subject
is aware that ideas and methods come into vogue and pass out, in his field as in
others, and that part of his business is to distinguish the evanescent fad from
permanent progress. In short, there is hardly a field of culture that is not subject
to some fashion variation.

It is difficult to say where fashion ends and where custom, or style in art,
begins, because custom and style also change. A possible differential criterion
would construe fashion as change for the sake of change, while style and custom
alter respectively under the pressure of inner developments or of outer circumstance. But the concepts are continuous, and sure distinction can be made only
at the ends of the scale.

[2] Not that any of these adult manifestations can be *directly* reduced to genetic and
physiological causes. They always have cultural antecedents and their immediate determinants are sociocultural behavior. It is only their ultimate basis that is organic and comparable to play.

When some detail of dress is given a new cut this year, and already begins to be crowded out by a new cut or trimming next year, there is no doubt that we are wholly within the domain of fashion, in fact in its very froth. If, however, in the second year the new cut or color or embellishment comes back into stronger favor and is more accentuated, and for the next three or five or ten years it becomes increasingly emphasized or exaggeratèd, and only then begins to be soft-pedaled, until it fades away after another three or five or ten years—have we here a fashion growth or style growth? As a matter of fact, in § 137-138 we have seen that there are features of dress fashion, such as proportions of silhouette or figure, which trend in one direction for fifty or more years, and are as long in moving back. Underneath the inconsistent year-to-year fluctuations, or those of a few brief years, women's skirts, for instance, do steadily become increasingly fuller or increasingly shorter for a half-century at a time. Such drifts in duration are somewhat like the economist's "secular trends" which underlie the fluctuations of the few-year business cycle.

Such long-term fashion swings are also comparable to growth in art styles. In painting, neoclassicism, romanticism, impressionism, expressionism, cubism, have each lasted no longer, or less long, than some of these trends in Western dress; and the degree of change effected by them is no greater. The total form and effect of Occidental clothing in 1815, 1865, and 1915 seem about as different as canvases painted in the classic manner in 1790 are different from the romantic ones of 1840 and these from the impressionisms of 1890 and surrealisms of 1940. The main difference is that we like to think of picture-painting and art exhibitions as serious and dignified, and of clothes and fashion shows as frivolous. But the behavior manifestations of the two sets of phenomena are much alike, so that we are justified in assuming that the processes at work are similar. One might even suspect the genuineness of the greater formal or avowed respect accorded the painter's activity. Presumably for every ten people in our civilization really exercised about a change in the manner of paintings there are a thousand who participate personally in changes of dress style, and who would be intensely perturbed if poverty or a sumptuary law prohibited them from conforming.

Landscape design or gardening is in an intermediate situation, as regards the attitude of our culture. It possesses a certain dignity because it is an expression of luxury and requires at least a measure of prosperity as a threshold. The tenement dweller contents himself with two or three geraniums in tin cans on the fire escape. The reasonably well-to-do, when the city is not too crowded, have a garden. The wealthy go in for landscaping a park. The same changes however occur. In one century gardens are formal in the Italian or the French manner. In another they are informal or rustic on the English model. Yet even a small garden cannot conveniently be entirely made over each year like a dress, so annual fashions are lacking. But there are fluctuations that are measurable in relatively brief periods. Rock gardens have a vogue for a decade or so, and then people become tired and pull them up. Pampas grass had its day, but is now scarcely any longer to be found except on neglected or avowedly old-fashioned properties.

Dress-designing being an art, even though not a very highbrow one, has style as well as fleeting fashions. It is distinctive in that everyone in the society is affected by it, and in that its products wear out and must soon be replaced. It is perhaps for these reasons that there is in it a greater element of rapid minor change than in the other arts, and that we are attuned to being highly aware of these superficial changes. The processes at work in dress styles presumably are not very different from those in other art styles. A dress fashion is in its nature datable from its appearance. But so are sculptures and paintings datable to art historians—within a century if ancient, usually within a decade if modern. This of course not only implies change, but that the change is more or less regular in the sense of being steady.

Why it should be in the intrinsic nature of style to change, ordinarily, is a complex problem, which is still largely unsolved, though at least part of the answer lies in the domains of cultural pattern and its control or achievement by virtuosity. At any rate, the essential instability of styles strengthens the indication of the genetic relationship of the arts to physiological play impulses. Pure fashion of course is an even more immediate manifestation.

165. VARIABLE PATTERNS OF MOTIVATION FOR ANIMAL BREEDING

Akin to fashion changes in dress and art are certain striking variations in the purposes for which animals were presumably first domesticated and for which they are still often bred by nonliterate or retarded societies. The range of this variability from people to people through space is similar to the range of fashion changes among one people in time. Also, many of the manifestations of this variability resemble fashion in being dependent on nonutilitarian motivation.

We look upon stock-raising as part of farming, as an industry or a useful business. That it is such among ourselves is of course no proof that it began as such, that the original motivation in the keeping of animals was utilitarian. There are in fact grave doubts that it could have begun that way. Too many cultures disregard too many of the potential utilities. All of southeastern Asia uses no milk, butter, or cheese; also no wool, except for whole sheepskins in the fleece. In most of their early distribution horses were not ridden until long after they were driven. The pig was an unclean animal and was not eaten in ancient Egypt, by the Hebrews, or in Islam. Practically all Negro tribes keep cattle, wherever the climate and the tsetse fly permit; but none make cheese, some churn butter for body ointment instead of consumption, and the majority are so eager to build up their herds that they rarely eat beef.

All in all, the utilization of domesticated animals in ways that seem rational to us was so incomplete in ancient times, and is so incomplete today among backward peoples, that Galton, Hahn, Laufer, and others have stressed nonrational factors—affective or sentimental considerations—as dominant in early stages of this activity. The motivations range from desire for pets, companionship, or play to the needs of ritual and magic on the one hand and wealth symbolism and prestige satisfaction on the other.

Among the South American forest Indians, monkeys, parrots, and almost all and any kinds of small animals were freely kept as pets, though there were no species domesticated for utility, and in parts of Brazil even dogs were lacking. In some parts of native California dogs were valued for deer-hunting; in others, they were kept chiefly to be eaten; in still others, they were merely tolerated and allowed to fend for themselves. In another California region, we have already seen (§ 159) that dogs were rare, imported as articles of luxury, pampered, and watched over. This regional Californian diversity illustrates neatly the vagaries of which primitive culture is capable—the workings in it of fashion and fad by locale instead of by period, we might say—and how motives of utility, of affection or display, or of indifference, can replace each other.

Negro kings have been known to keep whole packs or menageries of the greater game animals. The Romans imported them largely for slaughter in their circus games. The wild elephant has long been tamed in India and Farther India for work and transport, but still more for war and royal show. In Burma and Siam albino specimens had almost sacred status as embodiments of supreme kingship. Farther India, by the way, is another area in which pets are in favor: monkeys and young gibbons. On the contrary, in this its presumptive original home, the common fowl is little esteemed for its eggs, which are few, or for its meat, which is tough; but since two thousand years ago its thighbones have been in demand for divination. Bristles are stuck into the blood-vessel foramina of these bones and the directions of protrusion throw light on the issue in question. In the pagan parts of Indonesia, chickens are in primary demand for ritual sacrifice, including divination from their bile sacs; in the Islamic and Christian areas, the pitting of the cocks in fights overshadows other uses. Indonesia and the adjacent southeast corner of Asia, so far as it is still pagan, perhaps contain the principal contemporary survivals of the once much more widespread identification of ritual sacrifice to the gods with meat-eating by the worshipers—an association once in force as far west as the Mediterranean (§ 128, 192). It would be too much to assert that people first bred cattle and pigs in order that they might sacrifice them. Nevertheless, over a large part of the domesticating area an early double custom grew up of eating ordinarily only such tame flesh as had been dedicated to the gods, and of consuming every offering so dedicated. The civilized nations of today might still be following this custom if it had not been displaced by Christianity, Islam, and Buddhism.

It is perhaps the fact that kept animals multiply which has led to their being prized as reserves of wealth—not only among pastorals who own little else, but among settled farmers, as among the Greeks and Romans. The word "pecuniary" is from the Latin *pecus,* cattle, just as "monetary," "money," derives from *Moneta,* an epithet of Juno, in whose temple the Romans happened to mint their coinage; the two terms illustrate the passage from a livestock to a money economy. Negro East and South Africa has not yet effected this transition. In favor of cattle as wealth is the fact that they are visible and conspicuous and lend themselves to prestige display and gifts. Thus it is that their social valuation is definitely greater than their actual subsistence utility, among many Negroes.

With the Ruwala of Arabia, mares have acquired a similar prestige position, while the camel and its milk is what these Beduin (§ 120) live by. Except for occasional raiding, horses are quite useless in the desert, and would perish if turned loose. But they are carried along with barley that has to be bought from alien farmers and which they share with the household. In dry times, water for them has to be carried in by camels. Their pedigrees are kept. They are an untold worry and trouble; yet a single mare is valued at perhaps twenty riding dromedaries, and many a man owns only a fractional share in one. Once more, this Ruwala situation is obviously an excrescence of development, rather than a condition typical of the origin of stock-raising. But with the attached affects and motivations so varied now, they are unlikely to have been solidly and uniformly utilitarian in the beginning.

Thus it is clear that men do not live by meat and bread only. They breed animals for their flesh and milk and hide and wool and traction, but they also breed them for religion and sport and social climbing and companionship and show. And from people to people, and from time to time, these ends intertwine and replace one another in almost endless recombinations: the changes are literally the play of culture. We can understand even the most alien of the attitudes, but we cannot explain more than a part of them from utilitarian need. The livelihood and profit motives have no doubt mainly sustained the continuity of stockbreeding through history. But its many other associations and motivations lend the greater interest to the changeable activity, as we view it in world-wide retrospect.[3]

166. LABILE SOCIAL STRUCTURES

When we pass from dress and animals and arts to institutions, we encounter a flood of impermanences and variabilities which suggest that we may still be at times within the sphere of the play-derived, though unconscious,

[3] And of course many of the innovations and shifts in respect to domestic animals can also be included among the play inventions of § 148.

activity of culture. Among primitives, such lability or instability is most often extreme in social structure; among lettered peoples, in political forms.

Consider for instance the situation among the several Brazilian tribes of the Gê family. Among the Canella or Ramkokamekra there are four separate and crosscutting moiety organizations—a moiety being a half of a society formally set off against the other half for whatever reason or purpose. This is very much as if among ourselves there were a compulsory segregation of the population into first Democrats and Republicans; next, Catholics and Protestants; third, people born in odd-numbered and even-numbered years; and finally, partisans of the American and National baseball leagues, with distribution so regulated that Democrats and Republicans would be about equally distributed between Catholics and Protestants, and similarly all down the line, so that the membership of one complementary pair of moieties would never coincide with the membership of another pair, but would crosscut all the other moieties as much as possible. The first pair of Canella moieties is matrilineal and matrilocal—follows the mother in descent and residence—and regulates marriage exogamously. The second pair of moieties is concerned with racing and hunting during the rainy season. It is not concerned with marriage but is totemic—that is, certain animals or natural objects are symbolically representative of each moiety. And membership in the moiety is determined by names given by older individuals, theoretically the cross-uncle or mother's brother for boys, the cross-aunt or father's sister for girls. The totemism of this second pair of moieties is conceptually extended over all nature. The third set of moieties consists of two pairs of age classes, each age class comprising all males jointly initiated within a given period of years. This third pair of moieties also functions in competitive sports, but in the dry instead of the rainy season. The fourth set of moieties has membership again based on bestowed names, but the names this time are the property not of uncles or aunts, but of three groups or subdivisions within each of the moieties, and of two clubs or four societies. The groups own assembly houses that occupy prescribed situations in the circle in which the village is built; and they and the clubs function ceremonially in connection with men's initiations. So far the Canella tribe.

Among the linguistically related Apinaye, there is only one set of moieties, matrilineal and matrilocal, whose houses are localized in the village circle, but who are not at all concerned with marriage. They compete in sports and are concerned with ceremonial, and are characterized by possession of a series of personal names bestowed by uncles and aunts. Marriage is separately regulated by four unlocalized *kiye* or "sides," where A marries B, B with C, C with D, D with A, for men; but for women, the rule is the reverse, or really, complementarily the same, A marrying D, and so on. These "sides" are not clans, because clan descent is the same for boys and girls but boys belong to the "side" of their father, girls to that of their mother. Moreover, the four "sides" group into two implicit or unavowed intermarrying moieties, one consisting of A and

C, the other of B and D; for A and C both marry with B and D, but never with each other.

Still another Gê tribe, the Sherente, have exogamous moieties that are patrilineal and patrilocal and are divided into six clans localized in the village circle, which seem to correspond partly, but only partly, to the six subdivisions of the Canella ceremonial moieties.

Still another tribe, the Kaingang, associate with their exogamous moieties the totemic division of nature that the Canella associate with their nonexogamous rainy-season moieties.

It is evident that a long array of social forms have been luxuriantly developed by these Gê tribes: the moiety, moiety subdivisions, their localization within the circular village, their seasonal functioning, totemism, exogamy, unilateral descent (both patrilineal and matrilineal, or even both simultaneously according to the sex of children), group ownership of names, bestowal of names by individuals of the uncle or aunt relation, competitive sports, ceremonial associations, and grouping of initiates into age classes. Underlying all these forms is the principle of grouping of persons, whether dual or multiple. However, the very luxuriance of kinds of groups has led to a variety of ways of combining them, and probably to the constant devising of new kinds of groups, which made possible still further combinations, or transfer of functions from one set of groups to another. It is difficult to review the structures of these Brazilian tribal societies without a strong impression of their instability: of remodeling, innovation, and experimentation having been active.

Inasmuch as the four tribes speak varieties of the same Gê language, they must be connected in their histories. The diversity of their modern social organization must accordingly represent changes after a period when they were more alike. They still share conspicuous remnants of an indubitably common original pattern, but each has enormously altered or rearranged this. Evidently, once the interests of a culture become weighted in the direction of social structure, the culture may make the most unexpected combinations and even inventions of social forms.

In scattered parts of native America there was practiced the custom of the ant ordeal. This was a ritual discipline or test of fortitude, and consisted of laying the victim or novice on a hill of biting ants. The act itself was uniform; its setting, context, and motivations were quite diverse. Thus, the South American Rucuyenne applied the ordeal to boys undergoing their ceremonial initiation. So did some of the Tupi tribes south of the Amazon—as did the far-away Luiseño in California. But back in South America, the Saliva administered the ant ordeal to their new chiefs on assuming office. The Arawak of Guiana used it in mourning; other Guiana tribes, in hunting ritual. It is evident that a distinctive and rather invariable unit of practice, the ant ordeal itself, must have a history of quite varied associations—it has been bandied about from one religious ceremony to another almost like a shuttlecock. Again we see lability prevalent: looseness of organization rather than stability, fixity, or permanence.

However, elaborate forms need not appear simply because a society is primitive. The Eskimo, the Great Basin Shoshoneans, and many other societies are instances of simple structures free from formal organizational features. The factors at work in producing these relatively unstructured societies may be connected with subsistence difficulties; they need not be. Extremely interesting is the discovery among the same clanless Shoshone of the custom of pseudo-cross-cousin marriage,[4] in semblance of the cross-cousin marriage favored by so many other peoples: the favored Shoshone mates are stepcousins, no blood kin at all. This was certainly a strange practice to think up. Relatives continue to be avoided, but imitation relatives are sought as mates. Who could deny inventiveness to primitives?[5]

In fact, the ingenuity and imaginativeness of the social structure of much of primitive life is the essential moral of such facts. Many of the institutions are true luxury products. They almost certainly serve some function; but it may be a minor one, while major ends are left formally unprovided for. A great deal of the picture suggests the play of earnest children, or the inventive vagaries of fashion. This in turn strongly suggests the high instability of many of these social constructs. This instability cannot ordinarily be absolutely proved, because our historical knowledge of primitives rarely has much depth; but it is indicated by the totality of the data.

Political organization, on the contrary, is something that primitives have in general not achieved to any notable degree. When unlettered peoples have achieved it, as in Africa and Peru, we tend to exclude them from our concept of what is primitive. By complement, high civilizations have throughout history regularly been accompanied by considerable degrees of political organization. The causes of the difference are probably complex. But weakness of technological controls and therefore of economic resources among primitives may be suspected as an important factor. If so, a generic nexus of technological development through economics with political organization can be inferred. Primitives being weak in the former, they remained weak in the latter. Instead, they threw their cultural interests and energies into the forms of social structure, into the institutions concerned with the nearer interpersonal relations.

In the grand vista of cultural growth, accordingly, technological and political developments, which characterize the successfully more complex civilizations,

[4] Cross-cousins are the children of brother and sister—whose sex differs or "crosses"—as contrasted with parallel cousins, who are the children of two brothers or two sisters. We do not make this distinction in our culture, either in law, inheritance, or reckoning of kin—in fact are usually unaware that it can be made. But among many nonliterates, and even in India and China, the distinction is important. Cross-cousins are often favored as spouses where parallel cousins are forbidden.

[5] Some African cases of luxuriation are mentioned in § 312: coexistence of patrilineal and matrilineal reckoning.

are secondary and late products reared upon social forms or devices centering immemorially around kinship. Some measure of these kinship forms persists into higher civilization because kinship is biologically inescapable and perhaps equally inescapable psychologically. But the kinship structures of complex civilizations are often reduced, almost always divested of excrescences and luxuriances of pattern; they have become humble, simple, subserving real ends. We no longer practice pseudo-cross-cousin marriage nor descend from our mothers into moieties in which we receive names from our uncles. Instead, we buy automobiles on the installment plan and elect officials to police and tax us. The inventiveness and instability so evident in the social forms of primitive societies are largely transferred in higher civilization to the technological, economic, and political fields.

167. AFFECT IN CULTURE CHANGE

Is it right for a man to marry his stepdaughter? Here again there is great variability between cultures and at times considerable change within cultures. Christian countries in which established religion strongly influences the law of the land have generally barred the practice. Sometimes the prohibition has persisted after disestablishment of the state church. For the forty-eight American states the situation in 1940 is shown in the diagrammatic map, Figure 21. A century or so ago probably all American communities ruled such marriage irre-

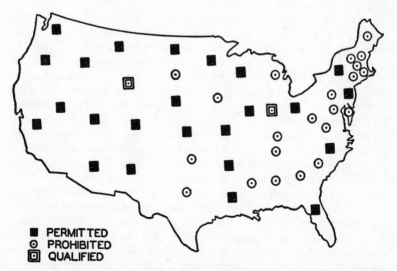

■ PERMITTED
◎ PROHIBITED
▣ QUALIFIED

FIG. 21.   LEGALITY OF MARRIAGE WITH A STEPDAUGHTER IN THE
48 UNITED STATES

ligious, immoral, and illegal. Most of the older and relatively conservative Eastern and Southern states still forbid it. But times have changed and twenty-six
of the forty-eight states no longer prohibit the practice—which means it is
legally tolerated. Yet two of these salve an uneasy social conscience by going
out of their way to specify extramarital relations with a stepdaughter as punish-
able.

Of 167 tribal and subtribal groups of Indians investigated between Vancouver Island and the Rio Grande, three-fourths definitely frowned upon stepdaughter marriage and presumably prevented it. Some 10 per cent disapproved,
but without attempting to do anything about occasional violations. About another 10 per cent of the tribes disliked but tolerated the idea; in other words,
were two-minded about it. Finally, perhaps 5 or 6 per cent of the groups admitted stepdaughter marriage as a recognized form; that is, gave it institutional
sanction. The custom is perhaps most common among the matrilineal and
matrilocal Navaho. If a man marries a separated or widowed woman who has
a small daughter, he often, with her mother's consent, adds the girl as wife
when she grows up. Each woman has less work, and yet the output of the
ménage is greater. The total tribal distribution of the custom, shown in Figure
22, is almost randomly scattering, with only slight tendencies toward areal segregation. Highly random local distributions of this scattered type can usually be
interpreted as the result of conflicting influences, and hence as indicating instability. While some tribes consistently banned the practice, others backed and
filled and kept changing their rules.

Why this variability and change? It seems to spring from a conviction that
is one of very few major premises common to all cultures: that one does not
marry close kin. But variation begins with the definition of who are close kin.
Some peoples bar even third cousins as wives; others permit aunts and half-
sisters. Some consider all clan mates kin, whether they are or not. Others not
only allow but favor the marriage of first cross-cousins, or again squeamishly
think they should be second cousins. Some religions, like the Greek Orthodox
Christianity, and until recently the Church of England, class affinals by marriage—such as sisters-in-law—as kindred, though they are not blood relatives
at all. This is reasonable enough because of the normally close association and
bonds with near affinal relatives; but it is scarcely logical, if incest has anything
to do with blood. It is of a kind with the Roman Catholic prohibition of marriage with a goddaughter, toward whom the relation is not even affinal, but
spiritual only. On the other hand, if the incest prohibition refers to blood kinship, permissibility of stepdaughter marriage is logical enough. Nevertheless,
many societies consider it unfit and shocking. Even where the practice is tolerated, there is often considerable individual repugnance to it; whereas in a few
polygynous groups it is institutionalized. The issue is evidently the sort of
problem one can argue and counterargue forever. In the end, it is settled by
some feeling or affect that one has or does not have. This feeling may be quite

strong, or it may be ambivalent. Being a feeling about ideas, it gets involved in logic. Nevertheless, the ultimate determination of the issue is affective, not intellectually realistic; and the motivation of affects is notoriously capricious. Culture features of this type are therefore likely to remain open problems, to which the answer keeps varying. Only when the point gets caught up in some larger organized system of feelings and ideas with big momentum is a consistent long-term answer expectable.

It is not to be assumed that strong affect necessarily produces stability and persistence. One can feel vigorously and yet have his feelings change. This is

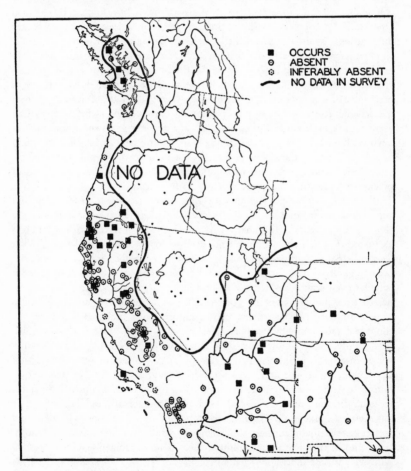

FIG. 22.   STEPDAUGHTER MARRIAGE IN WESTERN INDIAN TRIBES

true also of cultures. Disposal of the dead is a case in point. Human cultures have devised a great variety of methods: burial, cremation, water burial, setting away in vaults or canoes or houses, scaffold burial, exposure or simple abandonment, cremation with eating or drinking of the ashes by the relatives, temporary inhumation with either reburial or preservation of the bones—not to mention previous mummification, dismemberment, and other related practices. Now while some societies have adhered for long periods to one basic method of disposing of their dead—ancient Egypt to mummification and mediaeval Europe to churchyard burial, for instance—others have been changeable. We are ourselves in the midst of a drift toward cremation. This may die out again, or cremation may come to replace burial. Many primitives have apparently changed often, to judge from the variety of practices found in adjacent groups—"scatter distributions" again—in, say, Africa, or almost any other continent.

Here again affect seems to be involved. Death obviously releases immensely powerful emotions; and a funeral, as the final act of a group toward an individual, comes to participate in this emotion. Once a method has become a preference or a custom, there is likely to be a strong affect attached to it. Witness the vehement feeling of many people among ourselves in regard to cremation versus burial, even while a progressive change is going on in the community as a whole. Evidently the affect can attach to something new and remain as strong as before. There are also always likely to be parts of the population who are two-minded, and others who are indifferent on that particular point—perhaps precisely because they feel more strongly about other matters.

In short, that people feel strongly in connection with a custom does not per se mean either that they will adhere to it with persistence or that they are about ready to abandon it. That a cultural practice is invested with emotion is an important thing about it, but is not decisive for its stability or lability. What decides between continuance or change seems to be whether or not a practice has become involved in an organized system of ideas and sentiments: how much it is interwoven with other items of culture into a larger pattern. If it is thus connected, even though the rooting be secondary and late, it has good expectations of persisting, since large systems tend to endure. But a trait that is only loosely connected and essentially free-floating can be superseded very quickly—in which case its affect may simply pass on to the new custom. Mediaeval Christianity was such a large, well-integrated system of ideas and sentiments—with it both stepdaughter marriage and cremation would have conflicted. Neither innovation is therefore likely to make much headway in cultures in which Catholicism remains the controlling force. Calvinism and Puritanism would also certainly have felt both practices to be out of fit with their systems or points of view, and would have condemned them. In consciously secularized countries, on the contrary, and in many primitive cultures, there is no organized sentiment system with which these innovations would conflict. In such societies, accordingly, the practices may easily become established, only to be easily superseded again.

168. CULTURAL FATIGUE: TABOO IN HAWAII

In 1819 the Polynesians of Hawaii at one stroke abolished their religion. This was five months before the first missionary landed on the islands, and was therefore a voluntary act. To be sure, Captain Cook had discovered the islands some forty years before and had been followed by a number of explorers, traders, and whalers. Through these the Hawaiians had learned of the existence of Christian beliefs. But it is unlikely that they understood them at all well. They had however seen Europeans repeatedly violate religious prohibitions—taboos— without being even punished by the native gods, and that must have shaken Hawaiian faith. Among the natives, this taboo system had grown very powerful and no doubt was sometimes felt as onerous. Women might not eat certain foods, such as bananas and coconuts. It was absolutely irreligious and shocking for men and women to eat together. The king let himself be carried over private lands because contact with his divine body would make the land taboo and untouchable by its owner. There were religious festivals that the population celebrated by remaining inactive indoors, so as not to break the taboo. The system was heavily loaded in favor of royalty, aristocracy, and priesthood, but apparently was coming to be felt as irritatingly restrictive by these classes also.

Some years after Cook's discovery, an able chief began to rise to power and finally fought his way to undisputed rule over the entire island group. This was the famous Kamehameha I. He died without having departed from the faith of his fathers or altered its regulations. His successor, Kamehameha II, was a young and easy-going man. The group that surrounded and swayed him now decided to do away with the taboo system. This group included his chief formal adviser or prime minister; his mother; and another widow of the preceding king, named Kaahumanu. The latter was a bold and ambitious person and perhaps the chief mover in the conspiracy. As a woman she unquestionably had much to gain by abolition of the taboo. Strangely enough, however, the high priest of the islands was also active in the coterie, and in fact subsequently took the lead in extending the movement from mere abolition of the taboo to the overthrow of the gods whose representative he was. This man seemingly had everything to lose by the change, and it is difficult to imagine what he could have had to gain. It is known that he did not profess to be a convert to the Christianity which was in the offing. He evidently represented, therefore, an element in the population that was psychologically ready for a breach with established religion, from internal reasons. Whether such a frame of mind could have developed before any Caucasian contacts, among Hawaiians who were beneficiaries of the existing system, seems doubtful. The old Hawaiians, knowing of no religion but their own, would presumably have found it difficult to imagine or invent any radically different form of worship. Nevertheless it is also hard to understand the high priest's motivation, unless he, presumably with many others, was tired of the established religious order to a degree that made him ready even for a switch to something unknown. In addition, the whites enjoyed prestige for their guns, steel tools, and big ships; and, by extension, their only vaguely known religion was probably accounted superior.

It was finally arranged by the conspiring royal entourage that the taboo should be publicly broken at a great festival. This would amount to a religious revolution from the throne. As the hour neared, the young king became increasingly uneasy; but he was coaxed and steered to the final act. After the royal ladies had first eaten forbidden foods in sight of the gathering, the king came over and ate with them. At first incredulous, the multitude finally realized what had happened. Shouts went up, and were carried over the island—"The taboo is broken!" The high priest himself mutilated the images of the gods and set fire to the temple. This action was imitated everywhere in a sort of frenzy. It is difficult to say now what the real reaction of the population at large was. They were certainly shocked and excited. Many of them must have been pleased. Some surely felt outraged, and others were more stirred than participant. The king was himself divine, so that the act must have resembled a sudden voluntary abdication by the gods themselves. However, the king's power was also absolute, and it is therefore likely that the mass of commoners received the event with some docility.

The only overt opposition came from high quarters. Kekuaokalani, a nephew of the late great king and next in line of succession to the high priesthood, when he could believe his senses rescued one of the god figures and strode with it from the assembly. He rallied a following of the pious and raised a revolt. His adherents were numerous and determined. It is evident that the innovation was not unanimously approved of by the population. Before long it came to battle. Kekuaokalani was defeated, his following scattered, and the conservative protest came to an end. However, the fight is said to have been decided by the Christian-made firearms which the king's side was able to muster. A few months later the first missionaries landed, were received with open arms and royal favor, and Hawaii as a whole rapidly became Christian.

There can be little doubt that we have here, in part, a culture change due to new contacts. It is also evident that at least some of the reformers were actuated by motives of personal advantage or convenience, though this does not apply to all of them. But the main factor seems to have been a kind of social staleness; the Hawaiians had become disillusioned, and tired of their religion. To this extent the incident is illustrative of what may be called cultural fatigue. It is no doubt an extreme case of such an attitude. But it is probably not wholly aberrant, and reactions of similar though milder type may be occasional factors in cultural change. French defeatism in 1940 was perhaps an example. Nor would it be difficult to make out a case for social fatigue or staleness having been operative in bringing on the French Revolution, in addition to exasperation over abuses and cultural lag and the ferment of new ideologies. The attitude of the

American people toward the depression of 1929 after it became profound suggests the presence of a considerable factor of the sort, with the New Deal as a reaction to it. Once an attitude of the kind develops sufficient strength, novelty as such may come to seem a virtue and a boon.

One other consideration is worth mentioning. The overthrow of the Hawaiian religion could not have been effected so rapidly and thoroughly if the impetus had not come from a strong and respected government. Without this, there would presumably have been prolonged civil war, and only a gradual giving-way of the old order to the new. The Japanese Emperor's sudden and successful renunciation of divinity in 1945 is a somewhat parallel case. In this respect both events resemble those alterations or reforms of calendrical, writing, and other pattern systems produced either by grand revolutions or by complete autocracies, usually in their first flush of power, as discussed in § 170 below.

169. CHANGE THROUGH ORGANIZED RELIGION

Organized religion has a way of being influential in the overturn and the reconstruction of major civilizations. It works first toward cultural change and then for conservation. Especially is this true of religions which set out to overrun the world because they alone are "true" and all other faiths and cults false and likely to taint even secular activities with which they have become associated. Most primitive and national religions have also started out, naturally enough, with the assumption of their own verity and importance; but alongside this they have had naïve tolerance of other faiths as being also more or less true, though of course not quite as good and true, or at any rate not as appropriate for their own nationals.

If one were asked to specify the most important single characteristic distinguishing Ancient Mediterranean or Classical from our own Occidental civilization—the culture of the Greeks and Romans from that of mediaeval and modern Western nations—it would almost certainly be Christianity. Our civilization is patently derived, in large measure even descended, from the Graeco-Roman; but it contains very few specific carry-overs from the preceding pagan cults or faiths. When the fourth-century Roman emperors, like Constantine and Theodosius, turned Christian, the end of the old order, of the former world view, was in sight. Within a century we have Rome "falling," and the continuous stream of history is renamed "mediaeval" instead of "ancient," as a symbol of the transformation.[6] The mythology and worship of the Greeks had of course been all intertwined with their literature, art, philosophy, learning, and even manners. Consequently Christianity in its three centuries of uphill fight tended to become hostile, suspicious, grudging, or at best indifferent toward Greek and Roman

[6] In fact, until not so very long ago, historical convention had "ancient" history ending not in A.D. 476 but in 325 with Constantine, the founding of Constantinople, and the Church Council of Nicaea.

achievements in these activities. So it was natural for the Dark Ages to follow the final supremacy of Christianity; and it was nearly a thousand years before Christian Europe could even begin to rival the pagan Mediterranean world in urbanity, knowledge, intellectual penetration, aesthetic performance, and the graces of life—including bodily cleanliness. This is not saying that Christianity was responsible for the long recession. These big historical situations are not adjudicated so simply as that. Just as soundly could one contend that Classical civilization had exhausted its patterns, was dying away within an empty shell, and that Christianity moved in to fill the void, but required time to grow a whole new civilization. However, this is sure: Irrespective of whether it was more largely cause or effect, Christianity was the pre-eminent point of crystallization for the civilization that superseded the Graeco-Roman one.

A very similar influence in change of civilization could be made out for Buddhism and Mohammedanism, the two chief competitors of Christianity as "world religions." The three share the following characteristics:

1. They are world religions not because they have encompassed the earth, but because they aim to encompass it, to be world-wide and supernational, in distinction from ethnic or tribal religions.

2. Each is attached to a transcending personality, from whom the name for the faith is taken. The usual view is that these personalities as individuals founded and made their religions. It is however also possible to see the founders more largely as symbols necessary to this type of religion. Certainly more of the total content of Christianity—as distinct from its "essence," which is in its very nature attached to his person—was evolved or contributed by his followers and successors more than by Jesus himself. St. Paul alone is sometimes said to have added as much as Jesus did. The same is unquestionably true of Buddhism, and quite possibly of Mohammedanism. Moreover, the fact that all three religions originated in southwestern Asia within little more than a thousand years, and followed outwardly parallel courses, suggests a pattern, and that something like them was "in the air"—that is, that the cultural set of the region and times was pointing that way.

3. All three religions are exclusive, in holding their truth to be incompatible with any other, so that cobelief and coworship in another faith are impossible (§ 132). This doctrine seems to have been first worked out in human history by the Jews as a gradual and hard-won attainment during that part of their history represented by the Old Testament, between 800 and 400 B.C. From Judaism the attitude worked over into Christianity and Islam. Buddhism has been the least intransigeant of the three in this respect. It coexists in China with the state religion or Confucianism, and in Japan it even worked out certain accommodations with the native Shinto.

4. All three religions, and speaking broadly only these three, have been actively missionizing.

5. Each of the three world religions developed an ecclesiastical organization or church, which has been a potent factor in maintaining the religion and its gains. Culturally, the ideologies have probably had a much more profound effect than the churches; but the influence of the latter toward a firm anchorage through temporal fluctuations, and even within the developments of the mundane aspects of civilization, cannot be overestimated. Ethnic or national religions often had temples, but generally no church as a unifying organization.

6. Side by side with the features of world-wide aim, exclusiveness, and an authoritative church, there developed what may be called universal or world languages. In these were expressed the sacred texts of each faith; and each tongue became also the approved and classical medium of thought, learning, and often literature in a self-sufficient and largely self-contained sphere or "world" (§ 102). These languages are Greek for Eastern and Latin for Western Christianity—when northwestern Europe revolted against Catholicism in the Reformation, one of its most significant acts was the immediate substitution of vernaculars for Latin; Arabic—rigidly adhered to in ritual—for Mohammedanism; Sanskrit for the more numerous northern branch or Greater Vehicle of Buddhism, with Pali for the southern or Lesser Vehicle of Farther India. With each of these is associated also a distinctive alphabet. The only other language that functions today in its larger sphere in a way reminiscent of these "world" languages is Chinese, whose writing is nonalphabetic.

The foregoing is a summary formulation of an enormously large situation, whose exactly authentic description would require endless qualifications and requalifications. In particular, consideration would have to be given to certain crucial border-line cases, especially in the Iranian and Chinese religions;[7] since with enough transitions, the "world" type of religion just depicted would tend to dissolve away. Provisionally, however, the type seems to stand. And so far as it does, the influence of religion on total culture, in the direction of both formative change and fixation, is evident. The world of Islam has always been recognized as a separate sphere of cultural influence. European civilization, as we have seen, breaks primarily into a pre-Christian and a Christian phase. The culture of India changes similarly from the pre-Buddhist to the Buddhist to the post-Buddhist period. Even in China and Japan, where old native elements have persisted with unusual continuity and force, the greatest alteration perhaps is that between the early, purely native form of the culture and the later one with

---

[7] Iran had Zoroaster, probably a little earlier than Buddha; and China, Confucius, Buddha's contemporary. Zoroastrianism, also called Mazdaism or the Avestan or Parsi religion, differs from the big three in being nearly extinct, and in having never effectively established its supernatural church and language. But some of its minor and later offshoots or divergences, like Manichaeism, and perhaps Mithraism, have tried to compete with the great religions by rivaling them in organization and missionary activity. Confucianism has a minimum of religious content and is a state cult instead of an ecclesiastical church; else it too might have grown into a world religion.

its Buddhistic absorptions. It is in the fundamental reorientation of civilization, in redirective change, that the great religions are outstandingly influential.

170. CHANGE BY REVOLUTION

Change by revolution may be construed as change suddenly precipitated, with more or less violence, affecting a considerable total portion of a culture, and due to an accumulation of arrears, or lag, in progressive change. Generally, it is one or two fields or departments of culture that do the lagging. Thus the lag was primarily economic in the French Revolution, in religion in the Reformation and Cromwellian civil wars, in politics and religion in England of 1688, and was due to war distress on top of economic disintegration in Russia of 1918. Once the revolution breaks through, however, other and neutral areas of the culture are flooded too, sometimes with most inconsistent results, both intrinsically and as regards permanence: the metric system is instituted, religion abolished, Lavoisier executed. This extension of area of overturn was practically lacking in the American Revolution, which is thereby characterized as atypical of revolutions. In fact its main immediate achievement was the formal and complete acknowledgment of a political independence that had been partial but unacknowledged before. This in turn was followed by the union of the colonies, and the "invention" of a written federal constitution (§ 153). But these latter were constructive rather than revolutionary acts.

Several other features are characteristic of revolutions. One is that change tends to be excessive, and is then partly given up again in early reaction. After the revolution the French kept their metric system, but gave up their irrelevant new calendar and the Goddess of Reason. These represented zeal for change in the abstract, but there was no real call for them and they provoked resistance and made for inconvenience. One of the first resolves of the Russian Revolution was to abolish the death penalty! Then three letters of the alphabet were dropped. This reform was not in the Bolshevik program, but it was a simplification and it has stuck. It is familiar history how the pure socialist doctrine began to be increasingly modified in Russia after about 1935 with property ownership, differential salaries, piecework premiums, fees for schooling, and the like creeping back. Free divorce and legal abortion were instituted early, but were discontinued after the peak of change was passed. At first there was a strong sense that all the older national literature, music, and art, except that produced by avowed revolutionaries, must be capitalistically tainted: the revolution would therefore produce its own proletarian higher culture. This attitude tended to persist while Bolshevik Russia felt itself an outlaw among nations and none too sure of internal solidarity. But once the revolution seemed a permanent success, and especially after the Germans had been stopped in their tracks and it had real allies among the Great Powers, Russian nationalism rearose stronger than ever, and great Czarist poets, novelists, and composers were proclaimed great once more. All these are type phenomena of what may be called the overswing and backswing of revolutionary change.

It is necessary to distinguish between the cultural and the social change of revolutions, though these tend to come intertwined. In every successful revolution there is not only an improved reformulation of rules, but in addition certain people get property, power, or privilege that others had before. This last is what causes most of the heartburnings. It whets the appetite of many a changer, and makes prospective changees bitterly resist reforms that they might accept as fair and desirable if they could be made other than out of their pockets and status. Protestantism arose as a religious revolution from the ranks, with an ideology of return to primitive Christianity, substitution of conscience and Biblical text for hierarchical authority, and the like. However, most of the converted rulers, in and out of Germany, were surely influenced also by the opportunity to confiscate extensive church properties and to strengthen royal power. And no less the peasants in Germany: the Reformation's change of ecclesiastical authority suggested to them the hope of politicoeconomic changes in their favor. They rose and were put down with bloody massacres—not as Protestants but as social revolutionaries. At least one group of Anabaptist sectarians extended their renewed primitive Christianity to include communization of property and redistribution of wives. It need hardly be added that this movement was premature and its leaders short-lived. Here we have both forces at work: personal advantage of new classes of individuals, and revolution spreading to additional aspects or sides of the culture.

There is a class of changes tending to be regarded as desirable in themselves by everyone but nevertheless difficult to effectuate except by revolutionary or totalitarian power. These are reforms in systems, such as calendar, spelling, measurements, or law. With the passage of absolute time, or change in speech, science, and customs, such systems get to be increasingly differentiated from the actual conditions to which they relate, and therewith increasingly inadequate, patched over, and complicated. Nevertheless, a change is upsetting and inconvenient, objectively as well as sentimentally, and therefore is deferred and redeferred until made by force, usually when long overdue. Everyone is agreed that the gulf between living English speech and English writing is so great that a reform which would make spelling coincide with pronunciation would save millions of hours—and probably even of weeks and months—of education annually. What blocks such a reform is the immediate cost. Grownups would have to learn reading and writing all over again—which many could not afford and few would want to do. The young would be cut off from everything now in print until it had been reprinted new-style. Newspapers and magazines would probably have to print everything two ways for a number of years—and run half as much matter. The crux of the difficulty would be that the acutest inconvenience would fall on us, now, for the first ten years; the clear benefit would all be reaped by future generations. People in the mass don't come as altruistic as that—and perhaps it is just as well.

But a Czar, a Pope, a revolution, a despot floated into control by a revolutionary period, can and sometimes do jam such reforms through. Thus there is the Julian calendar reform effected by Caesar in 46 B.C., the Gregorian by Pope Gregory XIII in 1582. Incidentally, since this latter correction came from the head of the Roman Catholic Church, Protestant and Greek Orthodox countries tended to hold off from it; England accepted the Gregorian calendar only in 1752, Russia in 1918.

Somewhat analogous is British and American resistance to the metric system, which in the abstract is undoubtedly superior to the irregular national systems, as shown by the fact that physical science, which is supernational, has never wavered from it. Continental Europe, and then Latin America and most of the world, soon accepted the system. The Anglo-Saxon nations, self-sufficient through being in the lead technologically and industrially, have not yet done so. To "go metric" would make for international uniformity and universal future convenience; but it would also entail a double standard and some confusion for a generation, or some years, in daily life and business in the United States and the British Commonwealth.

An ancient reform of spelling, if that term can be applied to a partly ideographic system, was supported around 1370 B.C. in Egypt by the Pharaoh Ikhnaton and his anticlerical coterie of the intelligentsia. They introduced monotheism, realistic sculpture, and "truthful" writing. Only the last stuck. As regards motivation, it may be added that the priesthood of the sun god Amen-Ra had become wealthy and powerful, and blocked the king and his reformist friends as hard as these fought the priesthood.

In most ancient and in most Oriental cultures, revolutions from above had much the better chance of succeeding. Apart from some cases in Greek and Roman history, successful and important revolutions from below seem to be a specialty of recent Occidental civilization. The great and effective Meiji modernization of Japan beginning in 1868 was engineered wholly by elements in the upper classes surrounding the young emperor. The Chinese revolution dating from 1911 did not emanate so clearly from those in power and has brought perhaps as much confusion as progress. The Bolshevik revolution was a symptom of Russia's having been drawn increasingly into the Occidental orbit, as its Marxian ideology was a direct import from western Europe. By contrast, Peter the Great, two centuries earlier, was Westernizing his subjects by force, like any good Eastern autocrat. He produced less profound changes than the Soviets, but also much less upset and clash. A revolution from below in Peter's day would have been foredoomed to fail.

One of the most drastic revolutions was that which Kemal Atatürk poured on the Ottoman Turks after World War I. Once the spearhead of the last Mohammedan penetration into Christian Europe, the Turks had for several centuries tried to remain stationary with Islam while Western nations changed and strengthened. Atatürk took over at the end of two and a half centuries of recession, with the last provinces of the Turkish Empire gone, his people defeated and reduced to their homeland. He deliberately led them out of the Islamic camp of culture into the Christian, in everything but formal religion. Western government, law, dress, calendar, were adopted more wholesale and more rapidly even than in Meiji Japan. Perhaps his most unparalleled overnight change was from the Arabic to the Roman alphabet. This happened also to be an immense improvement in its much better fit to spoken Turkish. But above all it marked a clear-cut break with Koranic law and attitude, and symbolized the transfer of Turkish allegiance from the defensive culture sphere of Islam to the expanding Occidental and international one. Like any capital operation, such a major set of changes had to be carried out decisively and swiftly, if at all.

Theoretically, revolutions, as redistributions of cultural structure and social rewards within a society, are due to internal strains accumulating until a sudden shift or tipover occurs. However, the cases just considered show in increasing measure external influences behind the internal strains, until, in the last instance, all the build-up of pressure is from outside and only the final climax of conversion is interior.

Therewith we can conveniently pass over to our second main group of changes, those from without.

171. EXTERNAL CHANGE: DIFFUSION

When something new has been evolved in a culture, whether a tool or an idea or a custom, there is a tendency for it to be passed on to the culture of other societies. This is much like the passing on of culture to the younger generation within the evolving society, except for being foreign-directed instead of domestic. In other words, new culture is transmitted geographically as well as chronologically, in space as well as in time, by contagion as well as by repetition. The spread in area is generally called *diffusion,* as the internal handing on through time is called *tradition*.

When an invention passes from the inventor to other individuals, we call that its successful cultural acceptance. Diffusion may be viewed as an extension of the process, on a much larger scale, by which an invention or innovation—or sometimes even an older culture trait—spreads from the society in which it originated to new societies and becomes established in their cultures.

Conceptually, the simplest form of cultural transmission is tradition: transmission within a society through education by the elders and imitation and learning by the young. Normally, education and imitation are not in conflict, and therefore reinforce each other. Also, neither education nor imitation in itself involves any element of innovation or change, both being aimed primarily at perpetuation of the culture.

In the case of areal transmission or spread of culture, the fact that the diffusion takes place between different societies somewhat alters the processes at work. Imitation or learning of course is still operative, but education mostly drops out. Missionizing may take its place, but the impulse to missionize occurs only in some societies. Moreover, it can scarcely hope to be as effective as education. Indeed it is chiefly when the missionary succeeds in controlling secular education of the young that he becomes really influential.

Even more important is the fact that, diffusion being cross-societal, new elements of culture are involved—new at least to the receiving or learning culture. This novel culture material may meet with anything from eager acceptance to bitter hostility. But since it does represent innovation and change, the traits that are being introduced will expectably encounter some resistance. After all, they are foreign to the pattern of the culture on which they are impinging; and while some of the imported traits will happen to fit into the native pattern, or be neutral, others will violate or upset it. Or their acceptance may have unforeseen consequences that prove to be upsetting. It will accordingly be evident that intra-society transmission of culture in time must normally tend toward persistence, but intersocietal transmission in space tend toward change.

This difference can also be viewed from the angle of total human civilization. When cannon and, later on, steam engines were invented, they represented a new increment in the whole of human culture as well as in European culture. When subsequently cannon and steam engines were introduced into Japan, both devices represented as much of an innovating increment there as they had in Europe, and their effects on war and industry were about as great. Yet from the angle of human development as a whole, there was no invention or addition whatever involved in the transmission to Japan, only a spread of things already in existence. In short, from the point of view of the world as a whole, diffusions can also be seen as continuations or persistences plus spread.

Similarly, though invention and diffusion certainly are distinct concepts, yet the resistance which an institutional invention or innovation often encounters at home, both as to being made and as to social acceptance, may be identical with the resistance set up against a diffusion from abroad.

These illustrations will serve to show how processes that as logical or abstract concepts are wholly distinct tend to appear intertwined and intergraded in the actual phenomena of civilization as history unrolls them. The very same cultural act or event can be construed equally as a continuance or an innovation, according as it is viewed from the angle of the trait itself or that of the receiving culture.

However, whatever else diffusion does or does not involve, it does always involve change for the receiving culture.

The total part played by diffusion in human culture is almost incredibly great. This is a corollary of what has been said before, in § 113, to the effect that all cultures are largely hybrid composites of material that once entered them from outside. Naïvely, human beings do not realize this to any great extent. It is of no advantage to a society, ordinarily, to have its members aware of the foreign source of most of their culture; nor is it a satisfaction to most individuals to be reminded of this debt to aliens. So the facts tend to be forgotten, perhaps more rapidly even than most events of history.

In addition, there is a precritical impulse in us to look upon foreign customs as things that flow spontaneously out of foreign peoples: Chinese "naturally" worship their ancestors and defer to their fathers, just as they "naturally" talk in singsong and naturally grow long black hair. This goes with the normal naïve assumptions on "race" differences and inferiorities (§ 80-81). So totems and couvade and bows and arrows and shell money and sympathetic magic were long construed as more or less "automatic" emanations of the "natural" human mind in its more "childlike" manifestations.

This older view, or rather assumption, has had to be largely abandoned under analysis. If our own civilization is due mainly to elements introduced into it from without, there is no reason to believe that backward peoples would be more spontaneously creative, especially since they obviously also incline to repeat one another in certain grooves. Above all, more accurate study of the forms of culture traits, of their related variants, and of their territorial distributions has yielded so many instances of proved or highly probable diffusion of things like totems and couvade and shell money that the explanation of spontaneous emanation is rarely invoked any longer.

In short, the usual intersocietal functioning of culture is somewhat like most interpersonal relations. We more often learn from others than devise original things ourselves. Therefore, when record has been lost of how culture traits were acquired, a specific, part-for-part resemblance between culture traits, coupled with evidence of sufficient other relations between the societies that possess them, is now mostly accepted as presumptive indication of their spread by diffusion, rather than of their wholly independent reinvention.

Like anything else, this working rule or hypothesis can be carried too far. On the average, it proves to be the soundest inference to make, in the present state of knowledge. Yet some diffusionists have gone so far as to deny altogether, or practically, the possibility of separate reinventions; all likenesses are claimed by them as due to diffusion. This stand seems arbitrary and unreasonable. It is perhaps motivated by an urge for rigor and simplification of process, comparable to the simplicity of the precritical "spontaneity" explanation. However, this ultradiffusionist view has also been pretty well abandoned.

Nearly all of the inventions discussed in § 147-149 and 183-187 also have a history of diffusion. Most modern technological inventions tend to show a rapid world-wide spread. New institutional devices, such as the referendum and the Australian ballot of § 153, often are not accepted the world over: these particular ones, for instance, obviously require democracy as a precondition. But so far as institutions do have a history of widespread success, this is one mainly of diffusion with adaptive modifications. The same is true of philosophies, religions, ideologies. In proportion as these are influential they tend to win an international following, at least for a time. Democracy, communism, fascism, are familiar examples.

To these illustrations from the full light of recent history, there can be added endless cases of more ancient traits or systems: Christianity or Mohammedanism, for instance, or printing. In the case of older technological inventions, the precise circumstances of the first origin have often become somewhat misty, although much of the spread is usually well attested. Such are the arch, gunpowder, tea-drinking, bells in towers, Arabic numerals, chess, the 360° circle, spectacles, water mills, clocks, and dozens of others. With these can be included a series of plants first domesticated in the Americas, such as maize, potatoes, sweet potatoes, tomatoes, Lima beans, and tobacco (§ 193), the cultivation and use of some of which spread rapidly to certain parts of the Eastern Hemisphere. The result is that we often speak of potatoes as Irish, and that whole archipelagoes in the East Indies have come to eat more maize or sweet potatoes than rice, and so on. Double diffusion is indicated by our name for the turkey: the domestication of the bird was native American, but it was carried first to Spain and the Mediterranean, and from there reached England and then its colonies. In consequence, North Americans mistakenly call an American bird after an East Mediterranean country. The histories of wheat, millet, and sugar cane, of chickens and horses, of pottery, of bronze, iron, and steel (§ 282, 284, 296, 298) are also clearer as regards diffusion than as regards origin.

Finally we come to elements of culture the beginnings of which may remain forever hazy to us but the coherent distribution of which argues strongly for a spread from one center of origin. Thus, none of the American Indian nations possessed any authentic record of how or when they had learned to plant maize. but it was found being grown all the way from central Chile to North Dakota and Quebec, by perhaps 500 distinct tribes. It would be intrinsically absurd to consider the possibility of each of these 500 tribes having made the domestication as an original invention of its own. Even if the notion were abstractly tenable, it would be refuted by the unusual "artificiality" of the cultivated maize plant, its inability to propagate and maintain itself in nature, our ignorance of a direct wild ancestor. But if most of the 500 tribes learned rather than invented maize-growing, economy of explanation inevitably carries us not only to 300 or 400 who learned it, but probably to 499. Invention in one tribe or region, then a spread to the rest, seems much the most economical and reasonable interpretation. This conclusion is fortified by a botanical consideration: Genetic mutations and hybridization, one or both of which are believed to have been needed to transform unknown wild ancestors into maize, are definitely rare in plant history—more likely to occur now and then only than over and over again.

The case for diffusion, rather than independent invention, of native American pottery, whose distribution is slightly wider than than of maize, though roughly correspondent, is similar, though not quite as firm. Theoretically it would be quite conceivable that there had been two or three or four independent inventions of the pottery art in America, each with its own history of growth and spread, until several diffusions coalesced and came to look on the map like a single bicontinental one. At any rate, there is no known physicochemical reason, corresponding to the genetic-botanical one for maize, to weigh against such a view of multiple origin. Yet even if there had been four or five or six separate origins of pottery in the New World, the ratio of tribal diffusions to inventions would still have been about a hundred to one.

Even at the beginnings of all human record, from the early Palaeolithic well back in the Pleistocene, the discovered distributions strongly suggest diffusions of wide sweep. In western Europe, North and East Africa, Arabia and India, the earliest cultures we can define with thorough assurance are "core cultures" (§ 273) using massive, trimmed-down flints of bifacial "hand-ax" or "Chellean-pick" type. Contemporaneously, central and eastern Europe, and presumably northern Asia also, harbored "flake cultures," with tools of edged chips struck off from flint nodules. The indication is that the two technologies were devised separately, and that each had its own history of spread, though both spread intercontinentally. By the time of the last or Würm Glaciation, the two diffusions had met and overlapped in western Europe.

Similarly, toward the end of the Palaeolithic, the chipping of minute delicate blades of flint was evolved in North Africa during the Capsian period, spread to Spain, and in the following Mesolithic became characteristic of northwestern Europe from France to Scandinavia (§ 275-276).

As regards patterned systems of traits, the world-wide dispersal of several of these—the week, the alphabet, the zodiac—is outlined below in § 196-197, 206-221, 229.

172. RESISTANCE TO DIFFUSION

We can assume from the foregoing that any feature of culture once established will automatically tend to spread to the cultures of other societies, just as it will tend to persist in its own. The principle is empirical, but so great is the mass of experience, both contemporary and historical, on which it is based that it has the force of an axiom. However, the principle affirms not that there *must* be diffusion, only that there will be some impulse for it to take place. Roughly, we can assume that culture traits will spread unless there are specific factors to prevent spread, much as we assume that things once in a culture will continue in it until displaced or modified by some positive impingement. This is because, from the angle of the culture trait, spread is after all only a form of persistence: it is continuation in a new geography.

However, from the point of view of societies and their total cultures, the contrary is true, and is important enough to repeat: Diffusion is like invention in that it results in an innovation. When an invention is accepted, place is made

for something that has just originated in the same society. When a diffused trait
is accepted, a place is similarly made in a culture for something that previously
originated in another society and culture. In both cases there normally are ob-
stacles or resistance to acceptance. These may occasionally be actually greater
for an invention or a home innovation, if this seems to threaten established economic interests or an ideology with active sanctions behind it, or even only
bodily habits that have firm hold. But on the whole the edge is probably the
other way, since the farther it travels, the greater the risk that the diffusing element will encounter wholly new settings which may contain something definitely antagonistic to it. Nevertheless, any difference between the resistances encountered respectively by invention innovations and diffusion innovations is
more of degree than of kind, and, on the average, likely to be not very great
in degree.

Of prime importance to the fate of either kind of innovation are the patterns it encounters in the culture at whose door it is knocking. There are going
to be obvious difficulties about inducing Christians and Mohammedans to worship, say, river gods, or persuading Mohammedans and Jews to eat pork sau-
sage—about equally so whether the prophet or the inventor of the idea be a
native renegade or a missionary from another faith. This class of situations has
been touched upon under invention (§ 151), and further instances are mentioned in § 185, 199, 221.

Sometimes the resistances are selective, as when the Japanese gradually took
over most of Chinese civilization but resolutely refused to accept rhymed tonal
poetry, civil-service examinations, foot-binding, and a number of other particular
Chinese features. The reason for the first resistance is simple and in a way extra-
cultural: The character of the Japanese language is such as to make a rhymed
and tone-observing poetry almost impossible, whereas in Chinese, prose and
poetry would be difficult to distinguish except by rhyme and tone. Civil-service
examinations as the basis for officeholding, power, and wealth began to be
developed in China when the aristocracy was crushed in the great national
unification more than twenty-one hundred years ago. In Japan, however, aristocracy of descent always maintained itself, in fact has pretty consistently been
the dominant power in the country, and never submitted to bowing to the yoke
of a merit system of tests. In China, the emperor was the Regent of Heaven;
but a dynasty that became wicked was thought no longer to represent Heaven
and could justifiably be overthrown. The Japanese eagerly took over the idea of
the Chinese emperor's absolute authority, which was much greater than that
of their own early rulers. But with the native rulers claiming to be gods descended from the sun goddess, it would not do to admit that their line could
become corrupt or that they might legitimately be deposed. So the dynasty has
remained nominally unbroken, though most emperors have had little real power,
and many have been edged into abdication.

Foot-binding is of interest because it seems to have clashed with an unconscious Japanese pattern to which anything like mutilation was repugnant. Thus eunuchism, which persisted at the Chinese court until this century, never got a foothold in Japan; and the Japanese avoidance of all body jewelry is perhaps related psychologically. In this way the Japanese nonacceptances of Chinese civilization seem quite spotty, and yet are characteristically Japanese. After 1931 it gradually became evident that the Japanese had been equally selective in taking over Occidental civilization. But we of the West had felt so pleased at being imitated since 1868, and thought so well of the Japanese for imitating us, that we were overlooking how much of Western culture they were also firmly rejecting.

Items of culture that are isolated, not much woven into a pattern, and therefore relatively neutral in their social functioning, and yet of an indubitable practical value, are least likely to encounter resistances to their diffusion: matches, for instance, or potatoes. In fact, the flint-and-steel strike-a-light has maintained itself, if at all, chiefly among very remote or very poor groups who could not secure matches regularly. And why not? Matches conflict with nothing institutional. Here and there a priest might insist that ritual fire continue to be made in the old way, or even by drilling; but such exceptions would not in the least impair the spread of matches for ordinary secular use, where the main motivation inevitably is the pragmatic one of getting a light as quickly, surely, and easily as possible.

Tobacco, as a relatively harmless indulgence, habit-forming but not leading to incapacity, and reasonably economical at that, has had a rapid, world-wide diffusion (§ 193). It is also essentially neutral toward the ideology or value pattern of most of the cultures it entered. In native America it did often have religious associations; but these promptly got lost when its travels began.

Now and then an autocrat or a religion attempts to freeze a culture as of a given moment. In the main, the endeavor is of course foredoomed. But it may cause some strange, spotty retardations of diffusions. Mohammedanism is the most striking example. It forbade images, wine, usury, and gambling; and the Koran, or the custom law it accepted or implied, was to be the basic civil law of Islam for all time. Among the consequences one is that the Arabs, who had had no previous representative sculpture or painting, never developed any, though the Mohammedanized Iranians, who had had these arts, managed in time to revive them. Playing cards diffused from China; they struck quick roots in Europe, but seem to have passed Islam by. Insurance has been difficult to introduce in Mohammedan countries. The pious conservatives could claim that it partook of both usury and gambling. Even coffee-drinking was in jeopardy for a while because it is not mentioned in the Koran; though Mohammedans at large soon became coffee-lovers. Tobacco has also at times been forbidden by the very strict. Printing was under graver and longer suspicion (§ 199). It is not sanctioned in the Koran; it would expectably be applied to the text of the Koran, which Mohammed had dictated for writing down by hand; and it was an invention of Chinese and Christian unbelievers. The first attempt to print in Mohammedan lands—a history of Egypt in 1729, nearly three hundred years after Gutenberg—led to riots and prohibiton. It was not until 1825 that a Mohammedan Arabic press was established in Cairo, though Christians had printed in Arabic type in Italy as early as 1512. Printing of the Koran in Islam was specifically forbidden in 1727.

These several Mohammedan blockings of diffusions are perhaps most interesting for the common resistance they encountered in spite of being inherently disconnected. There is neither logical nor intrinsic nexus between sculpture, insurance, coffee, cards, and book-printing. What made these so dissimilar introductions meet resistance was a psychological attitude: a timorous legalism or puritanism (§ 248) that tried to protect the accidents of a system or code adopted by the culture. Obviously useful novelties that were indifferent toward the spirit or the letter of Islam, like the compass, cannon, matches, and automobiles, met no such resistance. Like Christianity, Mohammedanism has generally been imbued with a characteristic feeling of superiority and has tended to manifest aggressiveness. But a counterpart of this quality has been an inferiority sense and self-protectiveness whenever the culture was unsuccessful—as it mostly has been, in competition with Christianity, since about A.D. 1100, except for the interlude of the Ottoman Turks.

The resulting defensive attitude of Islam is somewhat akin to that which led China, Tibet, Korea, and Japan to try for two or three hundred years to shut out all Occidental contacts. The Far Eastern societies had been unaggressive, and now tried to isolate themselves and their cultures altogether. Islam could not make the identical endeavor, both because of being unusually far-flung and exposed in geography, and because of its fundamental militancy. But it could and did try here and there to effect a protective exclusion of culture features that were tending to enter. This might be construed as a sort of seclusion in spots.

173. MARGINAL CULTURES

The important concept that cultures are retarded because of their peripheral or marginal position in geography rests largely upon the idea that diffusion is a more or less continuous process. It also assumes that it is in the higher centers of civilization that the most numerous inventions and the most generally adoptable advances will be made, on the whole. As these new increments tend to spread, they will however spread most slowly to those societies which are most remote or most difficult to reach. Further, the innovations and additions that do reach the edges and peripheries may fail of acceptance by the cultures there, because they involve requirements the receiving culture cannot fulfill. Thus a marginal culture might be quite eager to use metal tools, and advanced enough in manual skills to learn metallurgical processes, and yet be forced to pass by the opportunity of acquiring them because it lacked, say, the gross tools, or the habits of industrial perseverance, necessary for mining ores.

In this way a growing gap may be created, theoretically and often actually, between the culturally productive center and the cultural margin. This gap tends to increase as the center piles up additional increments and the margin receives or accepts only a fraction of them. In theory, accordingly, peripheral cultures would tend to drop farther and farther behind. Finally some center, besides enriching its culture, may also extend it geographically until part of its society is transported to the marginal lands, comes in contact with the marginal cultures there, and proceeds to extinguish these, absorb them, or brush them aside. This is what has been progressively happening to most primitive cultures since 1500 at the hands of the increasingly expansive Occidental civilization.

But there is no necessary sequence in these matters. The high centers may recede or shift, or new ones may come up—finally even at the edges—until what was peripheral has become focal, and perhaps vice versa. In 3000 B.C., for instance, all of Europe was certainly marginally retarded as compared with nearer Asia and Egypt. In 500 B.C., Greece was within the center, but Italy still lagging, and western and northern Europe even more so. By A.D. 100, Rome looked like the focus, and certainly was part of it. At some later period—just when is debatable, but certainly by A.D. 1650—the nucleus of highest productivity in European culture had shifted across the Alps. During the past three centuries England has surely been among the small group of northwestern-European nations that constitute the central hearth of Occidental civilization. But previous to 1550, England was, equally obviously, retarded and marginal to western continental Europe, and the more so the farther back we go in history: in 1000 B.C., or 3000 B.C., England was no more than a feather edge of high culture, a margin of a margin.

Similarly with the radiation of culture out of the great Far Eastern center that began to glow and spark in North China three to four thousand years ago. This culture expanded, diffused over South China and Annam, also eastward into Korea, and from there to Japan. Of two peoples in Japan about the opening of the Christian era, the Yamato or ancestral Japanese held the parts of the islands nearest Korea, from about Kyoto southwest; the Ainu held Tokyo and the northeast beyond. The archaeological remains suggest no great difference of cultural level between the two races. But for century after century elements of the long-established civilization of China dribbled into southwestern Japan, culminating, around A.D. 400-700, in a rush of import of writing, learning, Buddhism, political organization, and hundreds of other things. Yamato Japanese culture now became fundamentally Sinitic. At the same time it was so placed as to cut off the Ainu from all immediate contacts with the higher Chinese civilization. The Ainu thus remained barbarian, the Japanese did not. They were gradually conquered, absorbed, or pushed by the Japanese to the extreme northeast of the archipelago, where some thousands still survive as an interesting racial relict, in a cultural and ethnic status recalling that of reservation Indians in the United States (§ 65). It was their geographical position of being marginal to the marginal Japanese that no doubt mainly accounts for the Ainu retardation until the present. But just so, and to about an equal degree, was Japan retarded fifteen hundred years ago as against China. And for the same reason. China on the mainland, in more or less contact with the rest of Asia and Europe, was profiting by this contact; but Japan lay beyond the farthest edge of the continent, in a little island world of its own, virtually beyond contacts in an age of limited and difficult navigation. Japan off the east of Asia and Britain off the west of Europe thus were in corresponding situations, and remained retarded for correspondingly long periods.

As for the Japanese, they sought for Chinese civilization at various times, and absorbed and assimilated it with skill, yet always managed to give the borrowed product a distinctive national individuality, until now and then it would have been difficult to assert that the teacher still remained more advanced than the pupil. Nevertheless, the flow of diffusion continued one-way. Whether it was coining money or drinking tea or printing books or a different Buddhist sect or a new style of painting landscapes, it was always China that originated, Japan that followed (§ 303). The lag might be one century or two centuries or six, but it was always Japan that was behind. The Japanese did exercise option about their acceptance, and simply rejected a good-sized series of Chinese traits, as we have just seen (§ 172). Where they had something of their own, however, as in the native Shinto cult, or where they gave something of Chinese origin a new twist or value, as in fine swordmaking, these originalities of theirs never passed out of Japan back into China. This does not mean that Japanese products and devisings were invariably inferior. They could hardly all have been so, and assuredly were not. Essentially it was Chinese self-sufficience, quiet arrogance about the superiority of their own culture, that prevented important return diffusion. Here, then, it was an attitude which was effective as a block; whereas the long retardation of Japan, like that of Britain at the opposite end of the great Eurasiatic land mass, was due primarily to its extreme marginal position. The historical relation of Chinese to Japanese culture may well be described as one of dominance, similar to that of parent on child, or between most persons in habitual relation to each other, or even, according to the psychologists, between most primate individuals.

Until 1500, the prevailing contacts of the whole Far Eastern or China-dominated center with the rest of the world were overland. Then came the ship-borne Portuguese, followed by Spaniards, Dutch, English, and French. After some unpleasant and disturbing contacts, both China and Japan—in fact Korea, Annam, and Tibet also—tried to shut these contacts out by policies of seclusion. During the nineteenth century these policies proved manifestly inadequate, were given up, and Western influences were once more admitted.

Here a difference developed: The Japanese now sought cultural imports from the West, the Chinese accepted them much more slowly, often reluctantly. Over the seaways, Japan now was no longer more remote from the new center of the Occident. In fact, as an island nation Japan was more accessible to successful diffusions, and more quickly permeated by them, than China with its hundreds of millions living mostly in the interior of a great land mass. So now, when advance for a while had largely become equated to Westernization, Japan at last took the lead, and before long not only defeated China in war but attempted to guide and instruct it. The roles of the two peoples reversed when the conditions changed, although the same processes continued at work.

This whole Chinese-Japanese relationship can also be seen, just as legitimately, as an example of acculturation. But acculturation is a more complex thing, from which diffusion must always be analyzed out as one of the elemental processes at work, as will be seen below, in § 176-179.

Marginal backwardness is manifest in total culture rather than in particular traits: it is essentially a cumulative matter. It is occasionally traceable in specific complexes, as when the Asiatic composite or three-ply bow of horn-wood-sinew appears in northwestern America as the simplified "sinew-backed" bow of horn and sinew or wood and sinew; and the associated thumb ring of Asia—for releasing the bowstring—is also lacking in America. Similarly, resist dyeing (§ 235), supposed to have originated in India and still flourishing in three forms in Indonesia—pattern, knot, and fiber dyeing—is represented as far out in the Pacific as Melanesian Santa Cruz Island by merely the last of these three processes. In general, however, retardation is obviously going to show in the total culture accumulated, rather than in special traits.

174. MARGINAL BIOTAS AS PARALLELS

Biologists long ago observed that the large backward or relict biotas—both faunas and floras—were those of the Southern Hemisphere. Africa south of the Sahara harbors a Pleistocene-like association of animals that is extinct in Europe. South America was never reached by many important groups of mammals; but as if to make up for this, it evolved a specialized fauna, such as the platyrrhine monkeys, and the noncompetitive sloths, armadillos, and other edentates of the Patagonian extremity. Australia of course is much the most retarded of continents biologically, its native mammals being virtually all of the primitive marsupial type. As compared with these three southern continents, Europe, North Africa, Asia, and North America form a virtually continuous land mass,[8] "Holarctica," within which species could migrate without much hindrance; and any new successful forms were likely to spread over the whole

[8] Continuous except for shallow Bering Strait, and this was repeatedly a land bridge in the past; whereas the existing Panama land bridge was more often a barrier strait in geological time.

great area. By contrast, the three southern continents are like three blind alleys running off from the much greater Holarctica, which stretches east and west four-fifths of the way around the globe. Newly evolved forms of life got into these three southern projections late, or not at all; old forms found shelter there, were preserved, or even underwent further local development. The net result has been that the three marginal southern continents—marginal to central Holarctica—have been evolutionistically retarded.

The cultural parallel is interesting. No very high civilization has ever developed independently south of the equator. The most advanced was that of ancient Peru. The native Australians are often cited as culturally the most primitive large block of mankind. Ultramarginal to the margin that the Australians constituted were the still more backward Tasmanians. The tip of South America was occupied by primitive Yahgan, Alakaluf, Ona, Tehuelche. In the far south of Africa were the Bushmen; scattered south of the equator, the Pygmy tribes; and Bushmen and Pygmies constitute the only two ethnic groups in Africa that still live wholly by hunting-and-gathering. The cultural retardation in the three southern continental extremities certainly seems similar to the faunal one.

At its northeastern end, the great Eurasiatic continent pinches into a nearly waste, unfavorable, Arctic tip, beyond which lies Bering Strait, and then nearly equally arduous Alaska, before the temperate and desirable parts of North America are reached. Here then is a bottleneck between the Old World and New World halves of Holarctica, between Palearctica and Nearctica. In the millions of years available for their dispersal since the Eocene, many species of mammals passed through this bottleneck at times when Bering Strait was dry land and the climate perhaps less raw than now. Among such were elephants, horses, bisons, camels, tapirs, wolves, bears, beavers, and many others. Some spread eastward, some westward; a few probably even flowed back. But other groups never did effect the crossing. Lions, tigers, hippopotami, rhinoceroses, true cattle and water buffalos, the whole group of true antelopes and gazelles, did not get into America, which can therefore be construed as faunally submarginal to Europe-Africa-Asia: semiperipheral to it, but not wholly dependent.

It is interesting as showing the influence of basic geography that for thousands of years America was submarginal in culture also. When this condition began to change after 1492, it was through the expansion of European societies across the Atlantic, not through enlargement or easing of the Bering Strait bottleneck. But pre-1492 America was culturally only semimarginal, not definitely peripheral like Australia. There was a demonstrable flow of culture from Asia into the nearer parts—about half—of North America. This diffusion included traits such as the sinew-backed bow just mentioned (§ 173), slat armor, snowshoes, the toboggan, bark boats, bark dishes and pots, basketry hats, the tepee or conical tent of skin or bark, scapulimancy, bear ceremonialism, the "magic flight" story (§ 227), and some others. But in the main, the more advanced and complex cultures of native America as a whole, both North and South, seem to have been independently evolved in the hemisphere rather than received by diffusion. This was perhaps the result of the opportunities offered by the large favorable areas well away from the Bering bottleneck, areas where agriculture was developed, population multiplied, and the arts of life increased. Most students of native American history believe that this development, which culminated in the stretch between Mexico and Peru, was essentially autonomous. It attained to cities, kingdoms, most metallurgical arts, some astronomy and calendry, and extraordinarily complex rituals. It did not achieve ironworking, writing, or a "world" type of religion (§ 169). It was thus retarded in type or level, by perhaps two or three thousand years, behind the highest centers in the Old World. But the retardation was through a separate and delayed start. Slowness and incompleteness of interhemispheric diffusions constituted only a remoter factor underlying the lateness of the beginnings of American Indian higher developments.

The Greeks had a name for the central area of higher civilization: *oikumenē*. Literally, this meant "the inhabited world"; but it had also the connotation of "civilized world," or civilization as a whole; much as an oecumenical council of the Church still means a council of the whole of Christianity. This *oikumenē* of the Greeks, which stretched from Gibraltar to India and dimly known China, was the region in which people lived in cities in organized states, plowed their fields and raised cattle, worked iron, and knew letters. What was beyond this civilization the Greeks were hazy about; they considered it either wasteland or land occupied only by unstable savages: for they much underestimated the size of the southern parts of Africa and the north and east of Asia, and of course Australia and America were wholly outside their ken. This concept of the *oikumenē* of the immediate pre-Christian and post-Christian centuries has a modern utility as a convenient designation of the total area reached by traceable diffusion influences from the main higher centers of Eurasia at which most new culture had up to then been produced.

175. INTERNAL MARGINALITY

It is important to remember that all this discussion of diffusion from centers to margins refers to prevalent directions of drift, and not to any rigorous or one-way determinism. To conceive the diffusion of culture as radiating out in concentric circles, like sound waves from a bell, is schematic; actual history is almost never so simple. In fact, even physical nature is likely to have winds and obstructions and conflicting noises interfering with the regularity of its waves. In culture, one of these complexities is manifest in societies that remain retarded although they are situated within the sphere of higher centers. Such cultures have been called "internally marginal." This phrase is literally appropriate when the habitat is a desert or a mountainous or undesirable tract inside a generally favorable region. In other cases the phrase is just a telescoped way of saying that the culture in question is backward, like cultures whose geography is marginal; that it is an incomplete form of some richer culture elsewhere and perhaps not far away. Often both conditions apply: The culture is retarded and is also crowded back into undesirable terrain that may shelter it from active diffusions almost as effectively as would distant remoteness.

Asia is particularly rich in tribal societies with "internally marginal" cultures. Examples are: the very primitive Veddas of Ceylon; the Todas and other nonliterate tribes of the Nilgiri hills in southern India; [9] most of the Munda tribes farther north in India; Palaung, Kachin, Moi, Semang, Sakai, and many others in the states of Farther India and Malaya; Lolo, Yao, Man, and so on in South China. None of these nationalities is situated on an actual outer edge of the continent. All of them constitute enclaves within a larger area and population of civilized people. Most often these latter, whether Hindus, Chinese, Burmese, Annamese, or Malays, have taken up the fertile plains and valleys. The primitives may now and then have pushed in to where they are, but more often they are an obvious remnant, now contracted to the hills, ridges, plateaus, higher mountain valleys, jungle, or "bush." This whole culture type is equally interesting from the angle of acculturation, which will be touched upon in the next section.[10]

In the East Indian archipelagoes, above all among the larger Philippine Islands, migration, travel, commerce, and enlightenment have moved easily by sea lanes, while land penetration is difficult, on account of both terrain and vegetation. The remote and backward places regularly are the interiors of the islands; the accessible and advanced tracts are their physical edges, the shorelands—as in post-Perry Japan. So we find, for instance, in Luzon the Negritos of simplest culture in the mountains most difficult to reach; next to them the pagan brown Filipinos in at least two distinguishable levels of culture and remoteness, exemplified respectively by, say, the Ilongot and the Tinggian; and then the lowlanders like the Tagalog and the Pampanga, long ago influenced by Hindu and then by Mohammedan and finally by Christian civilization.

It is evident that this Indonesian condition inverts the space relation of "center" and "periphery" with which we started. Culturally, centers are spots of high productivity; margins, spots of prevailing receptivity and retardation. Cultural centers may be geographically central also, or on geographical margins.

[9] They are sometimes misnamed "pre-Dravidian" in order to shunt the contamination of primitive affiliation away from the civilized Dravidian nations. Actually the Toda, Kota, and so on are fully Dravidian in speech, and their cultures seem to be somewhat specialized and retarded tribal or caste facets of general Dravidian or southern Hindu culture.

[10] Internal marginality is recognized also in the Smithsonian Institution's *Handbook of South American Indians,* and in the ethnographic classification of that continent developed below in § 319, 331.

Geography always enters into consideration in the matter, because it is diffusion that is at work and diffusion is geographical spread; but it is culture that is spread, or which fails to be spread and leaves certain societies retarded. Such retarded cultures are often spoken of as peripheral whether their situation be on the edges or in the interiors of land masses.

176. ACCULTURATION

Acculturation comprises those changes produced in a culture by the influence of another culture which result in an increased similarity of the two. The influencing may be reciprocal or overwhelmingly one-way. The resultant assimilation may proceed so far as the extinction of one culture by absorption in the other; or other factors may intervene to counterbalance the assimilation and keep the cultures separate. The process of acculturation tends to be gradual rather than abrupt. It is perhaps always gradual and long-range enough for acculturation phenomena to fall within the scope of history, even if the phenomena examined be contemporary ones. In fact, in so far as history is more than the story of particular events and particular individuals and deals with social and cultural changes, a large part of all history the world over, possibly more than half of it, deals ultimately with the results of intercultural influencing —that is, acculturation. This is clear as soon as we consider the findings of that part of history in which the role of particular events and persons is of necessity reduced to a minimum; namely, archaeology. Practically all the diffusion we have been considering either contributes to acculturation or can be viewed as an aspect of acculturation; and conversely, all acculturation is full of diffusion. The two are thoroughly interwoven in the phenomena: the distinction is a conceptual one of approach and emphasis of interest. When we follow the fortunes of a particular culture trait or complex or institution through its wanderings from culture to culture, we call it a study of diffusion. When we consider two cultures bombarding each other with hundreds or thousands of diffusing traits, and appraise the results of such interaction, we more commonly call it acculturation. Diffusion is a matter of what happens to elements or parts of culture; acculturation, of what happens to cultures.

In 1935, Redfield, Herskovits, and Linton, as a committee of the American Anthropological Association, formulated the following definition: "Acculturation comprehends those phenomena which result when groups of individuals having different cultures come into continuous first hand contact, with subsequent changes in the original culture patterns of either or both groups." They went on to distinguish acculturation from culture change, of which it is only one aspect; from assimilation, which at times is one of the results of acculturation; and from diffusion, which constitutes only one aspect of acculturation, but yet is always present when there is acculturation and sometimes when there is not.

In a concrete science like anthropology there is little gained by pushing conceptual distinctions very far, and some risk of sterility, because phenomena intergrade endlessly, especially in so highly plastic a thing as culture. A broad definition, centering on the core of the meaning involved rather than aiming at hairline logical definition of its edges, is therefore ordinarily the most useful. A definition of this kind for acculturation might be: the effect on cultures of contact with other cultures. In this would also be included the effect on the societies that carried the cultures. Viewed in this way, it is evident that acculturation takes in a lot of meaning. It has no doubt been operative since there have been separate human cultures. Ninety-nine per cent of all acculturation must lie in the past; and it involves the nature, the processes, and the patterns of culture as well as its changes.

If any modification of one culture by another culture is acculturation, why the sudden interest, almost excitement, beginning about 1920-25 and culminating perhaps in 1935-40, about a concept as wide, elusive, and protean as this? It must have had some special implications; some portion or corner of it must have been charged with particular connotations.

The principal factors that made for the whirl of vogue which acculturation studies were given for a while were the beliefs that such studies were immediately contemporary and that they were practically useful—plus, probably, a sense that they dealt with our own civilization as familiar to us and that therefore they involved less wrench to our natural ethnocentrism, by our not having to depart from it to examine other culture and times. With these considerations, there were mixed some subsidiary ones. For instance, as World War I closed, an "Americanization" movement swept patriotic, political, social, philanthropic, and educational circles in the United States. Poles, Italians, and other immigrants were to be amalgamated. The "foreigners" who were outside were to be kept out; those who were in were to be remolded, as quickly and effectively as possible, into reproductions of Anglo-Saxon Americans. Anthropologists and sociologists were to help appraise the methods and the degrees of their assimilation. In England there was a somewhat analogous movement, relating to the adjustments to European civilization that "natives" under colonial administration were facing or making.

Further, it had become an ethnological technique to study other cultures, especially backward ones, by investigating them in the field, on their own ground: perhaps the Arunta in Australia, the Toda in India, the Yoruba in Nigeria, the Dakota or the Hopi on their reservations in the United States. In every case, these primitive societies had begun to have their culture visibly invaded and affected by Western civilization; some only to a minor extent, others so far that the former native culture could only be recovered from memories of the older people, while the present-day population lived in a transitional hybrid culture—or sometimes a parasitic one—that was neither quite native nor quite Western. Often it was easier to describe this patent, obtrusive mixture than to reconstruct the native primitive culture before it went all to pieces. One could observe the workings of the hybrid culture instead of having to extricate or to infer the workings of the past. Further, the unconscious hold of ethnocentrism on all of us is strong; so that some students preferred dealing with a bastard partial derivative of their own culture to orienting themselves in one of radically different assumptions, patterns, and attitudes; the mental journey took them less far from home. Again, uncontaminated primitive societies still going their own way might possess fairly retarded cultures, but normally these would be adjusted fairly well to their own problems and making more or less of a success as going concerns. In contrast, when the much more massive and powerful Occidental civilization begins to impinge on backward cultures, it tends to disarrange or disorient these. Primitive societies in process of disappearance are therefore usually full of maladjustments, miseries, and unsolved problems. These sufferings stimulate students with philanthropic or reformist inclinations or those interested in social pathology, but tend to distract those whose interest lies rather in cultural patterns and their normal values.

At first, acculturation studies also held out an exciting promise of showing how the wheels of culture change go round. One saw what people had been, what they were, what they were turning into, and why. It was like catching the dynamics of culture change in the act, almost like setting up a laboratory. This is more or less true. Yet essentially the same thing holds for all culture changes due to contact, in the past as well as now, between two alien civilizations as well as when our own is concerned. The precise motivations of the people involved in these former and foreign situations will mostly not be as familiarly vivid; but in compensation the ultimate effect on their culture patterns will normally be much more fully visible after the act of acculturation has been completed than while it is still in progress; and the outcome should be more fully understandable in the perspective yielded by a more remote period or region. There is no difference of principle between the acculturation involved in the Hellenization of the Romans in Italy during the two or three centuries following 270 B.C. and that of the Americanization of Italians in the United States in the century following A.D. 1850. The chief unlikeness is that the ancient Italians were the dominant and majority group, the modern Italians a minority and socially dominated group. Which problem one prefers to investigate is largely a matter of taste and temperament. Those to whom foreign and historical phenomena easily carry a meaning, or do so only with difficulty, will respectively be interested in one or the other approach. The approaches are equally legitimate. Which alternative one chooses for himself is likely to be determined by the degree to which one is ethnocentric or allocentric, at home with a synchronic or a diachronic view, inclined to discharge ideas into action or to let them sink in deeper—rather than being a matter of better or worse scientific procedure.

At any rate, these reflections on method are of a certain importance because they show that the particular type of "acculturation studies" developed by anthropologists in the interval between the two World Wars does not so much represent the discovery of a radically new type of problem as the emphasizing of one special aspect of the long-recognized phenomena of culture change, and the application of investigatory techniques to somewhat nearer and possibly more "practical" situations.

What is distinctive in these special acculturation studies, as Linton has pointed out, consists of several features. First, they view acculturation almost wholly and one-sidedly from the angle of the impact of a dominant, prestige-laden society and culture upon a backward or dominated minority. Next, the changes investigated are almost invariably not spontaneous and automatic, but purposively directed or controlled, at least in part, by the superior society, through its Colonial Office, Bureau of Indian Affairs, Army, police force, authorized missionaries, and the majority public opinion behind these. Special attention has also been given to phenomena of nativistic revivalism. By this is meant defense efforts of the dominated culture to glorify its past and to re-establish at least parts of it. Finally, the acculturation has been studied as it is intended to work; namely, to result in ultimate disappearance of the minority—in its cultural and social fusion. Even where conspicuous racial differentiation and a sense of racial superiority tend to prevent social assimilation, as in the case of the American Negro, there is little doubt that the pressure of the majority population is in the direction of cultural assimilation. The studies made therefore incline both to take ultimate uniformity for granted and to accept it with a degree of equanimity.

All these characteristics of the conventional type of professed acculturation studies apply to only a selective part of the total phenomena of change resulting from culture contact, or acculturation in the broadest sense. The following sections will accordingly try to present some instances of culture-contact dynamics of a broader and more fundamental type.

177. ACCULTURATION WITH AND WITHOUT DOMINANCE AND ASSIMILATION

Since acculturation basically is the acceptance or borrowing of material from one culture by another, it always involves some approximation between the two cultures. But there is no reason why such approximation should continue into assimilation. Normally, we may expect assimilation only when the outlook of one society is inclusive and when this society is definitely the stronger and its culture the more advanced. In the majority of cases the populations somewhat balance each other in size, have separate territories, are mutually influenced, but expect to retain separate ways and customs, and do retain them. In other words, the acculturation is more or less reciprocal, but incomplete. Each people is also likely to be developing new peculiarities even while it is taking over culture from the other. This is perhaps the most common form of acculturation: across a frontier that remains a frontier, although not a closed one.

A familiar example is the boundary between Mexico and the United States, which is also the frontier separating the two principal facets of Occidental civilization in the Western Hemisphere: Latin American and Anglo-American. The border states from Texas to California show a series of influences from Mexico that are not found elsewhere: in names, architecture, foods, land grants, community-property marriage law, frequency of knowledge of the Spanish language, and understanding of Latin American ideology and attitudes. Complementarily for the Mexican states from Tamaulipas to Sonora, as compared with for instance Michoacán or Oaxaca or Vera Cruz: people and habits seem and are more like those of the United States. At the same time there is no question but that crossing the Rio Grande either way means entering a thoroughly distinctive form of modern Western culture.

This type of situation is exceedingly common. It recurs wherever Mohammedan and Christian peoples adjoin. Religion and language maintain a cultural barrier that may be stationary for centuries, but which is continually permeated by diffusion. Spanish civilization for instance has a larger heritage of absorptions from Islamic civilization than any other in western Europe. Witness as a sample just the following words with the article *al-*, which were among the many diffused from Arabic into Spanish, and from there passed through French into English: algebra, almanac, alkali, alcohol, alfalfa, alcove, cotton (*algodón* in Spanish), adobe. Primitive tribes who are neighbors are always partly accultured, as is evident from the fact that their cultures regularly resemble each other even though their speech affiliations may be quite diverse. But no two such tribal or national cultures are ever identical. Each people is aware that the other has some peculiarities which have not been accepted by itself.

Of course assimilation also takes place at times. The Norman and Saxon fusion after 1066 is a familiar instance. Within three centuries these two strains were assimilated in culture, speech, and mainly in blood. English civilization was greatly enriched by the infusion of the large Norman-French element into the Anglo-Saxon, so that by say 1400 it had come to approximate more nearly French culture in its level; but of course it remained definitely distinct from French. The Normans produced a decisive effect because their mainland culture was more advanced and more effective than the belated island culture of the Saxons; but their being fewer in numbers made the assimilation easy and natural. Also, they were in a sense professional "acculturators." Only a century and a half before, in fact, the Viking Norsemen had similarly conquered Normandy for themselves out of France; and they had since then been acculturing themselves into fairly close representations of Frenchmen.

The Manchu, the Mongols, and the still earlier Tungus conquerors of China lost their own cultures there. This was evidently because they were a small minority with a much more limited culture than the Chinese. The situation was almost as if the Apache or the Sioux had overrun the eastern United States seventy-five or a hundred years ago. We might in that event conceivably be paying taxes to a great Indian chief, while American civilization with its machinery, highways, schools, newspapers, movies, and slang would perhaps be going on not so very different from what it actually is. At least one might so infer from the repeated Chinese cases; and from the story of the Vandals, the Goths, the Lombards, and other tribes of the Germanic Völkerwanderung. This hypothetical example indicates that as regards what happens to civilization, the main results will be much the same, irrespective of who conquers or becomes "dominant," when a large population possessing a rich culture collides with a small, backward one. The difference between our imaginary Sioux Indians giving orders from the Capitol and collecting customs duties for themselves in New York, and the actual Sioux living submarginally beyond the Mississippi because they have made a poor go of farming and can't all join Wild West shows—this difference is one that affects very profoundly the success and fortunes of some ten thousands of Sioux. But that is the principal effect the imagined difference would have had. Native Sioux buffalo-hunting culture would almost certainly be as essentially disintegrated by now as it actually is, even if the Sioux had by some miracle conquered us; and American culture would perhaps have been modified only in minor respects.

Some United States Indians have worked out an interesting semiassimilation of their own. These are certain central tribes, such as the Winnebago, the Fox, and the Shawnee. They have accepted American money, dress, houses, furniture, and transportation—in other words, the tangibles and the economics of our civilization. But they have kept their old social institutions and rituals. This snatching of a half-preservation from the pervasive swamping which acculturation has meant for most Indians appears to be due to an intransigeant sense of superiority that these few tribes managed to retain even when defeated and crowded onto reservations: they never accepted spiritual dominance by the white man. The Shawnee have had an unusual history of migrating from west to east and then north and west again for three hundred years, and of repeatedly moving into contact with white men and a variety of Indian tribes, and out again. Exceptionally exposed in these long roamings to a multitude of possible diffusions, they have ended up by developing an anti-acculturation attitude, in order to preserve their identity. Thus they avoided or postponed the total assimilation with which their small numbers threatened them.

The Pueblo Indians of Arizona and New Mexico have also kept their society and religion intact, plus a good deal of their material culture and subsistence. This is because for two and a half centuries they were under Spanish rule, with enforced Christianity. They countered with an outward acceptance of this, beneath which they kept their old rituals and idea systems alive by a sort of semisecret passive resistance. They were aided in their conservatism by the sparseness of Caucasian immigration.

Somewhat similar is what happened in Latin American countries in which the Indian racial ingredient remains heavy, especially parts of Mexico, Guatemala, Ecuador, Peru, and Bolivia. Here the Aztec, Otomí, Maya, Quechua, or Aymará Indians were economically oppressed by their conquest, and were made Christians more effectively than on the remote Pueblo frontier of New Mexico. Hence their old religion was completely shattered and is now largely lost, even where they live in solid populations of hundreds of thousands. Mostly they are devout Catholics, but with considerable pagan absorptions. Their dress is not the old native one; but it often is distinctive of locality or class, like peasant costume. The rest of their life is a similar mosaic of indigenous and Spanish elements in complex and unpredictable combinations. There are millions of such "Indians" in these countries, with a culture that is not pre-Columbian, not Spanish or colonial, not modern Occidental, but some of each, plus local developments evolved from the mixture during four hundred years. There has been an enormous amount of acculturing going on here in these centuries. But the product is better characterizable as a hybridization than as an acculturation, if that word is allowed to retain its usual implication of assimilation into something superior or larger. These millions of Indians are not "assimilated," either nationally or culturally.

A third type of adjustment has been made by the Navaho, a branch of the Athabascan Apache, along with whom they entered the Pueblo territory in the southwestern United States an unrecorded number of centuries ago. For some reason, the Navaho took over more culture from the Pueblos than did the other Apache: corn-planting, cloth-weaving, probably matrilineal descent, certainly a great mass of ritual elements. Subsequently they borrowed sheepherding and silversmithing from the Spaniards. With these enrichments of their culture, they became definitely prosperous, by their own standards, in a habitat that is pretty meager in resources. But this very poverty of the land resulted in few Spaniards or Americans coming into it. Meanwhile the Navaho multiplied themselves severalfold in the eighty years between 1865 and 1945; so that instead of retracting as did so many other tribes, they overflowed their territory. The result is that they are largely self-sustaining, independent, proud, and willing to maintain their old ways. They are Navahos with Navaho habits, dress, and speech, not imitation white men; and the usual absorption by assimilation is not in the least in sight for them at present. The chief causes of this situation seem to be their old and skillful adaptation to a rather poor environment; their growth in numbers, which made them a regional majority instead of a swamped minority; and with this the preservation of assurance and even a certain sense of superiority.

This factor of assurance can be of the greatest importance if a minority wishes to maintain itself. The Gypsies were satisfied with themselves, wanted to remain separate, and did keep themselves intact in Europe for centuries. They changed in some measure along with the culture that enveloped them, as in shifting from horses to automobiles in the United States—but without thereby ever coming any nearer to social absorption, which they evidently did not desire. Perhaps the greatest dislocation of the semiautonomy of their caste society in the United States was due to WPA and other work-relief inducements of the 1930's. Since Gypsies ordinarily possessed only portable and tangible property, those who, previous to WPA, wished to escape could ordinarily have done so only at a low social level; for this it was hardly worth while trading their unshackledness. It was perhaps the half-realization of this fact which strengthened their old attitude of aloofness and professed self-satisfaction.

On the other hand, the fact that Jews remain a minority group is perhaps more largely due to Gentile majority pressure. As their enforced segregation and exclusion diminished cumulatively in the eighteenth and nineteenth centuries, the Jews began definitely to assimilate culturally, and even socially. They have been, on the whole, economically prosperous, so that those who wished to and did flow out of their old caste confinement had opportunity to do so on favorable social levels.

By way of contrast, it may be of interest to consider some cases where groups of Western origin have become minority populations.

178. JEWISH AND CHRISTIAN MINORITIES IN ASIA

In 1163 a colony of Jews from Persia settled at K'aifêng in Honan. Five hundred years later they were still there, as attested by a stone inscription, and had just rebuilt their synagogue under imperial sanction. Two centuries more, however, and they were preserving only a consciousness of being Jews and some scrolls of their Law. The last rabbi had died about 1830 and the synagogue was pulled down by 1850. The colony no longer knew Hebrew, could not therefore read their scrolls, were uncircumcised, had lost their pedigrees, and were indistinguishable in names, dress, and often in features from Chinese. They had become poor, and this may have contributed to the relative rapidity of their final assimilation.

Even older is a Jewish colony in Cochin in southern India, which was flourishing in 1020, as is shown by a grant of lands and privileges to one of its leaders, preserved on copper plates of that date. There are also Jewish tombstones dated 1269. Following the Hindu pattern, these Jews today are divided into three castes, which do not marry or eat together, though their religion and general culture are identical. The so-called "White" Jews number less than 150 and are all in one congregation, to which the "Black" are not admitted. These

Whites may include some descendants of the original Jewish settlers in India, but seem mainly to be of Spanish Jewish stock that arrived in the sixteenth century and kept itself separate. They are of about the same complexion as southern Europeans, and in blood they are very high in type A (§ 72), a distribution characteristic of the Iberian Peninsula. The "Brown" caste numbers only two or three dozen native servants or ex-servants of the White caste converted to Judaism. The Black caste is some ten times as numerous as the White and has seven synagogues. They resemble the Cochin Hindus in color and blood type, and in origin they must be either outright converts from the native population or the descendants of former cumulative intermarriages of Jewish immigrants with natives. The two main castes are old: in 1686 they were described much as now, and synagogues still in use by the Whites and the Blacks were built in 1568 and 1489, respectively. The Cochin Jews are at once well fitted into southern-Indian civilization and separate from it where they want to be, which is chiefly in religion and group identity. They live in a ghetto street, but from choice. They all learn to read Hebrew, the Blacks as sedulously as the Whites, for prayers and services, but talk Malayalam along with the rest of Cochin. Rice is their staple food, as it is in all southern India; but they will never mix curries of meat with those of milk, in conformity with the orthodox Jewish injunction. They chew betel, paint their nails, play rummy, but have preserved their Hebrew ritual and festivals scrupulously. There is much acculturation, but also a wholly successful maintenance of the integrity of a minority group and of a subculture around an intact nucleus of religion.

Equally interesting are the native Christians of Cochin, who legendarily stem from the disciple St. Thomas, and at any rate were found long-established when the Portuguese reached India in 1498. There are five sects of them. Two groups are Roman Catholics, one using Latin and the other Syriac as the ritual language. These both acknowledge the Pope, of course, but represent somewhat different degrees of secondary influence of Portuguese missionaries on the local Christians. The native Chaldaean Syrians are under the Patriarch of Babylon; the Jacobite Syrians, under the Patriarch of Antioch. From these latter, the fifth sect, the Reformed or St. Thomas Syrians, seems to have branched off, with its own local bishop as head, under the influence of immigrant Protestant missionaries; this sect rejects confession, relics, masses for the dead, and invocation of saints. To these five sects there correspond seven castes, which absolutely prohibit interdining and intermarriage, in conformity with standard Hindu custom. The Roman Catholics of Latin rite comprise three castes, whose basis of separatism is not clear. Otherwise, each sect is also a caste, except that the Jacobite and Reformed Syrians are jointly split—not on the basis of religious adherence, but of ancestral residence: the northerners, Jacobite and Reformed alike, claim to have arrived in India earlier, thus being superior, and accordingly refusing to marry with the southerners.

It is clear that the customary tolerance of Asiatics toward religions, strength-ened by the dominant Hindu leaning toward caste particularity, afford minority groups of foreign origin an excellent chance to maintain themselves without being extinguished by assimilation, and yet to acculture, outside of their re-ligion, as far as is convenient to them. At the same time, it is also evident that the Cochin Jews, and still more the Cochin Christians, have been aided in the preservation of their particularities by occasional relations with overseas co-religionists, resulting in their reinvigoration as minorities. The Jews in China, remote, inland, and secluded, were beyond such reinforcement, and both their social and their cultural identity washed away after some centuries.

179. VOLUNTARY OR SPONTANEOUS ACCULTURATION

It is true that much modern acculturation of minorities is directed by the majority culture, and that their assimilation is consciously furthered as some-thing desirable. Uniformity has a way of commending itself to majorities. How-ever, there is some importance in remembering that assimilation and standardi-zation are not inevitable outflows from anything in the nature of man or his culture. A whole lot of human history has unrolled without any notable en-deavors at uniformizing. The Persian Empire, the Hellenistic states, and Rome were all notorious for not attempting any total assimilation of their subjects. One obeyed the authorities, kept the peace, and paid taxes. Beyond that, one was free to follow the ways of his fathers or to abandon them. And there was a deal of acculturation nevertheless. Asia Minor and Syria largely turned Greek in culture and speech; the greatest Greek city in the world was Alexandria in Egypt; Gauls and Iberians became utterly Romanized—of their free will, be-cause it was to their own advantage or prestige, not because a ruler or a majority put pressure on them.

Ethnically at least, the attitude of the Middle Ages was much the same. Conformity to the Christian doctrine and church was exacted, but little else. In fact, controlled acculturation came late. Not until well into the modern period of European history, along with the rise of consciously nationalistic programs, did the inclination become strong to improve people of other culture and speech by inducing or forcing them to accept one's own. China and India have always been notoriously tolerant or indifferent in these matters. The list of "internally marginal" backward peoples that have been mentioned (§ 175)—who are of course only partly acultured populations—is evidence.

A few cases to exemplify this generalization—that much human accultura-tion has been voluntary—will now be cited. One instance will be recent, one older, the third in the primitive field.

Since the Meiji reform of 1868, Japan has obviously been making its culture over to conform progressively to Western civilization, at least in most respects. Thus, following the charter oath, with its clause that "intellect and learning shall be sought for throughout the world," in 1871 feudalism was abolished. Then there followed these introductions:

1872: compulsory universal education
1872: first railroad and telegraph
1874: Gregorian calendar
1875: girls' normal school
1881: Bank of Japan
1889: constitution with a parliament
1890+: new law codes
1897: gold standard
1899: abolition of extraterritoriality
1902: Anglo-Japanese alliance

All this "Westernization" or adoption of Occidental culture was voluntary. Perry had used a mixture of persuasion and threats to open the door and establish relations; but none of the actual Japanese acculturation was due to compulsion or even to pressure from outside—no more than there had been in the similarly large-scale Japanese taking-over of Chinese civilization between A.D. 400 and 800 discussed in § 172-173 and 303. Neither, of course, was there the least diminution of Japanese social, racial, or national integrity. The whole matter of minorities and absorption was lacking, as was direction or control from outside the group. And yet what happened is one of the most sweeping and important acculturations in history, even though much too brief to be complete.

The Lithuanians furnish the contrary example of a people voluntarily submerging both their culture and most of their identity. By about 1200 Europe had been Christianized, and therewith brought into Occidental civilization, except for the barbarous, independent Prussi, Litva, Latvi, Kor, and other tribes along the lower Vistula, the Niemen, and the Dwina. These peoples, often mistaken for Slavs, were not Slavs, but formed in speech an independent, co-ordinate division of Indo-Europeans, the Baltic or Lettic branch. To their east, the Russians had previously been Christianized from Constantinople to the rites of the Greek Orthodox Church. To the south, the Hungarians and the Poles had been converted to the authority of Rome. So had the Germans on the southwest and the Scandinavians to the northwest of the Baltic peoples. From Sweden, Christianity had been carried to the peaceful pagan Finns off to the north of our Balts; the latter thus formed the one remaining island of heathenism in Europe —a typical "internally marginal" retardation.

Then, in 1226, the Teutonic Knights, a militant monastic order, began a crusade for the conversion or extermination of the Borussians or Prussians. Gradually the whole coastal territory along the east side of the Baltic Sea as far as the Gulf of Finland was subjugated and appropriated by the Germans. Its inhabitants were either exterminated or Christianized by force. One group of tribes alone, the Litva or Lithuanians, a little farther inland than the rest along the Niemen, fought back for their freedom and managed to retain it long enough to learn about organized war and statehood from the encroaching Germans. Beginning with Mindvog in 1247, they developed a series of national leaders. They also commenced for the first time to found fortified towns such as Vilna. Soon they passed from holding their own to expanding, especially toward the south, where the recent Mongol storm had left the several Russian nationalities and states shattered. Gedymin overran White and Volhynian Russia; his son, Ukrainian Russia beyond Kiev; under the Grand Duke Jagiello, Lithuanian dominion reached down the Dnieper almost to the Black Sea. In 1386, the heiress to the Polish crown was persuaded to marry this Jagiello, on condition that he become Christian; and his people followed him. A personal union of rule thus bound together Poland, much longer civilized, and Lithuania, perhaps twice as large. The combination being voluntary and reinforced by joint successes against the German Knights, the Lithuanian higher classes eagerly Polonized themselves. They took over not only the Catholicism but the speech, manners, dress, customs, and education of the Poles; and by the diet of Lublin in 1569 they handed over the old Lithuanian conquests to Poland. That, incidentally, was the basis of the Polish-Russian disputes over eastern Poland after World War I and during World War II. The population of the disputed area still is prevailingly White Russian, as it was when annexed by Lithuania six hundred years before; but it had been under unchallenged and sole Polish rule for about two centuries. In the home district of Lithuania, the peasants and serfs continued to speak Lithuanian and to preserve Lithuanian folk customs; but the culture of the higher classes was Polish. A heavy proportion of eminent Poles in all fields of accomplishment were Lithuanian in ancestry, but thought of themselves as Poles. This was much as a Spaniard or a Tunisian of the early centuries after Christ would feel himself to be really a Roman in citizenship and civilization; his actual provincial origin was of no particular moment. All three of the Baltic states founded in 1919 had genuine difficulties to overcome in their careers, because they were really erected on a basis of the social submergence of their nationalities. The nationalities, as linguistic or ethnic groups, were unquestionably there. But their educated, prosperous, professional, and politically trained classes were prevailingly either Germanized, Russianized, or Polonized. Yet in the case of the Lithuanians, their acculturation and semiassimilation had really been thoroughly self-sought and self-imposed by a respect for an older civilization.

Another voluntary reorientation is that made by the Algonkin and Athabascan hunting and fishing tribes of the great transcontinental coniferous forest of northern Canada, as a result of European demand for furs. Their habitat was rich in fine pelts, though miserably poor in almost all other immediate resources. Deer, moose, or reindeer continued to be hunted for food by these tribes; but mink, marten, beaver, and ermine assumed a wholly new value in terms of what white men were ready to give for them: steel traps, firearms, tools and kettles, woolen blankets, trinkets, and tea, flour, and pork. A dependence of families, bands, and tribes on trading posts grew up. Caucasian contacts gave the Indians more comforts, but also entrenched them more firmly as hunters. Their canoes, snowshoes, and the like were retained because they had been successfully worked out to fit living off the country. Their present culture thus has a native foundation, but it also has a large Caucasian constituent and at least partial Caucasian motivation. And the acculturation was not due to conquest, to missionaries, or to dispossessing settlers swarming in, but to the fact that the Indians, who remain in the majority, changed their ways of their own accord (§ 327).

180. NATIVISM, REVIVALS, AND MESSIAHS

After two societies have come into sufficiently close contact for one to feel the other as definitely more populous, stronger, or better equipped, so that its own culture is in process of being supplanted by the other, a conscious preservation effort or defense is often produced. Such reactions have been called nativistic endeavors or revivals. They envelop with a sort of halo the culture that is passing away, and attempt to reaffirm or re-establish it, or parts of it.

An immigrant group in the United States or Brazil almost always forms an association of its nationals, not only to give its members aid, but to help preserve the folkways, customs, speech, and home life characteristic of the old culture. This may be done even though the immigrants are economically better off than they were in the homeland and would not think of returning to the conditions from which they emigrated. People in growing up do get attached to the ways of their culture, much as they become attached to their kinsfolk or their old home. By the time they begin to age, their memories of the culture have got tinged with pleasurable nostalgic sentiments and assume a symbolic value. Folk dances, for instance, or literary exercises thus may come to mean much more than they did in the old country.

Much the same effect may be produced when the territory of a more backward minority is being occupied by an alien dominant population; when a people is conquered and forced to change its ways; or even if it only feels its own culture peacefully giving way under the automatic weight of a neighboring larger and more successful one. Thus the ancient bardic gatherings called Eisteddfods were revived in 1798 for the conscious preservation and cultivation of Welsh speech, poetry, tradition, and music; these were almost all that remained of the national culture of Wales, since Welshmen had long been full participants in British citizenship, empire, and civilization.

With primitive tribes, the shock of cultural contact is often sudden and severe. Their hunting lands or pastures may be taken away or broken under the plow, their immemorial customs of blood revenge, head-hunting, sacrifice, marriage by purchase, or polygyny be suppressed, perhaps their holy places profaned or deliberately overthrown. Resistance is crushed by firearms or by superior military organization. Despondency settles over the tribes. Under the blacking-out of all old established ideals and prestiges, without provision for new values and opportunities to take their place, the resulting universal hopelessness will weigh doubly heavy because it seems to reaffirm inescapable frustration in personal life also. At this juncture a prophet is likely to arise and picture a wish fulfillment: a release from the human impasse by supernatural mechanism. The ancestral dead are to return and sweep the encroaching whites off the land. Bulletproof shirts will neutralize firearms. The game animals will pour out from the bowels of the earth whither they withdrew to evade the white man. The old customs, the old rituals, the old happy gatherings, will all be re-established. All that is needed, says the prophet, is faith in the impending miraculous event, and some slight token observance of faith, such as dancing, or destroying one's belongings of white manufacture. Therewith a revivalistic movement of return to the good old days is launched. The prophet's motivation may range from sincere delusion to desire for power, fame, or even money, or be compounded of these. His converts follow him because of the stress of their social unhappiness. Skeptical individuals or groups are ignored, or finally get caught in the mass infection too.

Some of these cults end in an armed clash and defeat. Such were, among American Indians, the Delaware Prophet's announcements of 1762 and the Shawnee Tenskwatawa's of 1805, which were followed by Pontiac's conspiracy and by Tecumseh, the Battle of Tippecanoe, and the Creek War, respectively. Other movements merely fade away when the date passes and the prediction is unfulfilled. More often they maintain themselves as a new, hybrid church combining elements selected out of the former tribal religion and out of Christianity—its hybridity conforming to the transitional character of the dissolving native culture as a whole. Of this character was the revivalistic cult established about 1884 by the Columbia River Sahaptin Indian called Smohalla, which ended in a permanent religion with church buildings, half after the Caucasian model.

In 1869 a Walker Lake Paiute of Nevada named Wodziwob began to preach locally the end of the world, destruction of the white man, and return of the Indian dead. This "First Ghost Dance" belief spread intertribally with increasing momentum. By 1871 it had the Indians of northern California in a ferment (§ 239); but from 1872 to 1874 it broke up into three movements. The first of these was the Earth Lodge cult, professing to protect the faithful from catastrophe by having them enter specially built subterranean houses. Next was the Bole-Maru, which arose after it began to appear that the world would not end just then, and which therefore relegated the impending catastrophe and return of the dead into the background; but its prophets or dreamers seized upon certain spectacular native dances, simplified these, and combined them with the use of patterned flags and modifications of white women's dresses. The third current was the Big Head cult, which drifted away to attach special importance to a certain type of feather headdress, which was passed on like a fetish to new converts. Of these three proliferations of the Ghost Dance, only the Bole-Maru lasted: it still was being practiced after seventy years at the outbreak of World War II. It thus represents a return from the convulsive character of a messianic revival or native millennium to the more stable adjustment of progressive acculturation.

Even more famous was the Second Ghost Dance of around 1890. This originated, in a sense, among the same Nevada Paiute that started the first one, the originating dreamer or prophet now being Wovoka or Jack Wilson, a son of the foremost convert of Wodziwob twenty years before. His doctrine was the same: cataclysm, reversion of the land to the Indians, return of their dead relatives. Because the First Ghost Dance had found its most ardent proselytes to the west among the California Indians, who were now disillusioned, this second movement stirred a new clientele of Indians to the east, mostly beyond the Rockies, among Dakota, Arapaho, Kiowa, and other Plains tribes. Its hysteria led to the battle or massacre of Wounded Knee, after which it subsided fairly rapidly, leaving as its chief relicts a few symbolic games and a couple of partly new dance costumes and steps—besides of course a more profound despair or resignation.

It is interesting that the rapid and wide spread of these Ghost Dances was itself due to a set of acculturation phenomena that had greatly increased the communication possibilities of the Indians. These were: English as a means of intertribal communication; railroads; and enforced acquaintance of diverse groups with each other on reservations.

Analogous stirrings, upheavals, and outbreaks are on repeated record from South America and South Africa, in Nigeria and New Guinea, wherever Caucasians have sufficiently crowded natives as to their land, subsistence, folkways, or religion. Usually the revolt—or the attempted escape into the miraculous—comes after the invaded culture has had its really mortal wound, when the natives as a mass begin to despair of its survival. Until then, they are troubled by the progressive disintegration of their fortunes and institutions, but not yet driven to relying on the supernatural for hope fulfillment. A few years later, disillusionment is profound enough to keep them in apathy—at any rate until a new generation has grown up. There seem always to be some pessimists and skeptics, and some passive resignationists. But when the emotional pressure on the mass becomes strong enough, even these individuals get caught up in the hope beliefs of the majority, or temporarily retire into side-line conformity: it is often difficult to tell which, subsequently.

The Jews have been particularly prone to such nativistic revival attempts. In 722 B.C. and again in 586, conquest and deportation by Nineveh and Babylon had ended, realistically and historically, the Hebrew dream of a great prosperous national kingdom. They possessed by then, however, a unique religion, more and more centering on belief in an exclusive deity with special interest in themselves. This belief led them in two directions. In part, they broadened their national monolatry and monotheism into a universal conceptual monotheism, and therewith laid the foundation for Christianity and Mohammedanism. On the other side, the narrower and cruder among the Hebrews took increasing comfort in the idea of the Messiah, the anointed one, descendant of David, who would restore the Hebrew kingdom to glory and perhaps supremacy among the powers of the earth. For more than two hundred years of Roman dominance, this Messianic idea kept goading the Jews into hopeless rebellions, the greatest being that led by Bar-Kochba, who actually took Jerusalem and a thousand villages before being destroyed by Hadrian's generals in A.D. 135. Thereafter rebellions were fewer; but claims to Messiahship kept being put forward through mediaeval and modern centuries, their frequency being fairly proportionate to the degree of misery or hopelessness the Jews were enduring at any given time in western or eastern Europe or under Islam.

The expectation of a Messiah definitely entered into the making of Christianity. Jesus' own immediate Jewish disciples considered him to be such: the epithet *Christos*, the anointed, is the Greek translation of *Mashiach*, the one anointed with oil—*mashach*—as a sign of sovereignty. It was denationalized Jews like Paul, and converted Gentiles, who in the generation after the Crucifixion swung the emphasis of the faith away from that of a Palestinian Jewish minority sect onto a basis that could serve for a universal religion. Blood sacrifice, circumcision, the exact Levitical law, were eliminated or made noncompulsory; belief, baptism, and communion sufficed to make non-Jews equal members of the church; and therewith the teaching of Jesus became possible of acceptance the world over. And with that, of course, the historically underlying nativistic revivalism was wholly transcended.

181. ETHNIC REVIVALS

Non-Messianic but literally revivalistic is a late development of Jewish history: Zionism, the movement to re-establish an independent state in Palestine, to serve at least as a center or a token of Judaism if not as a home for all the Jews of the world. Incidentally, the Zionistic movement is only a particular example of a world-wide drift toward autonomous nationalism: an independent Finland and an independent Poland emerging and re-emerging from World War I, Iceland breaking away from Denmark, the cry of "Indonesia for the Indonesians," and dozens of similar cases. The only fundamentally peculiar element in Zionism is that its proponent Jews are not a full nationality and have not been one for two thousand years. It is religion and religious customs, not speech or general culture, that have at the same time held the Jews together and segregated them from the rest of the world.

Some of the Jewish Zionists went one step farther, however, and decided to restore Hebrew as a national language (§ 107, 120), though it had been only a language of ritual and literature—a "dead" language as compared with a "mother tongue"—twice as long as Latin. It is believed that already in Jesus' time Aramaic had replaced Hebrew as the everyday idiom of Palestine. Now engineering and economics are being taught in Hebrew at a Hebrew university in Jerusalem, and some tens of thousands of Palestinian Jewish children speak nothing but Hebrew.

That we are really dealing here with only an example of a generic drift of the times is shown by the attempted revivification of Gaelic in Eire, and by the creation of a Norwegian national language in recent generations. Gaelic or Irish, of Keltic derivation, had sunk in the later nineteenth century to being the speech of a fraction of a minority population. In general, it survived only in western Ireland, mostly among the rural, remote, little-educated, and uninfluential. It has now been enacted into one of the two official languages of Eire, is spoken in the Dail, and taught in all schools.

Norway, while politically a part of Denmark, got along with Norwegian folk dialects on the part of its farmers and fishermen, though people with schooling and social pretensions had learned Danish, or rather a Norwegian sort of near-Danish. After the separation in 1814, this modified Danish assimilated more toward the homespun or folk Norwegian, and became known as Riksmaal, or "language of the realm," in distinction from standard Danish. This was not enough to satisfy the more ardent Norwegians, however, and soon after 1840 a linguist, Aasen, constructed a synthetic pure Norwegian out of local dialects. This, the Landsmaal or "language of the country," was accepted by some, opposed by others, suffered some changes, but was finally adopted as a second official and standard Norwegian language.

These cases are of some theoretical interest because it has been widely taken for granted that while a language in its written form might be embalmed and used indefinitely, as a living speech it was dead and unrevivable once it had no more mother-tongue speakers. It is evidently unsafe to predict too sweepingly about what any culture or aspect of culture can or cannot do. However, it would also be rash to predict that Biblical Hebrew, Irish Gaelic, and Landsmaal Norwegian have struck deep enough roots to flourish permanently and independently of propaganda, subsidy, and official support. They do look like experiments that so far are partly successful—which is a pretty good resuscitation for the seemingly moribund.

182. ASSIMILATION AND UNIFORMITY

The recent tendency and desire to see group minorities and cultural localisms assimilated into complete uniformity is much accentuated by the recent burst of technological development. Not only does a better machine quickly displace a dozen previous ones, but ever improving transportation and communications leave to all particularisms very little isolation in which to shelter themselves. Such particularisms may get temporarily caught up as an interesting novelty and have their nation-wide or world-wide day of vogue: the dirndl costume, for instance. Otherwise, they certainly tend to get obliterated by the increasingly uniformized general culture. It is precisely Austrian and South German dirndl-wearers who gave up peasant dress. In a country like the United States, everybody dresses alike, rides in the same makes of cars, reads the same dispatches, columns, and cartoons in similarly headlined newspapers, dances to the same music, in any given year or month. Much of this uniformization has begun to spread internationally. It is certainly convenient to find the same foods, drinks, houses, clothes, amusements, and reading matter anywhere in the world —if one knocks about the world. But, equally surely, it is also monotonous. And when there is no more place left to find something different, or from whose localism to derive a new stimulation, the world may conceivably awaken to a situation like that of the ancient Hawaiians when they found that their religion had staled on them (§ 168).

It is an old recognition that nationalistic effectiveness resides in union. Whether it be a matter of survival, expansion, or economic prosperity, a united English-speaking America was bound to count for more than thirteen colonial states; a German Reich, more than the sum of its twenty-six kingdoms, principalities, and free cities. And next to political union—in national efficiency—is social and cultural uniformity. A hundred million people living, acting, speaking, thinking, and feeling alike can normally move with a trip-hammer effect, whatever the undertaking, such as could not possibly be attained by a union of fifteen groups of ten million each, differing in customs, outlook, occupations, manners, and ideals—except perhaps occasionally in a transcendent crisis. In a shrinking world, which is therefore inescapably more competitive, there is an obvious premium, first for national size; next for tightness of political unity; third for cultural uniformity—at least while other things remain equal. India and China have the size, but neither the unity nor the uniformity; Japan and Germany, by 1935, had each begun to enforce their unity and uniformity, and therewith to threaten the world. The unusual cultural homogeneity of our 140 millions undoubtedly was a great help to the United States in enabling us to sustain the storm of World War II and to pass rapidly from defense to attack. Yet it is well to remember that this homogeneity differed from that of Hitlerian Germany chiefly in being spontaneous and unenforced, although its degree, after the United States was well in the war, was not so very different. The cause and the motivation of our homogeneity were different from those of the Germans and the Japanese. But it remains to be judged by what the future brings whether the net effect on ourselves of having had to uniformize ourselves, especially if we have to repeat the process, may not include the development of some attitudes similar to German and Japanese ones. There seems to be little doubt that a degree of differentiation by locality, profession, or custom, with the impingement of their varieties on the whole, affords a provocative stimulation and a wider scope of experiment toward fruitful change of culture forms, as well as greater inclination toward tolerance of differences.

In this connection the Russian attitude on acculturation is of considerable interest for its bearing both on uniformity and on its control. As a left-wing party developing in an absolute monarchy, the original Bolsheviki were naturally in sympathy with freedom for national aspirations. As socialists, their planning for a new organization of international culture, and their program of control of change, both tended toward their favoring uniformity. When they came into power in Russia, they set up, gradually, a long series of soviet republics, one for each larger minority nationality—Ukraine, White Russia, Latvia, Georgia, Armenia, Azerbaijan, Uzbek, Tadjik, Kirghiz, and so on—plus the inclusion in the Russian Soviet Socialist Federated Republic of subautonomous units such as Altai and Yakutsk. At first, subject or included peoples, such as the Georgians, the Uzbek, the Yakut, were to be liberated and unsubmerged, much like the Russian proletariat itself—also, much as Woodrow Wilson conceived of Letts and Lithuanians as free and autonomous nationalities. Alphabets were devised for the peoples if they had none; literature was translated into their vernacular; and everything was done to encourage each people to work out its own culture in line with its own past and its aspirations.[11] It was Czardom, the absolute and exploiting state, which had been crushing minorities and subject nationalities, just as it deprived the masses of liberty and opportunity. It was assumed by the Bolsheviks that each such group would spontaneously respond to the grant of its cultural liberty, and gratefully reciprocate by embracing the political faith of its liberators and supporting them. Some notable experiments were made in this direction of tribal cultural development, most interesting perhaps when they were applied to wholly specialized and backward peoples like the Chukchi, or some of the almost pure pastoral nomads.

After some dozen years the official Soviet attitude on these matters changed. The causes may have been a growing sense of security as to survival of the Soviet regime; the tendency to rechannel the emphasis of the Communist program from world-wide revolution to internal strengthening; or still other factors—the situation is complex, and it is unnecessary to account for all the precise causes in the present connection. At any rate, there was a shift in official policy away from international and multinational to strictly nationalistic aims. This shift was enormously strengthened by the successful resistance to the German attack after 1941. The overwhelmingly leading nationality in the Soviet Union being Russian, and especially Great Russian, this new attitude in effect was one of Russian patriotism. With this majority patriotism the minority nationalisms might interfere; but they could hardly strengthen it materially. The later Soviet policy has therefore tended to revert once more to de-facto Russianization, to promot-

---

[11] Except in the domain of religion, any form of which the early Bolsheviks saw as an inevitable enemy. Therefore they did what they could to prevent even the shamanistic practices of their primitive populations.

ing uniformity and homogeneity. The cultural autonomy of Tadjik or Lithuanians or Yakut or Ukrainians is evidently slated henceforth to consist mainly of folk dances and sports and suchlike matters, plus the use of their own tongue in local and provincial spheres. That is, the minority nationalities will presumably be submergent once more.

Quite likely this process is inevitable. Political fractionation would be endless over the world if every group with a culture and language that could be distinguished as separate were to split off into complete political autonomy at will. There is no attempt here to indicate a solution, or to say what rightly ought to be. The Russian situation is pictured in order to outline, a little more fully than one is likely to conceive it from the angle of one's own majority nationality alone, some of the involvements of acculturation, assimilation, and homogenizing to uniformity.

INDEX